Silenced

Silenced

The Forgotten Story of Progressive Era Free Methodist Women

Christy Mesaros-Winckles

LEXINGTON BOOKS / FORTRESS ACADEMIC

Lanham • Boulder • New York • London

Published by Lexington Books/Fortress Academic

Lexington Books is an imprint of The Rowman & Littlefield Publishing Group, Inc.
4501 Forbes Boulevard, Suite 200, Lanham, Maryland 20706
www.rowman.com

86-90 Paul Street, London EC2A 4NE, United Kingdom

British Library Cataloguing in Publication Information Available

Library of Congress Cataloging-in-Publication Data Available

ISBN 9781978714885 (cloth : alk. paper) | ISBN 9781978714892 (epub)

∞™ The paper used in this publication meets the minimum requirements of American National Standard for Information Sciences—Permanence of Paper for Printed Library Materials, ANSI/NISO Z39.48-1992.

Contents

List of Figures

Note on Transcription

Spelling and punctuation vary widely in *The Free Methodist*. When transcribing, I have opted to transcribe articles as they originally appeared. I have also maintained misspellings and punctuation conventions except when they impeded comprehension, as I believe that the voice of the author should be preserved as carefully as possible.

Acknowledgments

I began this project in 2010 as my dissertation and thought the research would stop there. However, I could not get these women out of my mind. Their lives were so exceptional, and no one knew who they were. I felt I owed it to them to continue researching their story. Without the help of numerous individuals, this book would never have been possible.

When I began this work, Clara Wetherald, Ida Gage, Anne Grant, Blanche Stamp, Eliza Witherspoon, Ada Hall, Laura Lamb, Minnie Beers, Bersha Green, and Anna Bright were no more than a footnote in Free Methodist history. At times I seriously questioned whether I would ever find enough information to understand the stories of these amazing women. Piecing together stories from newspaper fragments, family letters, census records, and family genealogy was no easy task. Without question, I would not have succeeded in this research journey without the help of these women's descendants. Special thanks go to Florene Turner, who faithfully preserved her grandmother Edith Gage Tingley's memoirs and provided me with a copy of this fantastic book. So much of what I know about Ida results from the Tingley family's thorough genealogical research.

Additionally, I must thank Norm Luppino, a descendant of Clara Wetherald's brother, Perry Miller. Thank you for working as my tireless, unpaid research assistant and sending me newspaper articles, family letters, and other valuable information about Clara Wetherald and her family. Furthermore, thanks to Betty Arford for her help transcribing the Miller and Wetherald family letters, Dr. Rev. Doug Showalter, who shared his research on Clara Wetherald's Congregationalist connections and was incredibly helpful in explaining the history of ordination in the Congregationalist Church, and Dorothy Spring, whose assistance during my initial research on Clara Wetherald was invaluable. Thanks also to Vanecia Davis, who kindly shared transcripts of Dr. Vivan Grant's memories of his mother, Dr. Sarah Anne Grant.

Furthermore, because *Silenced*'s heart and soul are issues of *The Free Methodist* and *General Conference Daily*, I wish to thank several archivists for their time and access to the amazing collection of treasures they oversee. Thank you to Cathy Fortner at the Marston Memorial Historical Center for opening up the Free Methodist archives and hunting down material during the early stages of research—special thanks to Spring Arbor University's White Library and Susan Panak, the archivist at White Library. Susan was always my go-to person for archival materials, helping me track down microfilm and periodicals. More than just an archivist, Susan was my sounding board. Her probing questions helped me think about the missing pieces in these women's stories.

The list of people who helped me in one way or another with this book is extensive, but I wish to especially thank two exceptional Free Methodist scholars whose research paved the way. First, thank you, Dr. Howard Snyder, for your groundbreaking history, *Populist Saints*. Your research about Free Methodist founders Benjamin Titus and Ellen Roberts helped me see that Free Methodism's impact extends beyond denominational history and is part of the history of social movements in the Progressive Era. Secondly, I thank Dr. Priscilla Pope-Levison for her extensive research into women evangelists. Her books *Building Old Time Religion* and *Turn the Pulpit Loose* were foundational in understanding where these Free Methodist women fit into the larger history of women pastors in the United States. Third, thanks to Dr. Paul Patton, whose ongoing passion for Benjamin Titus Roberts and his dramatic interpretation of Free Methodist history has brought this time period to life in a way that only the theater can.

Additionally, I must thank Rev. Dr. Mindi Cromwell, Larry Winckles, and Dr. Roberta Mosier-Peterson for reading the early drafts of this book. Without their feedback, this book would have taken much longer to complete!

Finally, thanks to my husband, Andrew Winckles, who acted as my editor and provided valuable, honest critiques of each chapter. He also willingly took on primary childcare responsibilities, so I had time to write. I also want to thank Adrian College for granting me a sabbatical in the fall of 2022, allowing me the time to edit and format *Silenced* for publication. I am indebted to each one of you for your help with *Silenced.*

Chapter 1

The Intersectionality of the Experiences of Progressive Era Women Preachers

This book is the story of forgotten Progressive Era Free Methodist women evangelists and the denominational debates surrounding their place within the Free Methodist Church. Their stories were lost in large part because they did not write the denominational history books—that privilege went to men. Instead, their accounts existed in the pages of the denominational periodical *The Free Methodist* and annual conference reports. Some worked alongside their husbands in ministry, others pursued ministry independently, and some even divorced their spouses to pursue their calling. They preached in backwoods towns on the American frontier, traveled extensively, held revivals, and founded churches. Because the only preaching role open to Free Methodist women was that of an evangelist, they could not marry, serve communion, or baptize their congregants. However, that did not deter them from pursuing a profession they felt called to follow.

The story of Free Methodist women begins in the late nineteenth century when a gender battle was brewing in the North American Free Methodist Church. Since the denomination's founding in 1860, women had been preaching and were slowly granted more governance rights. In 1874 women were allowed to become licensed evangelists, and at the 1886 General Conference, women received the right to become elected lay delegates at annual and general conferences.[1] With the support of Benjamin Titus Roberts, the denomination's founder and the first editor of the periodical *The Free Methodist*, women evangelists and their contributions were placed at the forefront of denominational publications, first in *The Free Methodist* in the 1880s and then in the quadrennial special publication *General Conferences Daily*. Under Roberts' editorial tenure, both male and female writers regularly published articles for and against women's ordination. These articles give historians a compelling narrative of women's role in Free Methodism. *The Free Methodist* debates on women's ordination also occurred at a crucial time in American evangelical history when other Holiness and Protestant denominations debated women's role in the church. In particular, it was a critical time in Free Methodism. The denomination could move forward and remain an example of egalitarianism or deteriorate into the dogmatism of early twentieth-century fundamentalism. The narrative of these debates and the stories of many of these early Free Methodist women, who often fought for their right to be more than just an evangelist, will be explored throughout *Silenced*. This first chapter will broadly situate the ministries of Free Methodist women evangelists within the denominational and cultural gender politics of the Progressive Era before outlining several theoretical and methodological approaches that inform the research in this book.

WOMEN IN MINISTRY DURING THE PROGRESSIVE ERA

The ministries of the Free Methodist women evangelists chronicled in this book coincided with a period in American history when traditionally male-dominated professions were beginning to open up to women. As a result, they also faced questions from detractors within the denomination about their physical ability to baptize and travel as circuit preachers.[2] Additionally, these early women preachers faced resistance to their participation in church governance as ordained male elders opposed sharing power with their female colleagues. The challenges Free Methodist women faced were not unique to their denomination but were signs of changing norms in American society. In other Protestant denominations, women preachers faced similar resistance; nevertheless, some did embrace women's participation in church governance and granted them ordination as elders. One of the first denominations to do so was the Congregationalists Church in 1853, followed by the Methodist Protestant Church in 1892,[3] though it was more common for denominations to grant women limited governance rights or a license to preach rather than ordination as an elder.

The hurdles Progressive Era women faced were daunting. In her book *Ungodly Women*, religious historian Betty DeBerg explains that "women who pushed for equality had to illustrate their competence and fight against the prevailing rhetoric of separate spheres and rhetorical warnings against the 'New Woman.' Within conservative Protestant culture, there was a decided push to encourage women not to support suffrage, attend college or seek professions outside the home."[4] Influential Progressive Era ministers reinforced this rhetoric, as in Charles DeWitt Talmage's series of articles in *The Christian Herald* on biblical gender roles. In his article "Duties of Wives to Husbands," Talmage admonishes women not to desire a life beyond the domestic sphere:

> My opinion is that a woman who can reinforce her husband in the work of life and rear her children for positions of usefulness is doing more for God and the race and her own happiness than if she spoke on every great platform and headed a hundred great enterprises.[5]

Sentiments such as Talmage's were common and often rhetorically used to justify limiting women's opportunities in the church. Within Free Methodism, the rhetoric of separate spheres was used to vote down women's ordination at the 1894 General Conference and establish a Free Methodist Deaconess Order in 1907.[6] Thus, the decisions the Free Methodist Church made regarding gender roles in the church were not unique and were indicative of more extensive, growing opposition to gender equality at the end of the Progressive Era as Holiness denominations, including the Free Methodist Church, forgot their radical beginnings and were swept up in the growing movement of American fundamentalism.

For example, the Methodist Episcopal Church North's views on women preaching constantly shifted in the mid-nineteenth century. In 1869, Maggie Newton VanCott was granted a license to preach. Free Methodist founder Benjamin Titus Roberts noted her successful evangelistic efforts in his 1872 tract "The Right of Women to Preach the Gospel." However, by 1880 the Methodist Episcopal Church North did an about-face and refused to grant Anna Howard Shaw and Anna Oliver local preaching licenses or their requests for ordination.[7] The 1880 decision to refuse women a license to preach directly resulted in some women pushing for greater gender equality both within and outside the church. As, in 1880, when Methodist evangelist Amanda Way was not granted a renewal of her license, she organized the first Indiana women's rights convention. Similarly, Anna Howard Shaw used her initial rejection to seek ordination in the Methodist Protestant Church and became the Women's Suffrage Association president in 1904.[8] Frances Willard was likewise influenced by the Methodist Episcopal Church North's refusal to license women and the 1880 General Conference's refusal even to seat women delegates. In an 1888 address to the Women's Christian Temperance Union (WCTU), Willard warned that if Protestant denominations continued to deny women ecclesiastical equality and leadership roles:

> The time will come . . . when if representation is still denied us, it will be our solemn duty to raise once more the cry, "Here I stand, I can do no other," and

step out in the larger liberty of a religious movement, where majorities and not minorities, determine the fitness of women delegates, and where the laying on of hands in consecration, as was undoubtedly done in the early church, shall be decreed on a basis of gifts, graces, and usefulness, irrespective of sex.[9]

Her vocal support of women's ordination led to Willard's continual ostracism from Methodist leadership positions, primarily due to James Buckley's efforts.[10] Buckley was one of the most vocal opponents of gender equality, opposing any role for women that took them outside the domestic sphere. As the editor of *The Christian Advocate*, the denominational newspaper, he regularly wrote editorials denouncing Methodist Episcopal women's right to participate equally in governance or pursue ordination. In an editorial entitled "Making Void the Law of God," Buckley clearly outlines his views on gender roles:

> Many good women have been misled by false principles of interpretation. Some of the best women, in agony over the wants and woes of earth's misguided, erring, and sinning millions, have fancied that if they had the power of rule in the State their numerical majority would "make all things new," and thus have been turned to superficial interpretations of God's word. Other noble women receiving a divine call to give their lives to working for Christ have confounded a spiritual impulse to work, which they had received, with permission, which they have not received, to disregard the limitations in God's word upon their mode of action.[11]

Buckley's editorials, including "Making Void the Law of God," were republished in an 1891 pamphlet by opponents of women's ordination; however, Buckley's views were not universally accepted. That same year, supporters of women's laity solicited the help of St. Louis Annual Conference minister George Hughey to write a rebuttal, and the Women's Christian Temperance Publishing Association published his pamphlet, which refuted Buckley point by point.[12] Methodist historian Carolyn De Swarte Gifford notes that the WCTU actively promoted the rights of women's laity through various publications.[13] The WCTU involvement is not surprising considering Willard's own experiences with Buckley and others who opposed her encouraging women to leave their homes and advocate for temperance and suffrage at a state and national level.

While some women such as Willard believed it was important to remain in denominations and advocate for their rights, others, such as Anna Howard Shaw, chose to leave and find more inclusive denominations. When the Methodist Episcopal Church North refused to ordain Shaw, she left and joined the Methodist Protestant Church, which did ordain her in 1869. Founded by Methodists frustrated with the ecclesiastical structure of the Methodist

Episcopal Church, the Methodist Protestant Church's governance structure favored laity and local church leadership over central denominational governance.[14] The autonomy given to the church and annual conferences allowed the denomination to be among the earliest Methodist offshoots to ordain women. The local autonomy favored by the Methodist Protestant Church also allowed women to organize a Women's Foreign Missionary Society (WFMS) independent of the main denomination. It was self-funded and controlled entirely by women. When the denomination attempted to bring WFMS under the control of denominational mission boards in 1884, the women resisted, and eventually, the denomination backed down and allowed WFMS to remain independent.[15] Some of the denomination's earliest ordained women emerged from the strong women-led missions movement in the Methodist Protestant Church, including Eugenia St. John, who was ordained in 1889. While the national Methodist Protestant Church did not recognize St. John and Shaw's ordination, these women would have been recognized as elders depending on the annual conference. The 1892 General Conference also shifted the authority to ordain to the regional authority. Sociologist Mark Chaves notes this was a "backhanded way" for Methodist Protestant leadership to remove denominational barriers to women's ordination.[16]

By the mid-century, the divisions within Methodism increased, and the Free Methodist Church was founded under the leadership of Benjamin Titus Roberts, a young Methodist Episcopal minister in Western New York. In 1857 Roberts published a series of articles in the *Northern Independent*, a newspaper published by abolitionist William Hosmer. In the articles, Roberts denounced the dominant leadership of the Methodist Episcopal Church for their worldliness and doctrinal laxity. He urged a return to what he called "Old School Methodism," which relied on the beliefs of Methodism's founder John Wesley and an emphasis on social reform.[17] His *Northern Independent* articles eventually led to Roberts' trial and expulsion from the Methodist Episcopal Church in 1858.[18] Together with other disillusioned Methodist ministers and lay leaders, he helped form the Free Methodist Church in 1860 on four fundamental principles of freedom: free pews, freedom of the slaves, freedom from secret societies, and freedom of both the clergy and laity to have equal say in denominational decision making. Each of these principles embodied the ideals of equality and the value of every person to God, and this connection to the holiness movement and social and religious principles of equality led to exponential growth in the denomination's first few decades.[19]

The Free Methodist principle of free pews originated as a response to pew subscriptions, through which wealthy Methodist churches raised money. According to Roberts, this system was not only un-biblical; it also created a divide between the rich and poor.[20] Therefore, "free pews" was more than just a church policy; it was a strong statement emphasizing the inclusion of anyone seeking a religious experience. Likewise, the Free Methodist Church took a strong abolitionist stance in response to the Methodist Episcopal Church's failure to harshly condemn slavery or sufficiently help African Americans improve their economic and social status. As Free Methodist historian Leslie Marston emphasizes in *From Age to Age: A Living Witness*, "The Christian principle of freedom for rich and poor, alike to gospel privileges, and as well as the slave's claim to civil and political freedom, was soon to play an important part in the formation of the Free Methodist Church and would principally determine its name."[21] It was for these reasons that Free Methodists also opposed secret societies. Many of the Methodist Episcopal leaders who expelled Roberts for his radical teachings were members of secret clubs and groups, and belonging to such societies required wealth and social status. Opposing secret societies was thus yet another way to draw a line between the poor and rich in church congregations.[22]

In addition to the early Free Methodist Church's emphasis on social justice and equal access, "freedom of the spirit," or the belief in Christian perfection (or sanctification), was central to the denomination's theology. Christian perfection was a theological belief dating back to eighteenth-century Methodism and the preaching of John Wesley. Wesley defined Christian perfection as "[a]s the elimination of all intentional sin," which he believed to be attainable in this life. However, by sin, Wesley did not mean unintentional wrongdoing but a "voluntary transgression of a 'known law' of God." Additionally, Christian perfection emphasized loving God and neighbor as a result of personal spiritual experience.[23] Thus, Christian perfection was directly related to Free Methodism's focus on social justice. If Christians truly desired to follow God's will, they would seek social and religious reform and devote much of their time to these efforts.

While all four foundational freedoms shaped early Free Methodism, Christian perfection was the guiding force behind Free Methodists' radical social positions. The popularity of Christian perfection extended beyond the Methodist tradition and into the larger Progressive Era culture. Radical social change was at the heart of an individual's quest for Christian perfection.

As the nineteenth century progressed, other religious movements also embraced the belief in spiritual perfection. The Transcendental Movement referred to it as a quest for "perfect love." Religious mystics of the period also sought new ways to connect on deeper levels with spirituality.[24] Social reformers of the time, like Harriet Beecher Stowe, were attracted to the Christian perfection preached by Methodists,[25] as was Charles Finney.[26] The belief that Christians could essentially become capable of living without sin through Christ was one of the greatest motivators for social reform in the nineteenth century.[27] With its "egalitarian gospel," the holiness movement brought together the philosophical ideas of the century and put them into a populist framework that the average American could understand.[28]

With its emphasis on popular theological principles, Free Methodism grew rapidly in its first few decades. By the first General Conference in 1862, there were 2,533 members; by 1866, there were 4,974. By the 1886 General Conference, when the debate about women's roles began to stir, there were 17,677, and by 1890, 21,161. The most rapid growth occurred between 1874 and 1890—about a 178 percent growth rate over 16 years.[29] The mass distribution of Roberts' independent magazine, *The Earnest Christian*, and the official denominational magazine, *The Free Methodist*, also helped rapidly expand the movement, reaching people from various denominational backgrounds and encouraging further revivals across the country. Both ventures quickly spread the denomination's rhetoric of equality and Christian perfection.[30] The deep connections between religious perfection and social reform were one reason Methodism has been credited with empowering women. From the very beginning of the Methodist movement under John Wesley up through the nineteenth-century reforms, women were heavily involved in the ministry and social reform movements associated with Methodism.[31] In particular, Free Methodism produced some of the earliest theological writings on biblical and social gender equality. Roberts strongly supported women's involvement in all forms of ministry, enfranchisement into public life, and egalitarian marriage. Since 1874, Free Methodist women were allowed to be licensed evangelists, who often spent weeks traveling, preaching in small towns, and developing new ministry fields for the denomination. By 1886 women could also be elected as lay delegates to their local annual conference and to the quadrennial Free Methodist General Conference, where denominational issues were debated and voted on by the delegates. By 1907 women could also be appointed as ministerial delegates at quarterly conferences, and by 1911 women were allowed to become ordained deacons in the denomination.[32] Despite this progress, women could not be ordained elders in the Free Methodist Church until 1974.[33] The delay in ordaining women was primarily due to a strong, socially conservative sect within the denomination that favored God-ordained gender roles and restricted women's roles within the public sphere. While Roberts was progressive in his views on race and gender, other denominational leaders were not.

Early Free Methodism's rhetoric and history also illustrate the cultural tensions between the contemporary suffrage movement and the cult of domesticity. It is no coincidence that Roberts' push for women's ordination in 1890 occurred during increased anti-suffrage activity in the United States. As historian Susan Marshall explains in her research on the anti-suffrage movement of the Progressive Era, opponents of women's advancement often relied on biblical arguments and imagery to support their position. It was not uncommon for anti-suffragists to argue that it was a God-given decree that women were subordinate to men, citing Eve enticing Adam in Genesis and their subsequent fall, as well as the writings of the apostle Paul in the Ephesians, where women are told to submit to their husbands as unto the Lord.[34] This "natural" inferiority of women was the basis of natural rights arguments against women in the pulpit and their disenfranchisement from politics and other professions traditionally held by men, such as medicine. Historian Catherine Brekus also notes that nineteenth-century American gender rhetoric emphasized the differences between the sexes as a way to make sense of an increasingly changing social order:

> This new rhetoric was mainly at a time when traditional family structures seemed to be threatened by the transformation of the market revolution. At a time when everything appeared to be in flux, when politics, economics, and the home were being fundamentally redefined, the belief that women were more virtuous than men—a new construction in and of itself—served a profound psychological need. If women could preserve the "feminine" virtues of selflessness and domesticity against the incursions of materialism and self-interest, then the modern world would not be as frightening.[35]

Perceiving women as both naturally morally superior to men while simultaneously physically weak and unable to perform ministerial duties was a way for anti-ordination advocates to feel stable in an ever-evolving society.[36] Thus, Free Methodist advocates of women's ordination faced an uphill battle that pitted them against the underlying philosophical beliefs of society. The "woman's sphere" argument was repeatedly seen at the 1890 and 1894 Free Methodist General Conferences and in the pages of the denominational publication *The Free Methodist* both before and after the General Conferences. As historian Nancy Gale Isenberg explains, gender constructs were still tied closely with religious terminology within the church and secular society. "If women challenged the social order, they required a dissenting stand toward the epistemology of traditional religion."[37] In other words, their fight was not only a political battle against denominational power structures but also a rhetorical struggle against a shifting narrative surrounding gender that was beginning to permeate every aspect of culture.

A NARRATIVE APPROACH TO RELIGIOUS HISTORY

History has always been a narrative of human interaction. At the heart of *Silenced* is the belief that narrative research methods are essential to understanding the nineteenth-century Free Methodist female evangelists' lives and contributions. Scholars cannot only study theology, religious history, *or* rhetoric. They must explore the contributions of historical figures through a layered perspective that considers numerous factors, including the rhetorical impact of the individual, the overarching cultural narrative of the period, and the theology that influenced various religious movements. As a rhetorical history, *Silenced* embraces theorist Walter Fisher's narrative framework. Fisher believed human communication should be viewed as historical and situational, as stories or accounts compete with others. The story is believable when it satisfies the demands of the audience to create a coherent narrative (narrative probability), and the audience believes the account (narrative fidelity). What narrative attempts to do is "[c]ome closer to capturing the experiences of the world, simultaneously appealing to various senses, to reason and emotions, to intellect and imagination, to fact and value."[38] Fisher's narrative philosophy allows for moral reasoning and spiritual practices to be considered valid forms of rhetorical argument and social belief. The narrative is both an individual and a social act. As an individual act, narrative allows people to have *free will* as everyone is responsible for crafting their own story. Narrative also provides context as to why some stories are forgotten within organizational memory and others are not. History is written by the victor and remembered from the victor's perspective. Those who are not included (such as the women in this book) were not considered essential to a particular view of denominational history, as well as the fact that the narratives of several of these women raise uncomfortable questions about gender and agency, as women such as Clara Wetherald and Ida Gage chose to divorce their spouses and continue in ministry. Anna Grant chose to focus on her careers in medicine and ministry, leaving primary childcare responsibilities to her husband. These women did not fit the standard early Free Methodist biographical narrative of a supportive, serene, and passive partner to a successful male leader.[39] What denominational histories do exist focus on the founding men of the Free Methodist Church and were either requested by denominational leadership or written by early Free Methodist leaders who were vocally opposed to women's ordination and full enfranchisement into denominational governance.[40] Fisher believed it was crucial to recognize the power of hierarchy in crafting organizational narratives and to give those outside the organizational leadership a chance to contribute. As he notes in his essay "Narration, Reason and Community":

> History records no community uncivilized or civilized without key story makers and storytellers, whether sanctioned by God, a 'gift," heritage, power, intelligence, or election. Narration implies, however, that the people judge the stories that are told for and about them and have a rational capacity to make such judgments. . . . Furthermore, the narrative paradigm does not deny that people can be

wrong. But then, so can elites, especially when a decision is social or political. There is no evidence that I know of to support the claim that the experts know better than anyone else when it comes to such decisions.[41]

Fisher's emphasis on narrative fidelity and coherence as an act of individual free will fits very well with Wesleyan theology's belief in personal autonomy. Within the Wesleyan tradition, God does not destine people to specific roles or create a group of "elect" who are the only ones who will get into heaven. There is choice and individual agency in Methodist theology, just as there are choices and variety in the rhetorical experience.[42] Regarding social factors that help determine the narrative, as Fisher explains, existing institutions, such as church denominations, provide the "plots" that help tell the stories. However, people are full participants in making and sharing the messages they create. Their embodied experience is front and center in the rhetoric. It is not a secondary aspect.[43] The Methodist emphasis on embodied experience ties directly into the belief in Christian perfection found in the nineteenth-century holiness movement. Central to this nuanced approach is understanding how Free Methodist women evangelists viewed and framed their call to ministry. Including their spiritual experiences is essential to understanding how these women developed their voice within Free Methodism.

While religious historians have not widely used the narrative paradigm, the framework provides helpful terminology that can be used to define the conversion experience, particularly in the Methodist tradition, where personal conversation narratives have been an intrinsic part of the Methodist ethos. The Methodist conversion narratives changed little from Wesley's time in the eighteenth century to the mid-nineteenth century when the Free Methodist Church was formed. Beginning in the eighteenth century, Methodist preachers would receive letters from individuals they had converted. These letters were often published to encourage conversion and to reassure the faithful.[44] At the turn of the twentieth century, the rise of denominational publishing houses, such as the Free Methodist Publishing House, widely distributed denominational tracts and books heavily influenced by the conversion narrative framework to promote the church's mission. Nevertheless, while denominations used the conversion narrative as an outreach tool, it also illustrates a dialectical tension still present in the Methodist tradition—a strain between a populist movement that appeals to the average citizen and a desire to remain apart from the world. As Methodist historian David Hempton explains:

The relationship between Methodism and popular culture is two-sided. On the one hand, Methodism did chime in with the popular culture in its conversionist theology (the age-old desire to make a fresh start), providential interventions, religious entertainment on a cosmic scale, underlying anti-Catholicism, and in its function as a religious association in the age of associations. On the other hand, Methodism confronted popular culture in opposition to drunkenness, bawdiness, rough music, wife sales, popular sports, and race meetings.[45]

This rhetorical tension of being "in the world, but not of the world" focuses on the individual nature of conversion, the knowledge that one's sins were forgiven, and a need to share one's faith with the world.[46] Charismatic joy and a desire for Christian perfection are also prevalent themes in the narratives of this book. Christian perfection was an essential tenet of early Free Methodist conversion narratives and is evident in early Free Methodists' writings as they also emphasize outward signs of Christian perfection, such as temperance and service to the poor. Those who believed in spiritual perfection felt God revealed his will directly to individuals. Free Methodist women evangelists argued that God had placed them in certain locations and given them specific roles to share the gospel.

During the Third Great Awakening (1890–1930), religious enthusiasm, such as the more charismatic members of Free Methodism experienced, was sometimes seen as a "feminine" reaction. However, at the height of the Third Great Awakening, emotional fervor was a common rhetorical device used by both male and female evangelists. Billy Sunday and Dwight Moody both induced religious enthusiasm at their revivals. As Jeremy Young notes in his research on Billy Sunday's revivals, within that context, the "feminine" emotion of weeping both in joy and repentance was embraced even by men who saw the emotional expression as part of their conversion narrative and socially acceptable within a religious setting.[47] In particular, the conversion narrative became a way for both men and women in the Progressive Era to detail their emotional and religious experiences in a socially acceptable manner. Many Free Methodist women evangelists used robust and emotional language and conversion experiences during this period in their ministry reports.[48]

In a period of American history when the cult of domesticity was prevalent, the concept of personal liberty in the form of religion captivated women. While the conversion narrative often contained strong emotional expression, the conversion experience also appealed to women who used the rhetoric of conversion to bridge the divide between dependence and freedom. As historian Phyllis Mack explains, it would be easy to view the conversion narrative as relating to the stereotypical concepts of romantic love or infantile attachment to a divine being. However, reducing the spiritual experience of Free Methodist women to such a framework would significantly diminish the sense of agency that religion offered these women.[49] Mack notes in her book *Heart Religion in the British Enlightenment* that eighteenth-century Methodist women used personal narratives and testimony in their sermons more than their male counterparts. Narratives appealed to the masses, who could see their flaws and similarities through the narratives of women evangelists.[50] Free Methodist women continued preaching into the nineteenth and early twentieth centuries. Their ministry reports and fragments of sermons still emphasize personal testimony and narrative rhetorical techniques. However, while understanding Christian perfectionism and the conversion narrative are undoubtedly essential elements in reconstructing these women's lives, they still cannot fully account for the complexity of the interpersonal experiences these women faced in their personal and professional lives. Unable to receive a regular salary or railroad discounts[51] as ordained male elders could, these women often relied on both the income and the tolerance of a sympathetic spouse as they left home to travel from town to town preaching and establishing new churches.[52] The strain on marital relations was intense for these early female evangelists, as evidenced by Gage and Wetherald's first marriages ending in divorce.[53]

What happens to the contributions of women who, through various life circumstances, suddenly struggle with what Christian perfectionism looks like in crumbling marriages? I would argue that it is their struggles and their gender which have resulted in the many early Free Methodist women, such as Gage and Wetherald, being overlooked in Free Methodist history. While the contributions of women evangelists have largely been absent from denominational narratives, the ability of these women to successfully transcend into the increasingly masculinized space of preaching while at the same time raising a family is impressive. *Silenced* integrates the rhetorical concept of passing when looking at the years these women *were* recognized and thriving within the Free Methodist Church. Especially in chapters three and six, this framework plays a vital role in understanding the experiences and rhetorical savviness of some of these female evangelists.

RHETORICALLY "PASSING" IN MINISTRY

The concept of passing (or, as it is sometimes called in rhetorical studies, "the fourth persona") looks at the lived experience of the rhetor and all the underlying factors that influenced their choices to provide context to their rhetorical contributions. The framework has most typically been utilized in queer rhetorical scholarship and the rhetoric of individuals who pass as "straight." Developed as a rhetorical construct by Charles Morris III, rhetorical passing focuses on the speaker's ability to maintain a double consciousness to survive and resist oppressive cultural practices. Oppressed speakers balance both secrecy and disclosure in their rhetoric.[54] Early Free Methodist women like Gage, Grant, and Wetherald had two personas: wives/mothers and evangelists. In a professional and symbolic sense, these women had to self-portray as men. They had to illustrate to their male colleagues that they, too, could travel long distances to preach and have vibrant ministries by starting churches. They downplayed their domestic role as ministers and focused on their successful ministries in their public persona.

While Morris uses the concept of passing as a construct for queer rhetoric, rhetorician Sarah Wells takes the concept of passing and applies it to nineteenth-century women physicians. Like nineteenth-century preachers, women physicians were entering a male-dominated profession during this period. They had to prove they deserved the respect of their male counterparts. As Wells notes, early women physicians, such as Putnam Jacobi, "urged her students [women] to see themselves first as physicians and then as women."[55] Thus, both groups of professional women had to maintain a double consciousness, remaining silent about the aspects of their lives that would limit their ability to stay in their chosen professions. Morris explains that in the act of passing, silence is constructive and used to maintain an individual's status in society.[56] In the case of women, evangelists passing was only successful *if* they were also seen as contributing members of their respective denominations. Once they were no longer physically present, either through leaving the denomination or through death, they were forgotten.

This rhetorical silence is seen in how their contributions have been preserved in denomination history. Annual conference minutes list their names as licensed evangelists and appointment of women to various ministry circuits. Still, those same records just as often reduced the women to little more than supportive spouses, listing female evangelists as "Mrs." or if their spouse was also a minister by removing their identity and only referring to them as "Rev. and spouse." Consequently, making it difficult to fully retrace the contributions of many nineteenth-century female evangelists in Free Methodism.[57] To fully understand the complex nature of women's roles in nineteenth-century religious culture, *Silenced* attempts to rediscover these women who now exist only as a name in conference minutes.

While Morris views silence as an active construct, rhetorician Dana Cloud takes a different approach, viewing silence as an oppressive construct. Referring to it as a silenced persona or null persona, rhetorical silence draws attention to issues of race and gender-based oppression.[58] The connections Cloud draws between hierarchy and silence can extend to include issues such as ideology and church hierarchy. As rhetorician Robin Patric Clair explains in her book *Organizing Silence*:

> The power of narratives in organizations' cultural and ideological development and reproduction is well documented. In the past, researchers frequently selected and interpreted organizational stories easily obtainable due to their public status. . . . It is essential to investigate those stories that do not receive the same public

exposure, legitimation, or respect within the organization that more commonly reviewed stories reach and receive, that is, sequestered stories.[59]

By the term "sequestered," Clair means stories set apart from the mainstream, such as narratives of women evangelists. As a rhetorical history, *Silenced* has a decade of archival research informing the narrative. My exploration of archives was not simply to see what I could find. I approached the denominational archives at Marston Memorial Historical Center and Spring Arbor University from a feminist archival approach to interrogate who wrote early Free Methodist history and their motivations for leaving out the narratives of many Free Methodist women. Historian Barbara Tuchman emphasizes this point with her research—history can and should be studied as a record of human behavior. It does not always have to focus on famous individuals or groundbreaking historical incidents. The purpose of history is much broader.[60] Particularly in women's history, when so many nineteenth-century women's contributions are still being contextualized, it is crucial to provide new approaches and access to largely unexplored archives, such as the Free Methodist Church's archival records, to situate these women's contributions within larger social narratives of the period. Cahill, Feimster, and Hamlin note in their essay "Expanding the Suffrage Archive" increased access to digital databases, family records, period newspapers, and tools such as searchable digital texts have brought attention to scores of women and their contributions which have been previously overlooked.[61] By exploring the narratives of nineteenth-century Free Methodist women, these women gain credit for their work. Their stories provide a more nuanced understanding of women's roles within Progressive Era organized religious life. However, because their stories were not preserved coherently, uncovering their narratives has been a complex, time-intensive process, and even after years of research, some facts may never be known.[62]

A CRITICAL APPROACH TO ARCHIVAL RESEARCH

The fragmented nature of their stories required an archival approach where, as Neil Lerner notes in "Archival Research as a Social Process," I felt all I did was live and breathe the research process, immersing myself in the period and whatever information I could gather. My unanswered questions leave room for others to continue exploring this topic and, as Lerner explains, also provide an excellent example of the complex nature of archival research:

> The histories that emerge from archival research are never simple, never complete. This conclusion should not be surprising because good historical narratives

are about the people, the programs, and the practices they have shaped. It does not take an advanced degree in psychology to know that people are very complex. The records to be found in archives only hint at that complexity.[63]

Lerner notes that the length of time a researcher spends with historical individuals often creates a sense of connection with those who passed away years ago. Their story becomes our story. The research becomes a personal quest for the scholar to find his/her own narrative in the study and give an overlooked historic individual a chance to have his/her contributions told. As historical rhetorician Elizabeth Birmingham notes, the archivist develops a "sixth sense." Dead people come alive through the archivist's search to learn more about them. The mystery and research quest to find more information spur the scholar forward. As Birmingham explains:

> My argument for the researcher's sixth sense is not that it will enable us to recover and converse with the lost dead, but that it will help us recover ourselves, help us discover that we did not know that we were dead, inhabiting the crypt, repeating dead histories in dead languages.[64]

As I spent days reading news articles, sermons, and personal correspondence, these women have become individuals I know despite the hundred-plus years separating us. My research has been a multi-year process spanning the past decade. I have collected original newspaper articles and speeches female evangelists wrote in defense of their ministries, along with numerous regional newspaper reports on nineteenth-century Free Methodism, U.S. Census records, and family genealogical research to understand the world of these women better. Genealogical research has helped me piece together many facts that I would never have discovered without the help of these women's descendants. I know there are still missing pieces from these narratives, but as historian Barbara Tuchman points out, the key to good scholarship is knowing when to stop because the story is never really finished.[65]

Other scholars must continue this research, as there are countless women in the holiness tradition whose stories have never been told. Both rhetoricians Kathryn Kish Skylar in her article "Organized Womanhood."[66] Furthermore, Susan Zaeske notes that scholarship from this period often focuses only on the rhetoric of suffrage on an organizational level and a particular woman's ties to the organized suffrage movement.[67] However, such an approach overlooks countless women. The women in this present book *did* promote women's rights. Their tactics might not have been the same as suffragists, and they were not part of any national organization promoting suffrage. Still, their objectives were the same—empowerment for women outside the home.

EXAMINING HOW RHETORIC IS
ORGANIZATIONALLY SITUATED

In addition to a more nuanced approach to Progressive Era religious history and suffrage history, there must also be an increased emphasis on combining organizational research with rhetorical and historical scholarship. There continues to remain a restrictive organizational climate in many evangelical communities, prohibiting women from serving in visible leadership roles.[68] If rhetoricians acknowledge that rhetoric is *culturally* situated,[69] is it not also fair to note that rhetoric can be *organizationally* situated? Regarding religious rhetoric, both a cultural and an organizational (denominations and theology) element influences the language of gender. Rhetorical scholars Lisa Ede, Andrea Lunsford, and Cheryl Glenn emphasize the need to recognize that rhetorical scholarship lives on the borders of numerous other disciplines,[70] including organizational communication and theological research. More exploration of these connections is needed to understand better how language, cultural norms, and organizational rules interact. It is not a revolutionary statement to acknowledge that even today, evangelical culture struggles to embrace biblical egalitarian principles. Complementarianism is both consciously and unconsciously embraced in many churches. However, understanding why this theological view of gender is so entrenched *is* something new to explore. Our efforts to understand the rhetoric of the present must be situated in an understanding of the past.

Therefore, *Silenced* not only plays with narrative scholarship but in chapters that outline debates on gender roles in Free Methodism, Earnest Bormann's Symbolic Convergence Theory (SCT) is used to explain how a narrative captures the imagination of its audience and then proceeds to be dispersed and widely accepted within that group.[71] The fourth and null personas provide a way to explain individual rhetorical experiences, as does the narrative paradigm. However, as Walter Fisher envisioned it, narrative also provides a framework for understanding individual behavior in an organizational context. Early Free Methodist leaders such as Edward Hart, George Coleman, and Wilson Hogue are complex figures whose contributions to Free Methodism have primarily been remembered in glowing terms. However, their legacies are far from straightforward. Hart voted for women's ordination 1890 only to vote against it at the 1894 General Conference, and Coleman and Hogue were adamantly against it from the start. Cultural trends beyond Free Methodism were highly influential in the 1890 and 1894 General Conference debates. Fisher notes that when organizational leaders with power and prestige "pursue values external to them," the organizational culture suffers, and their character also suffers. Earlier Free Methodist histories do not devote extensive coverage to women's roles within the denomination, contributing to the glowing personal narratives of these founders, which have been passed down within Free Methodist culture for decades. Nevertheless, when their lives and decisions are viewed holistically, their story becomes much more complex and problematic. As Fisher would say, "One's membership in multiple, competing communities [narratives] means that one can be an upstanding character and a rogue at the same time."[72]

When Fisher's concerns regarding competing beliefs that could sway community leaders to promote a narrative counter to the mission of their organization are put into conversation with SCT, scholars have a framework to help explain both how rhetoric is organizationally situated and the power of group leaders to gain acceptance for specific social and theological views. Chris Underation's research into the powerful rhetoric of Four Square founder Aimee Semple McPherson provides a framework to apply SCT to religious movements. Underation argues that SCT provides a framework to examine personal motivations that allow individuals to promote specific concepts in an organizational vision.[73] The rhetorical influence of leaders is a powerful tool that can dramatically shape and reshape the values of a group. In early Free Methodism, there were several competing rhetorical visions that various leaders embraced and then tried to persuade other Free Methodists to buy into their views. Roberts' strong egalitarian beliefs were central to his beliefs in what Free Methodism could become. However, other leaders such as George Coleman and Wilson Hogue held polar opposite views, writing numerous editorials in *The Free Methodist* supporting separate spheres of influence for men and women. As Underation explains:

> Culture, according to SCT, does not develop from a single *task.* Culture develops from an *idea* that group members generally accept and that brings a general direction to their actions. In that action, though, community members must be able to see their particular connection to an idea, own it, and allow it to become a part of their life and thought.[74]

In Free Methodism, this rhetorical buy-in to a more complementarian view of gender roles happens slowly over decades. During Roberts' lifetime, tension existed between Free Methodists who supported his egalitarian vision and those who supported the separate spheres argument of Coleman and Hogue. As Free Methodists who bought into Roberts' vision passed away or moved on to other denominations that would ordain women, the dominant rhetorical vision became one of the women ministering alongside men in distinctly female forms of ministry such as the Free Methodist Deaconess Order or ordination as a deacon, which for women carried a caveat that ordination as a deacon in no way was to be considered a step to ordination as an elder—which it was in the case of their male colleagues.

Scholars must begin to recognize the importance of rhetoric in shaping denominational history and culturally situating denominational history in the larger narrative of Progressive Era American history. Understanding how Free Methodism moved away from the ideals of its founder is complex, and no one variable influenced the move. *Silenced* employs multiple theoretical approaches to explain the denomination's evolving beliefs about women's roles in the home and ministry. In the proceeding chapters, *Silenced* outlines how the Free Methodist organizational narrative on women's right to preach and serve in church governance shaped the construction of gender roles within the movement and interacted with the broader cultural conversations of the Progressive Era surrounding gender. The story of Free Methodist women's struggle to become ordained and recognized as equal with their male peers is thus not simply a story about Free Methodism or evangelical religion, but one about the shifting social and cultural mores in nineteenth-century America. In this light, the fight for ordination should be read as a fundamentally feminist act. As Nancy Hardesty notes in *Women Called to Witness*, feminism, such as Free Methodist women espoused, was simply the belief in the fundamental equality of men and women and the right of each person, regardless of gender, to choose their own path.[75] Notably, the Wesleyan concept of free will and entire sanctification served as ways for supporters to justify their arguments theologically.

Chapter two tells the stories of three prominent Free Methodist female evangelists, Clara Wetherad, Ida Gage, and Anna Grant. The three women were prolific writers, published regular ministry reports in *The Free Methodist*, and voted in favor of women's ordination at the 1890 or 1894 General Conferences. Chapter three begins a chronological exploration of the Free Methodist Church's internal debates regarding women's role in the denomination. Chapter four explores the editorial tenure of Roberts as editor *of The Free Methodist* from 1886 to 1890. During his tenure as editor, Roberts used the publication to promote women's ordination and participation in church governance. In the months leading up to the 1890 General Conference, where women's ordination would be debated, Roberts was actively publishing articles by both men and women in favor of women's ordination. Chapter five begins at the 1890 General Conference, where Roberts' resolution supported eliminating barriers to ministry by gender, race, and class was defeated. Ultimately, the decision was sent back to annual conferences and would be taken up at the 1894 General Conference, which voted down women's ordination. Chapter six covers the years after the 1894 General Conference saw the denomination shifting away from the egalitarian beliefs of Roberts towards a more complementarian interpretation of gender that was favored by leaders such as Wilson Hogue, who was editor of *The Free Methodist* in the years immediately after the 1894 General Conference. During his tenure, the front page featured snippets from anti-suffrage advocates. The editorial section also featured articles idealizing women's role in the home and separate spheres of influence for men and women. In 1903 Hogue was replaced by Charles Ebey as editor. Under Ebey's leadership, the tone of *The Free Methodist* shifted and began to include pro-suffrage news articles regularly. *The Free Methodist* editor had tremendous influence over the tone of the publication. In 1907 J.T. Logan took over from Ebey, shifting the focus away from gender to topics about Christian living.[76] However, even Logan could not wholly escape gender debates. In the lead-up to the 1907 General Conference, when the denomination was considering establishing a deaconess order, women evangelists had an increased role in quarterly and annual conference governance. The topic again received considerable attention in *The Free Methodist*. Chapter seven explores this period of Free Methodist history, including the early years of the Free Methodist Deaconess Order and the 1911 General Conference decision to allow women to become ordained deacons.

The long-term impact of Free Methodist leaders voting down women's ordination as an elder in 1894 and the influence of gender essentialism and anti-suffrage sentiments in *The Free Methodist* cannot be overlooked. *Silenced*'s epilogue discusses this impact and ongoing concerns regarding the acceptance of ordained women and access to leadership roles within the Free Methodist church and, more broadly, evangelical culture.

NOTES

1. Karen Offen, "Defining Feminism: A Comparative Historical Approach," *Signs* 14, no.1 (1998): 151.

2. Brooke Freeborn, "Do Women Preachers Ever Wear Out?" *The Free Methodist*, May 30, 1911, 3.

3. Mark Chavez. *Ordaining Women: Culture and Conflict in Religious Organizations* (Cambridge, MA: Harvard University Press, 1997), 16–17.

4. Betty DeBerg, *Ungodly Women: Gender and the First Wave of American Fundamentalism* (Minneapolis, MN: Fortress Press, 1990), 44–58.

5. Charles DeWitt Talmadge, *The Wedding Ring: A Series of Discourses for Husbands and Wives and Those Contemplating Matrimony* (New York: Louis Klopsch, 1896), 88.

6. Lynn Webb, 1907 *General Conference Daily* (Chicago: Free Methodist Publishing House), and J.G. Terrill, ed., *General Conference Daily* (Greenville, IL: 1890).

7. Janette Hassey, *No Time for Silence* (Minneapolis, MN: Christians for Biblical Equality, 1986), 49–50.

8. Chavez, *Ordaining Women*, 77–78.

9. Christopher Evans, *Do Everything: A Biography of Frances Willard* (Oxford: Oxford University Press, 2022), 203.

10. Ibid., 204.

11. Carolyn De Swarte Gifford, *The Debate in the Methodist Episcopal Church over Laity Rights for Women* (New York: Garland Publishing, 1897), 11.

12. Ibid., 9.

13. Ibid.

14. Hassey, *No Time for Silence*, 50–51.

15. William Noll, "Women Clergy and Laity in the 19th Century Methodist Protestant Church," *Methodist History*, no. 1 (1977), 107–21.

16. Chaves, *Ordaining Women*, 246–47.

17. The original articles were entitled "New School Methodism," which critiqued current practices in the Methodist Episcopal Church. As a member of the Genesee Methodist Conference, Roberts faced political backlash from a group of conservative leaders called the "Regency Group." His first trial relating to his articles was at the 1857 Genesee Conference where he was convicted 52 to 43 of "unchristian and immoral conduct" for publishing "New School Methodism." His punishment was a vigorous reprimand from the bishop and a warning not to engage in similar actions in the future. His expulsion came in 1858 after George Estes republished "New School Methodism" and Roberts was accused of helping publish the tract which was a direct violation of his 1857 sentence. Roberts denounced the accusation that he was responsible for Estes' track but the conference still voted 54 to 33 to expel him from the Genesee Conference and the Methodist Episcopal Church. Howard Snyder, *Populist Saints: B.T. and Ellen Roberts and the First Free Methodist* (Grand Rapids, MI: Wm. B. Eerdmans Publishing Co., 2006), 402–5 and 426–45.

18. Ibid., 444–47.

19. Ibid., 505.

20. Leslie Ray Marston, *From Age to Age: A Living Witness: Free Methodism's First Century* (Indianapolis, IN: Light and Life Communications, 1960), 344.

21. Ibid., 505–38.

22. Snyder, *Populist Saints*, 520.

23. *Minutes of the Methodist Conferences, Vol. 1* (London: Mason, 1862), 713.

24. David S. Reynolds, *Mightier than the Sword* (New York: W.W. Norton & Company, 2011), 26.

25. Ibid., 27.

26. Donald Dayton, *Discovering an Evangelical Heritage* (Peabody, MA: Hendrickson Publishing, 1976), 15–24.

27. Benjamin Titus Roberts and Ellen Roberts were influenced by Phoebe Palmer, a Methodist lay leader whose writing and meetings encouraged others to follow Wesley's tenants of Christian perfection. She and Charles Finney are credited with promoting Christian perfection. Mark Noll, *Old Religion in a New World* (Grand Rapids, MI: Eerdmans Publishing Company, 2002), 96–100.

28. Donald Dayton, *Holiness Tracts Defending the Ministry of Women* (New York: Garland Publishing, Inc., 1985), viii.

29. Snyder, *Populist Saints*, 666.

30. Ibid.

31. Mark Chaves, *Ordaining Women: Culture and Conflict in Religious Organizations* (Cambridge, MA: Harvard University Press, 1997), 61–63.

32. B.T. Roberts, ed., *The Doctrines and Disciplines of The Free Methodist Church* (North Chili, NY: 1879), 84; B.T. Roberts, ed., *The Doctrines and Disciplines of The Free Methodist Church* (North Chili, NY: 1887), 69–71; Free Methodist Church, *The Doctrine and Disciplines of The Free Methodist Church* (Chicago: Free Methodist Publishing House, 1908), 97–98; & Free Methodist Church, *The Doctrine and Disciplines of The Free Methodist Church* (Chicago: Free Methodist Publishing House, 1912), 49.

33. R.L. Page, ed., "First Lady Elder in Free Methodism," *Pittsburgh Conference Herald* 35, no. 1, September 1974, 1.

34. Susan Marshall, *Splintered Sisterhood: Gender and Class in the Campaign against Women's Suffrage* (Madison: University of Wisconsin Press, 1997), 19.

35. Catherine Brekus, "Writing Religious Experience: Women's Authorship in Early America," *The Journal of Religion* 92, no. 4 (October 2012): 172.

36. Richard Hughes, *Christian America and the Kingdom of God* (Chicago: University of Illinois Press, 2009), 139.

37. Nancy Gale Isenberg, "Co-Equality of the Sexes: The Feminist Discourse of the Antebellum Women's Rights Movement in America" (PhD diss., University of Wisconsin Madison, 1990), 183.

38. Walter Fisher, *Human Communication as Narration: Toward a Philosophy of Reason, Value, and Action* (Columbia: South Carolina Press, 1987), 17.

39. Ibid, 75.

40. Both Free Methodist denominational histories published in the twentieth century were requested by denominational leadership. Leslie Marston's *From Age to Age: A Living Witness* was requested by the board of bishops to complete a record of denominational history from 1915 to 1960, beginning where Wilson Hogue's two-volume *History of the Free Methodist Church* left off. David McKenna's *A Future with a History: The Wesleyan Witness of the Free Methodist Church* picks up in 1960 and covers denominational history through 1995. Like Marston's book, McKenna's history was also requested by the board of bishops and funded by various Free Methodist patrons. The denominational publishing house Light and Life Press also published both from Leslie Marston, *Age to Age: A Living Witness* (Indianapolis, IN: Light and Life Press, 1960), 5–7, and David McKenna, *A Future with a History: The Wesleyan Witness of the Free Methodist Church* (Indianapolis, IN: Light and Life Press, 1995), vii–xvii.

41. Walter Fisher, "Narration, Reason and Community," in *Writing the Social Text: Poetic and Politics in Social Discourse*, ed. Richard Harvey Brown (New York: Aldine De Gruyter, 1992), 210.

42. Donald Bastian, "Does Theology Matter?" (Indianapolis, IN: Life and Life Communication), pamphlet.

43. Among the early Free Methodist biographies are Ellen Roberts, wife of the founder of Free Methodism B.T. Roberts; Mariet Hardy Freeland, one of the first

women evangelists; Adella Carpenter, who worked at Chesbrough Seminary and was active in promoting Free Methodist Missions; and Free Methodist Missionary to China Clara Leffingwell. Roberts was not an evangelist, choosing to stay in the background most of her life. Carpenter was a licensed evangelist, which is not emphasized in her book. Instead, the book briefly overviews her work at Chesbrough Seminary and with the Free Methodist Women's Missionary Society.

Freeland's biography does devote chapters to her call to ministry and desire to preach and the public resistance she faced in the Methodist Episcopal Church, but within the Free Methodist Church, she was much more devoted to education, working with the Wessington Springs Seminary, and did not choose to use her evangelist license for circuit preaching.

Clara Leffingwell's autobiography does feature a mention of her work as a starving evangelist who was assigned to a schoolhouse and given little financial support, but the biography was written by Free Methodist Bishop Walter Sellew, who was outspoken in his views that women could serve in missions, as part of the deaconess order, and as deacons but were not equipped for senior-level leadership positions or to become ordained elders. So, Leffingwell's biography should be read keeping the author's views in mind. Woman's Foreign Missionary Society, *Mariet Hardy Freeland: A Faithful Witness* (Chicago: Free Methodist Publishing House, 1913); Emma Hogue, *Adella P. Carpenter: In Memory of a Beautiful Life* (Winona Lake, IN: Light and Life Press, 1939); Adella Carpenter, *Ellen Roberts: Life and Writing* (Chicago: Free Methodist Publishing House, 1926); Walter Sellew, *Clara Leffingwell: A Missionary* (Chicago: Free Methodist Publishing House, 1907); Christy Mesaros-Winckles, *Data on Free Methodist Women Evangelists 1876–1920* (March 2022), distributed by Christy Mesaros-Winckles.

44. Bruce Hindmarsh, *The Evangelical Conversion Narrative: Spiritual Autobiography in Early England* (New York: University of Oxford Press, 2008), 321–27.

45. David Hempton, *Methodism and Politics in British Society, 1750–1850* (London: Hutchinson & Co., 1984), 29.

46. Hindmarsh, *The Evangelical Conversion Narrative*, 59.

47. Jeremy Young, "Transformation in the Tabernacle: Billy Sunday's Converts and Emotional Experience in the Progressive Era," *The Journal of the Gilded Age and Progressive Era* 14 (2015): 369.

48. Phyllis Mack, *Heart Religion in the British Enlightenment: Gender and Emotion in Early Methodism* (New York: Cambridge University Press, 2008), 133.

49. Ibid.

50. Ibid., 133–135.

51. Daniel Woods, "Spiritual Railroading? Trains as Metaphor and Reality in the Holiness and Pentecostal Movements, ca. 1880–ca. 1920," in *Holiness and Pentecostal Movements: Intertwined Pasts, Presents, and Futures*, ed. David Bundy, Geordan Hammond, and David Sang-Ehil Han (Union Park: The Pennsylvania State University Press, 2022), 130.

52. Sister Wetherald, "Fourth Sitting," *General Conference Daily*, October 13, 1890, 61.

53. Edith Gage Tingley, *Memoirs I*, unpublished manuscript, and "Circuit Court," *Flushing Observer*, July 9, 1891; "He Sold Buckwheat," *The Democrat*, July 4, 1891.

54. Charles Morris III, "Pink Herring and the Fourth Persona: J. Edger Hoover's Sex Crime Panic," *Quarterly Journal of Speech* 88, no. 2 (2002): 230.

55. Sarah Wells, *Out of the Dead House: Nineteenth-Century Women Physicians and the Writing of Medicine* (Madison: University of Wisconsin Press, 2001), 192.

56. Morris III, "Pink Herring," 230.

57. Morris notes that the act of passing is not a "beacon of safety" but, as Wells also notes in her research, is constraining and often ends up excluding the speaker. Ibid.

58. Dana Cloud, "The Null Persona: Race and the Rhetoric of Silence in the Uprising of '34," *Rhetoric & Public Affairs* 2, no. 2 (1999): 179.

59. Robin Patric Clair, *Organizing Silence: A World of Possibilities* (Albany: New York University Press, 1998), 74.

60. Barbara Tuchman, *Practicing History* (New York: Ballantine Books, 1981), 20.

61. Cathleen Cahill, Crystal Feimster, and Kimberly Hamlin, "Expanding the Suffrage Archive: Chronology, Region, Ideology, Biography, and Memory," *The Journal of the Gilded Age and Progressive Era* 19 (2020): 536.

62. One question I have been unable to answer is where Sarah Grant went to medical school. I discuss this more in chapter three.

63. Neil Lerner, "Archival Research as a Social Process," in *Working in the Archives: Practical Research Methods for Rhetoric and Composition*, ed. Alexis Ramsey, Wendy Sharer, Barbara L'Elplattenier, et al. (Carbondale: Southern University of Illinois Press, 2010), 203.

64. Elizabeth Birmingham, "'I See Dead People': Archive, Crypt, and an Argument for the Researcher's Sixth Sense," in *Beyond the Archives: Research as a Lived Process 2008*, ed. Gesa Kirsch and Liz Rohan (Carbondale: Southern Illinois University Press), 145.

65. Tuchman, *Practicing History*, 20.

66. Kathryn Kish Skylar, "Organized Womanhood: Archival Sources on Women and Professive Reform," *The Journal of American History* 75, no. 1 (1995): 176–183.

67. Susan Zaeske, "The 'Promiscuous Audience' Controversy and the Emergence of the Early Woman's Rights Movement," in *Walking and Talking Feminist Rhetorics*, ed. Linda Buchanan and Kathleen Turner (West Lafayette, IN: Parlor Press, 2010), 234–236.

68. Hassey, *No Time for Silence*, 137–138.

69. Robert Shuter, "The Cultures of Rhetoric," in *Rhetoric in Intercultural Contexts*, ed. Alberto Gonzalez and Dolores Tanno (Thousand Oaks, CA: Sage Publications, 2000), 12.

70. Lisa Ede, Cheryl Glenn, and Andrea Lunsford, "Border Crossings: Intersections of Rhetoric and Feminism," in *Walking and Talking Feminist Rhetorics,* eds. Linda Buchanan and Kathleen Ryan (West Lafayette, IN: Parlor Press, 2010), 55.

71. Earnest Bormann, "Fantasy and Rhetorical Vision: The Rhetorical Criticism of Social Reality," *Quarterly Journal of Speech* 68 (1982): 396–407.

72. Fisher, "Narration, Reason and Community," 214.

73. Chris Underation, "Seeding the Vision: Symbolic Convergence Theory and Aimee Simple McPherson," *Atlantic Journal of Communication* 20, no. 5 (Nov. 2012): 275.

74. Ibid., 276.

75. Nancy Hardesty, *Women Called to Witness: Evangelical Feminism in the Nineteenth Century* (Knoxville: University of Tennessee Press, 1999), 79–82.

76. Marston, *From Age to Age*, 489.

Chapter 2

Trailblazing Free Methodist
Women Evangelists

While there were at least fifty licensed female evangelists in the Free Methodist Church by 1890,[1] only four women had the power to vote in favor of their own ordination at the 1890 and 1894 General Conferences. In 1890 the East Michigan Conference sent Clara Wetherald,[2] a licensed evangelist, and friend of Benjamin Titus Roberts. At the 1890 General Conference, Roberts and Wetherald worked together to push for ordination. Both gave evening sermons during the conference on the topic, and with only four ministers invited to preach special sermons, Wetherald's inclusion seems an intentional rhetorical move by Roberts. Dr. Anna Grant was also sent to the 1890 General Conference by the Northern Indiana Conference. Like Wetherald, Grant was not the typical Progressive Era woman. She was a mother of ten children, a trained doctor, and a licensed evangelist. Both women voted in favor of ordination, but the decision was ultimately tabled until the 1894 General Conference so the annual conferences could vote on the matter.[3] Free Methodist women received slightly higher representation at the 1894 General Conference with four women elected as delegates, including Ida Gage, a successful evangelist from Ohio who spoke and voted in favor of women's ordination.

This chapter will focus on the lives of these three extraordinary female evangelists—Wetherald, Grant, and Gage. Grant's dual careers in medicine and ministry were highly unusual and only possible with the help of her spouse, John Grant, who regularly took primary childcare responsibilities. Like Grant, Wetherald and Gage were also mothers and had successful ministries, but their first marriages did not survive the stress of their careers. Wetherald left the Free Methodist Church in 1892, soon after her divorce from John, but Gage and Grant remained in the denomination, preaching until their deaths.[4] These women led multifaceted lives, constructing their public ethos in a manner that allowed them to gain social acceptance and success. To fully understand how these women came to be successful evangelists, drawing large crowds and leading revivals lasting weeks at a time, it is crucial to understand how their childhood, marriages, and family relationships helped construct their rhetorical identities.

As rhetorician Charles Morris III would say, they lived a life of double consciousness. They resisted the dominant Progressive Era narrative that women's God-ordained role was only in the home. They had to balance both secrecy and disclosure in their rhetoric, especially Gage and Wetherald who had complex family lives. Their double consciousness consisted of both a public and private persona. As preachers, they downplayed their domestic roles and focused on their capability as ministers.[5] They had to demonstrate to their male colleagues that they too could travel long distances to preach and have successful ministries starting churches. In a professional and symbolic sense, these women had to self-portray as men. While no diaries exist from these three women, they have left behind a rich history of personal letters, family stories, and professional correspondence in *The Free Methodist*. They stand out for their support of women's ministry at general conferences where men vastly outnumbered the women, boldly standing toe to toe with male counterparts who opposed their ministries. Gage and Wetherald demonstrated they could debate just as well, if not better, than many of their male colleagues. Therefore, it seems only right to give these three extraordinary women their own chapter, beginning with Wetherald's and Grant's lives and ministry, both of which chronologically preceded Gage's work in the Free Methodist Church. As their narratives are explored, emphasis will be placed on illustrating how they balanced a double consciousness. Yet while they did attempt to control their narratives, ultimately, their legacy was determined by others. Particularly in Gage's case, her daughter Edith's memoirs intentionally downplay aspects of her mother's ministry and the life she did not agree with. Because all three women did not leave diaries behind, it was left to their children and their colleagues to recount their accomplishments, as others chose to intentionally write out or emphasize certain parts of these women's lives. Fortunately, through census records, regional newspaper stories, family narratives, and other historical records, their stories have slowly been reconstructed for this chapter. There are still fragments of their lives that remain mysteries and might always remain that way, but as historian Barbara Tuchman points out, the key to good scholarship is knowing when to stop because the story is never really finished.[6]

CLARA WETHERALD: 1890 GENERAL
CONFERENCE DELEGATE AND EVANGELIST

Clara Miller Wetherald was born June 20, 1849, in Erie County, Pennsylvania.[7] Her parents, Esther and Harvey Miller, moved to Michigan when she was three and settled near Montrose, Michigan.[8] Wetherald had three other siblings, an older brother, Perry Miller, an older sister, Sarah Miller, and a younger brother, Frank Miller.[9] Wetherald credits her mother, Esther Miller, with influencing all four of her children to go into ministry. Wetherald's sister, Sarah (Miller) Smith, also became an evangelist.[10] Her older brother, Perry Miller, served as a pastor in several different denominations, including the Free Methodist Church. Perry Miller became an ordained Free Methodist elder in 1868.[11] Perry's involvement most likely influenced Wetherald and her first husband, John, to join the denomination in 1875. Wetherald's close relationships with her siblings and her mother demonstrate how influential family relationships were in forming her identity.

Esther and Harvey Miller's Influence on
Wetherald's Identity

Esther Miller was highly influential in her children's spiritual development, but her life was not without hurdles as Wetherald's father, Harvey Miller, did not share Esther's religious conviction. The couple had a difficult marriage. Harvey was a successful land speculator, buying and developing more than 100 acres in Michigan's Genesee and Saginaw counties, and in 1858 served as constable and highway commissioner in Montrose, Michigan (located in Genesee County). While he was a successful local leader and businessman, his marriage to Esther was not as successful. He abandoned Esther Miller and his children to move to Missouri in 1861 where he remarried.[12] His infidelities led Esther Miller to file for divorce in 1862.[13] Wetherald was thirteen when her parents divorced, and the divorce had a profound effect on her. Her brother Frank credits their parents' divorce as the primary motivation for her entering ministry, remembering Wetherald first felt a clear call to ministry by sixteen.[14] According to Frank, at sixteen she pleaded with God to save her "wicked father," and if he would save him, she would devote her life to his service. The divorce also left her as the sole caretaker for Esther.[15] Her oldest sister had married in 1861, a year before her parents' divorce,[16] and Wetherald's older brother, Perry, had enlisted as a drummer in a Michigan regiment during the Civil War.[17] Clara and her younger brother, Frank, were separated, with Frank being taken to Missouri to live with Harvey and Clara remaining in Michigan with Esther.[18]

Fig. 2.1. Clara Wetherald, undated photo. Courtesy of Norm Luppino from the Miller and Trask Manuscripts Kansas State Archive, Topeka, Kansas

While her siblings dispersed to different parts of the country, Wetherald stayed at her mother's side and witnessed her second marriage in 1862 to Wm. H. Smith.[19] Despite the hardships she faced, according to her children, Esther had a strong backbone and was not a woman to cross. Her strong example influenced Wetherald to develop a self-sufficient personality. In Esther's obituary, Wetherald shares an account illustrating her mother's strong-willed personality. According to Wetherald, when her mother was eighteen and living in Marbletown, New York, she was converted to Christianity. Her oldest child, Perry, was just six months old, and despite it being winter, Esther insisted the ice be broken so she could have her infant son immediately baptized. She was not fazed by protests from other members of the congregation saying it was too cold for Perry. As Esther aged, her religious zeal only increased.

Wetherald recounted her mother would always convince ministers to come out to the rural locations the family lived. Once, while living in Kansas with her second husband, they traveled one hundred and fifty miles to bring a minister to their area. The couple supported him financially so he could stay in the area.[20] Wetherald's deep connection with her mother not only shows how influential her example was on her, but Esther's obituary, written by Wetherald, is another indication of her dramatic, rhetorical style and ability to portray her mother's life in a socially acceptable manner. Esther's divorce is only briefly mentioned. The two-column obituary reads as a tribute to a spiritual woman whose life influenced scores of people. In describing her mother's final moments, Wetherald expounds:

> Notwithstanding her many years of useful, faithful service, as her life drew towards its close, she looked up and said, "Clara, my righteousness appears to me as 'filthy rags'; nothing can save me but the precious blood of Jesus." When dying, she called each child present by name and said "Pray," which we did, and then sang "Jesus Paid it All," "Happy Day," and finally "Safe in the Arms of Jesus," and while we sang the spirit passed away. . . . By her mother's request, her daughter Clara preached from the words, "She hath done what she could." Mark 14:8.[21]

By the time of her mother's death in 1903, Wetherald was an established preacher and an ordained Congregationalist minister. While all Wetherald's siblings were in ministry, it is significant that she was asked by her mother to preach her funeral sermon. Her mother's request shows Esther's respect for her daughter's accomplishments. In both of Esther Miller's marriages, at least from Wetherald's recollections, her mother was a robust and influential leader. Therefore, both Wetherald and her sister were brought up in a unique home environment. Through their mother's example, they saw that women could take leadership in the home and in the community. They also saw that women could be advocates for themselves. Their mother's divorce came at a time of increased divorce rates in the United States, but divorce still was relatively rare. By the end of the Civil War, divorce rates had risen sharply as, out of necessity, gender roles within the home had been redefined during the war. Women were left to financially care for the household as men served in the front. Upon the return of men after the Civil War, the changing family dynamics often led to permanent divides. However, divorce was still difficult to come by and in most northern states only allowed in cases of infidelity, bigamy, or desertion.[22]

Wetherald's Methodist Roots

Wetherald's mother, Esther, ensured her children were raised in the Methodist tradition, and all of Wetherald's siblings would eventually go into some form of ministry.[23] Thus, the Wesleyan emphasis on her conversion experience was central to her desire to be a pastor and was foundational to how she viewed her purpose as an evangelist. Wetherald's conversion narrative has been pieced together from her speeches at the 1890 Free Methodist General Conference, her obituary written by her brother Frank Miller, and the necrology report from the Michigan Congregationalist Conference in 1922 after her death.[24] In Wetherald's narrative, there is no precise date or turning point of

Fig. 2.2. (top row, left to right) Sarah Miller and Clara Miller (Wetherald); (bottom row, left to right) Frank Miller, Perry Miller, and Harvey Miller. Courtesy of Norm Luppino from the Miller and Trask Manuscripts Kansas State Archive, Topeka, Kansas

conversion. Instead, her testimony begins with her call to ministry. The fragmented nature of her narrative is just another illustration of the silencing of women's contributions as ministers. Few records of Wetherald's conversion and call to ministry exist in her voice. Instead, we see her brother Frank and the Congregationalist Church reconstructing her life and ministry and framing it from their perspectives. The Congregationalist necrology report of her conversion favors the Congregationalist Church's organizational narrative. In contrast, Frank Miller's account of Wetherald's ministry focuses on her impact as a national evangelist. He almost omits anything about her personal life, aside from her impact on his own life and her concern for her father's soul. The necrology report for the Michigan Congregationalist Conference credits the Congregationalists with Wetherald's conversion. According to this report, she

> [w]as converted before she was sixteen in the meetings conducted by the father of Rev. Chester C. Omans, one of the ministers of our Conference. She preached her first sermon in the pulpit of Mr. Oman's father. At the age of sixteen, she began the kind of ministry in which she has been so singly successful, namely, preaching as an evangelist and conducting revival meetings. In her first service, three adults were converted.[25]

The report does not allude to the personal motives behind Wetherald's 1865 call to ministry. It also claims she was connected to the Congregationalist Church since her conversion, when she was raised in the Methodist Episcopal Church, married a Methodist minister, and officially began preaching as a licensed evangelist in the Free Methodist Church.[26]

Despite pressing concerns about her father's salvation, she seems to have had little contact with him after the divorce. By 1861 her father lived in Missouri and died in 1866 from a gunshot wound. The death of Wetherald's father is tinged with a hint of sensation. According to numerous family accounts, in 1866 Harvey Miller was shot in the head by the Jesse James gang and died three months later from his wounds.[27] The family stories vary about what happened. Wetherald said he was shot because the gang hated all Yankees.[28] Frank, who was with his father when he was shot, said he was shot over a misunderstanding. According to Frank, their father was attempting to sell part of his Missouri farm. He had gone about town, telling the local merchants about the land sale in hopes of stirring up interest. The gang members, who were in town at the time, thought he was warning the community about them. So, later they rode out to the farm and shot Harvey while he offered them a drink of water.[29] While the story's facts are murky, there are too many independent family testimonials about the incident to doubt it occurred, even if it was not the Jesse James gang that shot him but another group of bandits.

Harvey's death came about four years after his divorce, around the time Clara felt her call to ministry. Though separated from her father, Frank recounts that Harvey still converted to Christianity before his death, largely due to Wetherald's efforts.[30]

The Only Path to Ministry Is through Marriage

Between the loss of her father and her zeal to find a way into ministry, Wetherald decided the best route to further her career was to marry a minister. Reflecting on her marriage during her sermon at the 1890 General Conference, she explained that while growing up she did not know of any woman preachers. She assumed the only way she could preach was if she

Fig. 2.3. (right to left clockwise) Frank Miller, Clara Miller (Wetherald), Esther Miller, Sarah Miller, and Perry Miller. Courtesy of Norm Luppino from the Miller and Trask Manuscripts Kansas State Archive, Topeka, Kansas

married a preacher. So, in 1866, at seventeen, she married John Wetherald, a Methodist Protestant minister.[31] Even at a young age, she developed a rhetorical identity not typical of the period. Wetherald resisted the accepted definition of nineteenth-century womanhood and in the words of rhetorical scholar Walter Fisher created her own "plot."[32] She was developing her persona as a preacher first and foremost. Even as a newlywed, she chose to self-identify not as the wife of John Wetherald but as a "missionary" when called to testify in court during a family land dispute.[33] Wetherald's marriage is one of many acts of rhetorical passing. She learned very early that to rhetorically pass meant marriage to a man devoted to the same profession as her. It was a necessary choice to gain access to a role still largely closed to women. Together, she and John formed a ministry partnership spanning twenty-five years.

Between 1866 and 1874, Clara and John Wetherald worked within the Michigan Methodist Protestant Church. John was an ordained elder and during their time in the denomination John was appointed to churches in Ingham, Macomb, Fremont, St. Clair, and Tuscola Counties in Michigan. However, in 1874 John requested the Michigan Annual Conference of the Methodist Protestant Church not appoint him to a circuit. It was around this time the couple transitioned to the Free Methodist Church.[34] By 1875, they had formed a friendship with Benjamin Titus Roberts' cousin, Septer Roberts, who was charged with bringing Free Methodism to Michigan. The Wetherald family, along with Clara's brother Perry Miller, were among the early pioneers of the denomination in the state.[35]

Wetherald's involvement in the Northern Michigan Conference's formation is shown through her participation in meetings in the Hadley Free Methodist Circuit. Rather than merely being a pastor's wife, she appears to have been a full member of the circuit leadership, serving as secretary at the early meetings. Additionally, throughout her time as a Free Methodist, she and John were often co-appointed as ministers.[36] While women had held evangelist licenses since 1874 in the Free Methodist Church, during this period only ordained men had their appointments recorded in conference minutes. From 1876 to 1880, no women are listed with a ministry appointment. It was not until 1881 that annual conference records show women serving as circuit preachers. A Miss Hagle, Miss Hoffman, Mrs. Warren, and Nancy Schantz were all appointed to circuits in the Canadian Free Methodist Annual Conference.[37] Since it was so unusual for women to have solo appointments,[38] the Wetheralds' appointments would appear in conference records as "Rev. John Wetherald and wife" or sometimes by the name "John and Clara Wetherald."[39] Often these appointments included several small churches where they were expected to preach. To cover their circuit the couple would split up and take on solo responsibility at various times. As illustrated in the October 10, 1888, ministry report Clara sent to *The Free Methodist*, Clara noted she had traveled alone to dedicate a new church in Royalton, Michigan. Upon her arrival, she found the congregation still needed to raise $369, and the building was not completed. "It was a great cross to me to go to dedicate a church, as I consider myself a poor hand to raise money."[40] Despite her qualms about her poor fundraising skills, on Saturday, September 29, 1888, she led the congregation in a time of prayer. As the congregation prayed for donations, people began screaming out the amounts of money they could give. "The Spirit of God fell with power upon the people. The sister who had subscribed five dollars was so blest that she stood up shouting glory; holding up both hands, she said, 'I'll sign five more for my husband; he's not here.'"[41] The fundraising was a success, and $400 was raised for the building.

The Royalton report suggests her magnetism. She turned a fundraising service into a mini-revival. Furthermore, the report illustrates her power to stir a congregation to action and proves she was successfully "passing" as a minister.[42] In her Free Methodist ministry she never self-identifies as a married woman; she is a preacher first and foremost.[43] When the ministry partnership of the Wetheralds is examined, it is quite evident Clara was the dynamic speaker, the one with a prophetic voice who used emotional fervor to draw in her audience. John was also a gifted preacher, but he remained in the background and allowed his wife to take center stage. In John Wetherald's 1902 obituary in *The Free Methodist*, a colleague from the East Michigan Conference reminded Free Methodists of John's ability to mentor many young men who wanted to be preachers. The same article also notes that wherever John and Clara traveled together to preach, massive revivals followed them. The more scandalous moments in John's life such as his infidelity and divorce in 1891[44] were not mentioned.[45] Yet, Clara did not depend on John's presence to pave the way. By 1885 she was being asked to travel independently and preach, for example, traveling to Indiana to preach at a Free Methodist church.[46] Her brother Frank also noted she traveled independently from coast to coast, conducting revival services.[47]

Wetherald's Role as a Mother

While motherhood remained largely in Wetherald's private life and not her public persona, it did play a role during her time in the Free Methodist Church. In 1868, her daughter Henrietta was born,[48] and in 1872, her daughter Mary Esther was born.[49] No one would have expected her to continue in ministry after her daughters' births. Nevertheless, Wetherald defied social norms and continued to minister and travel extensively. Based on family records, it appears Wetherald maintained a close relationship with her mother throughout her life and most likely relied on extended family to care for her daughters when she was unable to take them with her on her travels. This was not uncommon for nineteenth-century women evangelists. Many hired their children out as domestic servants to strangers, or left them with family, and would travel for months at a time without seeing their children at all.[50] The call of God was most important and required a willingness to sacrifice all in pursuit of ministry. Her role as a minister seems not to have been stunted by her relationship with her daughters. Her daughter Mary discusses her mother's impact on her faith in a testimonial sent to *The Free Methodist* in 1888.[51] Mary does not describe her mother in domestic terms, showing even in her relationship with her daughters Wetherald rhetorically passed as a minister.

In Mary's published testimony she shows her mother's gift as a revivalist:

> My folks were on the Hudson and Addison circuit, and I was permitted to be with them through a protracted meeting at Hudson. One evening mother had entreated sinners to turn to Christ. I arose and, with the Lord's help, asked them too, and the Lord Almighty blessed me. Of course, after sunshine the storm had to come, and the devil planned just right how to overthrow me, for it worked so. After church my father stepped up to me and said he was very sorry I had done as I had; I was too forward for one so young, and the Devil said: "Well, there; if a Christian thinks so what does the sinner think?" I went with it to mother, and she told me it was the enemy trying to overthrow me; that she knew and felt that I had the Spirit with me, but Satan suggested a great many things, and I gave up in despair and served the devil faithfully for three years the most of the time.[52]

Wetherald's encouragement led Mary to return to her faith in 1888, the same year her testimony was published in *The Free Methodist*. Mary's testimony also illustrates the marital roles John and Clara Wetherald played. Clara was the dominant one in the relationship. She was the one who was able not only to persuade large crowds at revivals to convert but also to persuade her daughter to return to the faith. Mary's testimony was published during a period Wetherald regularly wrote to *The Free Methodist* and was becoming a well-known Free Methodist evangelist. Others also wrote in during this time citing Clara's influence on their faith. For example, the March 2, 1887, *Free Methodist* includes testimony from Hiram Montgomery of Topeka, Kansas. Montgomery said, "Last fall Sister Wetherald was holding meetings here, and I went to hear her twice. I believe, and I was convinced I had no religion. . . . I was determined to break away from the grasp the devil had on me . . . and praise the Lord! I found it."[53] As with Mary's testimony, Montgomery's testimony illustrates the power Wetherald had to lead individuals to repentance and her continued rise to prominence within the denomination.

Further adding to her influence, was her relationship with Benjamin Titus Roberts. While only one letter survives from their correspondence, it reveals the close connection between the two. Writing to Roberts about a funeral she had conducted for the Lincoln family, missionaries to Africa, Wetherald describes the funeral setting:

> The house was thronged with people, and the deepest sympathy was manifest toward the bereaved friends, and great reward was shown for the deceased. By request, we stayed and preached in the evening. God came in power. Three arose for prayers, and we had a melting time. Eternity will reveal how much of a success Brother and Sister Lincoln's going to Africa has been. May God help us to "judge nothing before the time."[54]

Wetherald had been asked by Mrs. Lincoln's father to preach the sermon at their home in Smith's Creek, Michigan. Not only did Wetherald preach the funeral sermon for the couple, but she also called for an offering at the end of the funeral sermon for the Lincolns' child, who was reported to have been left in Africa with other missionaries. She raised $57 in donations for the child's return to the United States. Even at a funeral, she could not merely preach; she had to include a call to action in all her speeches. Wetherald's writings allude to additional correspondence with both Ellen and Benjamin Roberts.

In an 1892 health report to *The Free Methodist*, she thanks the Roberts for their letters and support during a period of intense mental and physical illness.[55] By 1887 she was moving in the highest circles of Free Methodist culture, gaining recognition as an evangelist and publicly supporting Roberts' quest for women's ordination. It is clear Roberts saw Wetherald as a strong advocate for women's ordination and an example of a successful woman in ministry.

However, despite her burgeoning ministry, after the 1890 General Conference, personal problems would cause her to disappear from the denominational history. Between 1888 and 1891, the Wetherald family resided in Clio, Michigan, on a farm they owned. After returning from the 1890 General Conference, problems in the Wetheralds' marriage came to a head. In February 25, 1891, the *Saginaw News* reported John Wetherald had gone to the city with the intent to sell grain but had fallen for the "gay ladies" of the city. When he returned to Clio, he confessed his actions at a Clio Free Methodist church prayer meeting. "The confession led to such a scandal in the neighborhood that his wife has asked the circuit court for a divorce," the paper noted.[56]

John's choices led to his expulsion from the Free Methodist Church. Clara, whose past experience with her own father's infidelity and her mother's initiative to not stand by and accept such behavior, chose to remove herself from the relationship. After John Wetherald's scandal, there are only two more references to Clara in *The Free Methodist*. The May 17, 1891, *Free Methodist* includes a ministry report from Holly and Germany, Michigan, where a recent

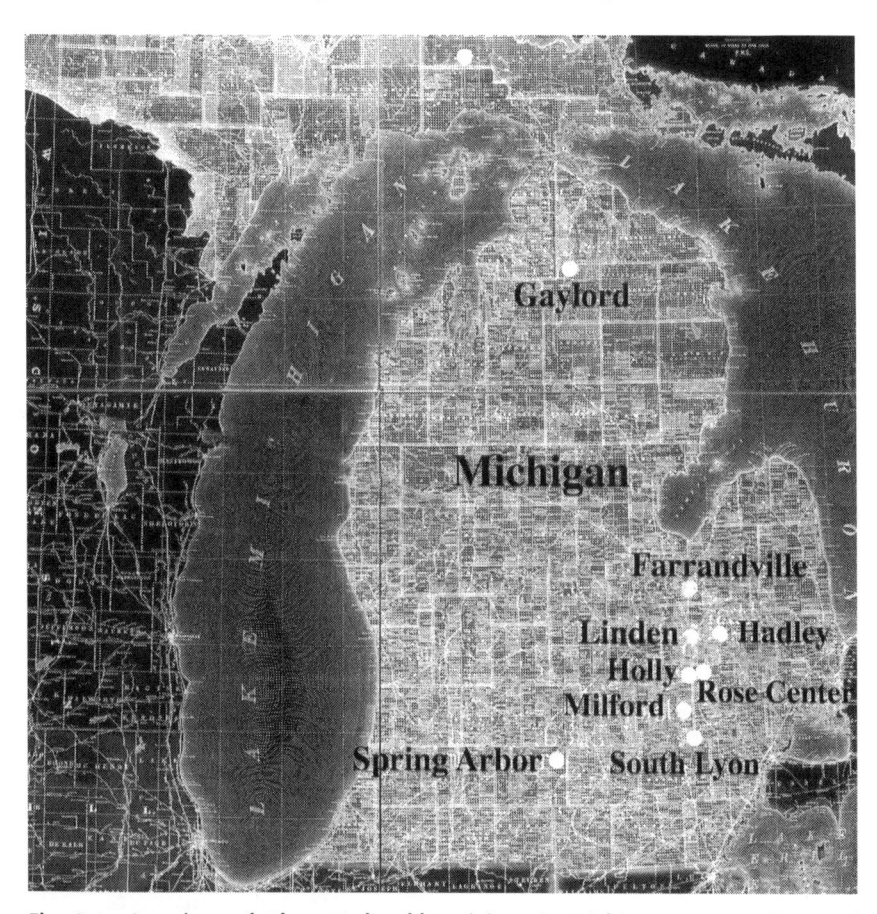

Fig. 2.4. Locations of Clara Wetherald's ministry in Michigan. Source: Library of Congress, Geography and Map Division; ministry illustrations by Alley Shaffer

revival campaign had concluded. The report credits Wetherald with preaching the Sunday morning service to a large and responsive crowd.[57] *The Free Methodist* article is significant because news of John's actions would have been well-known by this time, as well as the fact that Clara had filed for divorce.[58] Regarding church policy on divorce, the 1886 General Conference had ruled that no divorce except for adultery was biblically lawful and "any person guilty of a violation of this rule shall have no place among us."[59] As the innocent party, Wetherald could have remained within the denomination and continued to serve as an evangelist. The May 1891 revivals show denominational leadership did not hold her responsible for John's faults or condemn her for filing for divorce. Clara was still passing, but she also knew her desire to gain acceptance and become an elder in the Free Methodist Church was unlikely to be fulfilled.

After the 1891 revival, Wetherald disappears for nine months, reappearing on February 17, 1892, almost two years to the day after Wetherald's husband John was accused in the *Saginaw News* of falling for the "gay ladies" of the town.[60] In a letter to the editor of *The Free Methodist* addressed from Holly, Michigan, she explains her absence from the revival circuit, noting she has been ill:

> I have labored almost constantly for twenty-five years, never having been laid aside for six months at any one time, until two years ago this month, when I was taken with nervous convulsions, caused by over labor and sorrow. The doctor who attended me forbade my laboring at all until all the strange feelings should have entirely left my head. I was confined to my bed for some time, and have not been able to hold a protracted meeting of any length since, except the meeting held here one year ago, when I assisted what I could during a three month's siege. When the last trouble came upon me, my physical strength gave way and I was again prostrated. Since then I have been unable to labor.[61]

The letter confirms the Holly and Germany revival was her last public address. The location of that final revival is also significant in that she was living in Holly at the time of the revival and was not required to travel a long distance. As she notes, despite her participation in the "three month's siege," she was physically struggling. Wetherald also thanks numerous Free Methodists, including B.T. and Ellen Roberts, for their support during this difficult time. Her dynamic nature is quite visible when she addresses her ongoing trials and inability to continue in ministry despite her desire over the past two years to do so:

> I consented to dedicate the church at Scranton City, Iowa and took pains to rest and be ready so if possible I could continue meetings after the dedication, and go to the other places they desired me in that state; but the day before I was to take the train I was taken violently ill and could not leave my bed. Many times have my dear ones gathered around my bed to see me pass into eternity; but still I am spared. God, through all these months of affliction and sorrow and trial, has marvelously sustained me, I cannot tell you what a cross it has been to be obliged to retire from the field, where I have labored so long; but I am enabled still to whisper, "As God will; And in the hottest fire hold still."[62]

The line Wetherald quotes, "As God wills," is taken from an anonymous German poem, "God's Anvil,"[63] which addresses the pain and suffering Christians face in this world, while at the same time trusting that God knows best and is with them despite their suffering. After her update in *The Free Methodist*, Wetherald leaves the denomination. It is clear from her letter she believes her ministry is over. On February 29, 1892, the same month her health update was published in *The Free Methodist*, she married her second husband, LeGrand Buell, in Holly, Michigan. Her marriage to Buell marks the end of her time as a Free Methodist.[64]

She resumes her ministry and serves as a minister on trial at the Gaylord Congregational Church, a church that was willing to ordain women and ordained Wetherald in the fall of 1892.[65] Wetherald never directly addresses the exact reasons she leaves the Free Methodist Church, but several factors could have prompted the move. First, the ordination debates at the 1890 General Conference and the likelihood that women's ordination would be (and was) defeated again in 1894, and then the death of her friend B.T. Roberts in 1893.[66] Perhaps what is most rhetorically fascinating about Wetherald's time as a Free Methodist was her ability to craft her denominational identity. She was so well accepted in the denomination that despite her husband's infidelity, there is no indication she was forced out of the ministry because of her choice to divorce John. After her divorce, her personal life continued to fascinate the press. She made regional news again in 1892 when she was ordained by the regional Congregationalist Council in Gaylord, Michigan.[67] Then, when her second husband, Le Grand Buell, died in 1895, she made headlines in the Midwest and East Coast for preaching his funeral sermon and turning it into a passionate speech for the temperance cause.[68]

Wetherald's Marriage to Buell

Wetherald's brief second marriage is entirely written out of her narrative in the Congregationalist necrology report and *The Free Methodist* obituary written by her brother Frank. The Congregationalists report she was married to John when she was ordained in the Congregationalist Church, even though church records clearly have her ordained under the name Buell.[69] Her choice to marry Buell was an interesting one. Buell was a native of Holly, Michigan, the town Wetherald resided in as she recovered after divorcing John. Buell was also the one who submitted the Holly/Germany, Michigan, revival report in 1891[70] so the two clearly knew each other soon after her divorce. Unlike John, Buell was a songwriter, not a minister, for various publications. The son of A.W. Buell, a prominent businessman in Holly, Michigan, who also served in the Michigan House of Representatives, the Buell family was credited with bringing the Detroit and Milwaukee Railroad to the area.[71] What information exists about Wetherald's and Buell's relationship focuses on Buell's struggle with alcoholism, which began during his service in the Union Army during the Civil War. Upon his death in 1895, *The New York Times* and other newspapers speculated Wetherald only married Buell to reform him and his drinking habits.[72] Whatever the reason, the marriage was brief as Buell died in 1895, only three years into their marriage. *The Jackson Citizen Patriot* described a packed church at the funeral service, which Wetherald preached. According to the paper, Clara walked to the front of the crowd to preach a specific sermon Buell had asked her to share. It was not just a memorial; it was his public testimony.

> My dear friends, you will realize, as I do, that I am not standing here of my own individual strength, but with the help of God. Were it not for His gracious help, I would never be able to face this ordeal. But friends, there is a great responsibility to be performed, one from which, with God's help, I cannot shrink. I promised my dear husband, whose body lies here cold in death before you if I outlived him I would preach his funeral sermon and point out the lessons of his life. I am simply fulfilling that promise. How it pains me, you will never know.[73]

Clara concludes the sermon with a passionate plea for others to resist the temptations her husband had struggled with most of his life. "I implore you, I entreat you, young men, old men, yes, boys of the coming generation to suppress this traffic. Fathers, sons, brothers, I pray to you, save your dearest relatives from the awful curse. Put a stop to it, I beseech you to stop it."[74] After preaching, Wetherald collapsed into a chair, letting the local pastor conclude the service.[75] While the marriage was short-lived. Buell clearly had an impact. He was part of three of the most crucial years of her ministry. He saw her gain ordination, something she had wanted since being a Free Methodist evangelist, and his struggles with alcohol most likely fueled Wetherald's passion for temperance work.

After Buell's death, Wetherald eventually remarried a Congregationalist minister, Edward Harbridge, in 1899. The Harbridge marriage is noted in both denominational obituaries.[76] The couple shared appointments in numerous Congregationalist churches around Michigan. As a Congregationalist, she remained active in temperance and prohibition efforts. Her Congregationalist necrology report notes her involvement in the Woman's Christian Temperance Union (WCTU)[77] and *The Journal of the Michigan House of Representatives* also refers to a rally at the state capitol in February 1913 where Clara, the Holly, Michigan, WCTU president, and a group of seventy-five chapter members filed a petition asking the state government to vote in favor of prohibition. Wetherald remained active in ministry and reform efforts until her death in 1921.[78]

Fig. 2.5. Clara Wetherald Harbridge and her third husband, Edward Harbridge. Courtesy of Norm Luppino from the Miller and Trask Manuscripts Kansas State Archive, Topeka, Kansas

DR. SARAH ANNE GRANT: 1980 GENERAL CONFERENCE DELEGATE AND EVANGELIST

Like Wetherald, Sarah Anne Grant was among the earliest women evangelists in the denomination. She was born July 19, 1845, in Canton, Ohio, to Sarah and Henry Brown. Even though she was her mother's namesake, Sarah Anne spent most of her childhood without her mother, as the senior Sarah Brown died when her daughter was eight. After her death, Henry relocated the family to Columbia City, Indiana, where she grew up and met her husband, John.[79] The couple married on March 29, 1866, and over the course of their marriage had twelve children, ten of whom survived into adulthood.[80] Grant's son Vivian wrote several narratives about her life, ministry, and career as a nineteenth-century female physician, which help piece together Grant's story. According to Vivian, Grant was converted to Christianity by a Free Methodist minister and both she and John joined the denomination.[81] While Free Methodist ministry reports and family narratives provide details on her time as an evangelist, it has been difficult to trace where Grant received her medical training. Many nineteenth-century medical colleges existed only for a few years and records were not preserved in any coherent fashion.[82] Grant began her career in medicine and as a Free Methodist evangelist in northern Indiana, most likely in the late 1880s or early 1890s. According to Vivan Grant, in the late 1860s or early 1870s Sarah approached John, requesting to leave their family farm and become a trained medical doctor because God was calling her to that profession. The couple already had two children, but John was supportive, staying behind to care for the children and the farm.[83] His willingness to allow Sarah to travel alone, as well as his willingness to take on primary childcare responsibilities, was highly unusual for a period where all domestic matters were considered a woman's domain.[84]

Grant's Medical Career

The decades in which Sarah likely pursued her medical training were a difficult period for women seeking medical careers. They faced numerous professional hurdles. Many medical schools would not accept them as students, leading to the founding of the Female Medical College of Pennsylvania in 1850 so women could receive training and hands-on experience with patients.[85] It was also still common for women wishing to become physicians to complete private studies or have an apprenticeship with a trained doctor.[86] This is perhaps what Grant did, since her name hasn't been found in records of medical college graduates of the time.[87] Even with a medical degree women physicians faced continual hurdles for professional acceptance. Newspapers ridiculed them and patients often refused to go to them. It was not uncommon to see derisive jokes and stories, both fictional and credible, scorning female physicians. One fictional example is a July 17, 1877, story called "Cousin Nell: A Love Story" that appeared in numerous papers across the Midwest.[88] In it, Nell, a sweet young woman whose father is a physician, is put in charge of caring for his patients. The young woman assures her suitor she has no intention of being a woman doctor as she has "no desire to step out of a woman's true sphere." She just hopes to become a good nurse. Even news stories tended to feature the most sensational or humorous accounts of women doctors. On September 24, 1877, an *Indianapolis Journal* article included a story about a woman physician in Ann Arbor, Michigan, who "meant business."[89] According to the article she had a sign on her office door that read "Gone to my husband's funeral; back in thirty minutes." Another story published on June 21, 1884, noted a young woman became "demented from the excessive study of medicine."[90] In a similar vein *The Sullivan Democrat* published a report on March 17, 1885, about a female doctor in Vincennes, Indiana, whose character was questioned. According to the article, the female doctor traced the source of the gossip and called out the man responsible. The doctor supposedly bought a rawhide whip and upon meeting the man "applied her latest remedy, to the mortification of the patient."[91] The cartoonish nature in which women physicians are portrayed in these articles was typical, as women interested in medicine were perceived to be an oddity, willing to forsake their feminine nature in the pursuit of science.

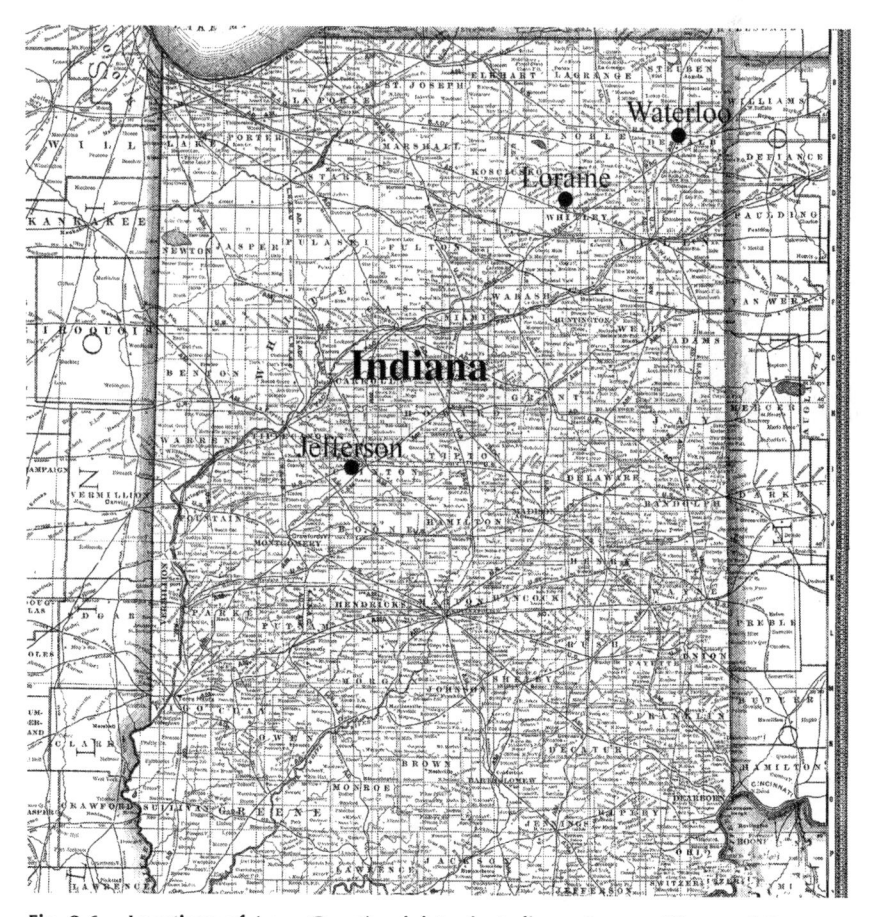

Fig. 2.6. Locations of Anna Grant's ministry in Indiana. Source: Library of Congress, Geography and Map Division; ministry illustrations by Alley Shaffer

Grant was not exempt from social ridicule. Vivan Grant recalled the local pharmacist would not fill prescriptions for Dr. Anne Grant. So she resorted to signing prescriptions as Dr. S.A. Grant, and raised her own herbs and medicine when she had time.[92] According to Vivian, early in her practice people were often rude to her and the patients who were willing to come to her practice were women and children. Like Wetherald's early career, Grant was forced to have dual personas. In her professional persona she performed as a man when necessary, and when that was not an option, she resorted to alternative means to help her patients. According to family stories, Grant had a regular route of towns she would visit and on one circuit was able to stop an unidentified illness that had been killing infants. After that incident, Grant did gain more respect in the community and her practice became a success. However, success came with an increased workload, and in her obituary, her son F. Grant noted she retired from medicine before retiring from ministry because "it was injuring her health to such an extent that she was obliged to retire."[93]

Grant's Evangelistic Career

While her careers as a doctor and evangelist do appear to overlap for a few years, ultimately it was her career as an evangelist that lasted until her death in 1916. Grant first appears as an evangelist in the Northern Indiana Conference records in 1890 and 1891 as a lay delegate at the annual conference.[94] During this time Grant writes ministry reports to *The Free Methodist* from Loraine, Jefferson, and Waterloo. Her enthusiastic reports emphasize spiritual sanctification, and normally describe protracted revival meetings she and other Free Methodists would help lead with an ordained Free Methodist elder. Her March 16, 1892, report from a Waterloo, Indiana, revival illustrates her vivid language choices and enthusiasm:

> The Lord is pouring out his Spirit and many are being saved. Young and old are under conviction, but especially the older class of people. Over twenty have been to the altar as seekers. Seven gray-headed men, nearly all over fifty years of age, and some over sixty have been saved. Some of them have been saved from the habit of strong drinks. They had a hard struggle but are now rejoicing in God. Praise his dear name![95]

Around 1894, the Grant family moved to Ida Grove, Iowa, but Grant continued assisting in revivals and camp meetings, only now in Iowa and not Indiana. The Grant family made a habit of moving into regions where the Free Methodist Church was just beginning ministry, helping establish Free Methodism in Iowa and Oklahoma. Grant traveled extensively while in Iowa as an August 21, 1894, report about a Free Methodist camp meeting near Lamars, Iowa, illustrates. Grant notes Free Methodists had only been active in Lamars for a few years but "our people are well indoctrinated and are solid, self-denying Christians. Let all who read this breathe a prayer that God may make us efficient workers for Christ."[96] While Grant continued to assist other Free Methodists in their ministries, she also planted churches herself. In a November 8, 1897, report in *The Free Methodist*, she recounts traveling alone to Aurelia, on the northwestern edge of Iowa, holding a week-long revival service at the invitation of some in the community.

However, not everyone in the community wanted the services, as it was a busy time of the year. So, Grant asked for a vote and the group overwhelmingly voted for the "holiness experience" to continue. She recounted that in a week, six individuals had experienced either the "blessing or the pardon of

Fig. 2.7. Locations of Anna Grant's ministry in Iowa. Source: Library of Congress, Geography and Map Division; ministry illustrations by Alley Shaffer

purity" as men repented from tobacco and women from their vanity. "I find hungry souls everywhere," she said. "They are as a sheep without a shepherd, and this doctrine and experience of holiness is as foreign as though it came from heaven lately." She concluded her report hopeful that she could organize a Free Methodist class in Aurelia before she left, and urged other Free Methodists to follow her to Aurelia, as she is the only one working in the area.[97]

In 1901 the Grant family moved again, this time to Granite, Oklahoma. Around this time there was a denominational push to get Free Methodists to move to the newly opened Oklahoma territory.[98] In 1901 the United States government opened thirteen thousand 160-acre tracts for settlement. The tracts had been located within the Kiowa Comanche Apache reservation and the Wichita Caddo Delaware reservation. Individuals wanting to settle in Oklahoma entered their names into a lottery for land in either the El Reno or Lawton districts. John's name appears in 1901 homestead applications for Seward, Oklahoma, but he appears not to have won a homestead in the lottery.[99] Instead, the family settled in Granite, Oklahoma, where they opened a hotel and remained active in Free Methodist evangelistic efforts. A 1903 *Free Methodist* article illustrates how well known within Free Methodist circles the Grant family was, as fellow Free Methodists would go out of their way to visit them in Granite. Referring to the family as "an itinerating family, and every move they make me think the evangelist work must follow them to help open a new Free Methodist work."[100] The conference report noted it was the third time district elders responded to the Grant family's request to hold revival services in Granite and were currently engaged in a two-week revival at the local Presbyterian Church. In both Iowa and Oklahoma, Grant is never listed in conference records as an evangelist, but it is clear she stayed active in ministry.

The next time she appears as a licensed evangelist is in the Southern California Conference in 1911. She and John had moved to California in 1911 because Sarah was in declining health, but instead of retiring and resting, she takes up active ministry, serving as the appointed pastor for the San Diego church from 1912 to 1913. In 1913 San Diego had a population of 60,000 and was a destination for men who wanted to visit the red-light districts of the city.[101] Grant was active in local reform efforts, working with women in the red-light districts. In a March 11, 1913, *Free Methodist* report, Grant recounts revival services held at her church, and the rugged nature of San Diego is apparent in her narrative. The four-week revival featured a guest evangelist and over "thirty-souls, directly or indirectly, found their way to sound conversion and entire sanctification." The revival faced opposition as Grant recalled:

A spiritual battle "waxed hot at times, reminding me of the inquisition in the dark ages, when men and women were put to death for their fidelity to God and nothing but the strong army of the law prevents us from receiving violence, as several nights a crowd would gather in front of the church. They sent a Catholic in with concealed weapons to kill the preacher, but he was hindered by one of God's little ones. He even followed him to the parsonage to antagonize him there, but two of their members were converted and one Catholic preacher was sanctified."[102]

During Grant's tenure with the San Diego church, revivals seemed to be the norm. Yet, despite the congregation's revival efforts it remained small. A 1912 *San Diego Sun* article reported the church had between five to six members and held four weekly services, averaging fifteen to twenty attendees at each service. Because the membership was so small, the*Sun* notes Grant's salary was also extremely small (although she commented to the paper that she never counted the offering). Her adult children are credited with supplementing her salary so she and John could get by.[103]

Grant's appointment as pastor of the San Diego church came during a time in Free Methodism when women were pursuing evangelists' licenses and serving in ministry. In 1910 there were three hundred and eighty-seven women licensed as evangelists, and by 1911 that number had increased to four hundred and three women.[104] After her appointment ended at the San Diego church, Grant remained in the area and retired around 1913 from active ministry. She died June 5, 1916. The Southern California Annual Conference report noted she was honored during their recognition of ministers who had passed away that year, an indication of the level of respect the denomination had for her work.

Yet, like Wetherald's obituary, her legacy was reshaped soon after her death. Her *Free Methodist* obit, written by her son F.F. Grant, noted, "With her many, many duties and labors as a physician and evangelist, her family was never neglected. The little ones in the home were always cared for with the touch of that mother's hand and the tender sympathy and love of a true mother."[105] In her reports, Grant never emphasized her role as a mother, only alluding to possible travels with children when she occasionally uses the pronoun "we."[106] F.F.'s insistence on referring to Grant's domestic role first and foremost was not something all her children did. In recounting memories of his mother, Grant's youngest son, Vivian, emphasizes his mother's medical career. He creates a picture of a capable independent woman whose medical career inspired him to pursue his own career in medicine.[107] F.F. Grant's emphasis on Grant's domestic life perhaps indicates an attempt to defend his mother's pursuits outside the home and illustrate she was able to be a mother, doctor, and preacher successfully.

IDA GAGE: 1894 GENERAL CONFERENCE
DELEGATE AND EVANGELIST

Unlike Wetherald, Ida Harley Gage did not experience conversion or a call to ministry until after she was married and already had two daughters. Much of Gage's life before marriage is unknown, but the memoirs of Gage's daughter, Edith Tingley, provide glimpses into her life pre-conversion. Ida Harley was born in Geauga County, Ohio, on March 30, 1861, to Sarah and A.F. Harley.[108] She married Charles Gage in Maple Valley, Michigan, on July 8, 1879. At the time of their marriage, Gage was eighteen, and Charles was twenty-seven.[109] As individuals, Ida and Charles were quite different. Edith notes that her father was illiterate, while Gage had worked as a schoolteacher before marrying Charles.[110] Ida was also the more dominant personality in the marriage, with Charles willingly following her from ministry appointment to ministry appointment and looking for work wherever the family lived.[111]

From early in their marriage, a pattern appeared to develop; the couple would travel as Charles tried to find work. In the first year of their marriage, the couple lived as boarders at a home in Kent County, Michigan.[112] Then, in 1881, two years into their marriage, Gage had her first child, Edith.[113] Her second daughter, Almeda, was born in 1884.[114] Edith was four years old when Gage converted to Christianity and felt called to ministry.[115] Edith's memoirs note her mother was converted at age twenty-three through the ministry of another woman preacher, Almeda McShay.[116] So, unlike Wetherald, who entered ministry having never met another woman minister, Gage saw women in ministry from conversion onward. After conversion, Gage quickly joined the Free Methodist Church and began preaching in Michigan. While Gage had a clear conversion experience, there are no records in either the denominational history or the family history mentioning a specific conversion experience for Charles. Gage's decision to go into ministry with two young daughters and a husband in tow is indicative of her personality. Her conversion narrative, which she shares at the 1894 General Conference, makes it clear she faced obstacles to pursuing full-time evangelistic work:

> Some years ago, God sent some blessed salvation planks floating down my way when bound by infidelity and atheism. I experienced religion and enjoyed it for fifteen days. God saw fit to lay his hand upon me. I lost my strength and there he saw fit to make me go forth and preach the gospel. When I arose from under the influence of the spirit and left the room, I settled it for time and eternity. I do not think the brethren intend to say things that hurt, but really my heart has been hurt to the core. My relatives all opposed me, I waded through my mother's opposition. I reached the place where it was this way or Kalamazoo. I was living in Michigan at this time.[117]

Fig. 2.8.   Ida Gage, undated photo. Courtesy of the Tingley family

More so than Wetherald or Grant, Gage's experience provides a complete conversion narrative. Salvation was symbolic of both spiritual freedom and freedom from the domestic sphere. Gage alludes to infidelity and atheism. It is unclear if she refers to Charles or herself as unfaithful early in their marriage and perhaps is referring to both as being atheists before conversion. Either way, Gage relies on the strong, emotional language often used by Methodist women evangelists to demonstrate the dramatic personal reform salvation brought. Wetherald, Gage, and Grant all use emotionalism in their writings. However, Wetherald's writings tended to emphasize results more than religious fervor, while Gage and Grant's writings are filled with examples of charismatic joy.

Gage's Evangelistic Work and Institution Building in Ohio

Gage's narrative implies she began her evangelistic career soon after conversion, preaching in remote parts of Michigan. Yet, in conference records, she first appears in Ohio, not Michigan. In 1891 Rev. W.B. Olmstead, an Ohio district elder, heard Gage preaching at a Michigan camp meeting and urged her to move to Ohio, where evangelists were desperately needed.[118] Gage agreed and moved the family to Bowling Green, Ohio, to begin a church plant. She was appointed to the Bowling Green area from 1892 to 1893 where she held Sunday afternoon meetings in a hall above Cooley's Grocery on North Main Street.[119] In 1893 Gage sent several ministry reports to *The Free Methodist* of her time in Bowling Green. Her first report from February 1, 1893, illustrates her concern for temperance:

> We came to this point from Conference, looking for victory, and we have had it. Bless God! The work is on the upgrade. We held seven weeks of meetings, when I first came, did more sowing than reaping. God has opened our way. We have a large hall on Main Street and our meetings are blessed with the presence of the King. Our quarterly meeting was a success. Brother Olmstead was helped of God. We felt it was good to be there. Two joined on probation and two by letter. Our watch-meeting was grand. The spirit of the meeting rose from the commencement until between eleven and twelve o'clock showers began to fall and the saints rejoiced "with exceeding great joy." God came down our souls to greet and glory crowned the mercy seat. Souls are seeking God here. Some have found and there are more to follow. Pilgrims remember us here. This is an important point. There are about 5,000 inhabitants, six churches, and twenty saloons. Death and formality reign. We meet with opposition but we are marching on, calling, "Come back! Come back! To the old paths." Pray for us.[120]

Gage's preaching style and personality shine through in this report. Using numerous exclamation points, dramatic language, and a detailed description of the sins still plaguing the community, she shows her tendency towards the theatrical, fiery writing and preaching that are often present in her writings and speeches. Still, despite her passion for evangelism, she was willing to go only so far in compromising her views. Her daughter Edith commented on this trait in her memoirs noting, "It was plain that mother 'ruled the roost,'" both at home and in her ministry.[121] Particularly in the area of fashion Gage held her own opinions on what modest attire meant. It was common for Free Methodists to embrace simple dress with no jewelry or adornments. According to Edith, Gage was fond of her lace collar and refused to stop wearing it. For many women evangelists in the holiness tradition, modest dress had doctrinal significance, as simple attire symbolized inward sanctification.[122] Gage's refusal to give up her lace collar is just another indication of her independent personality. Choices like this caused her to face criticism from parishioners who saw her mother's wardrobe choices as a sign she was not fully committed to renouncing worldly temptations.[123] Despite parishioners questioning her commitment to her faith, in a personal testimony published in the February 8, 1893, *Free Methodist*, her commitment is apparent.

> I am saved and cleansed by the blood of Christ. I know I am in the order of the Lord. God saves me now. I desire the prayers of all the pilgrims, especially those I have become attached to in Michigan. My coming to Ohio was of God. Bless his name! I have the victory now.[124]

Gage's ministry in Bowling Green was just the first of many appointments in the Ohio Conference. After 1893 she was appointed to Hume, Deshler, and Santa Fe, Ohio.[125] After three years in the Ohio Conference, she was gaining a reputation as an evangelist who could draw crowds and successfully start churches. While all ministers regularly switched circuits on a yearly or bi-yearly basis, the fact Gage was trusted to bring Free Methodism to new communities with no established church illustrates the conference's faith in her abilities.

During her appointment in Hume, Ohio, she also was elected a lay delegate to the 1894 Free Methodist General Conference. She was the only female delegate recorded to speak in defense of women in ministry at that conference, and while the 1894 General Conference did not grant Gage or other women evangelists the right to be ordained elders, the decision did not cause her to leave the denomination. In many ways, it accelerated her popularity and success. Before the 1894 General Conference, Gage was just beginning her career as an evangelist. Her speech at the 1894 General Conference and her ministry reports brought attention to Free Methodist efforts in Ohio. She became a long-serving evangelist in the conference until she moved back to Michigan in 1908. Like Wetherald and Grant, Gage never noted her domestic duties in any of her ministry reports, rhetorically maintaining a double consciousness as she was viewed publicly only as a minister equal to her male counterparts in both preaching and the physical demands of itinerant ministry.

By 1895 Gage was holding revivals that lasted for weeks at a time. An article in the February 6, 1895, issue of *The Free Methodist* commented that Gage's revivals in Hume, Ohio, were so successful that other ministers had to assist because the response was so great. As W.B. Olmstead noted, "Sister Gage is in the labors abundant, and has the confidence and esteem of the people."[126] A March 1895 ministry report from Gage also illustrates the success of the revivals:

> We have had a sweeping victory at Hume. . . . We began to preach a living Christ and invite the people into Beulah land. We down before God for the anointing were kind to all the men; and, glory to God! The wall began to melt. The meetings were deep and spiritual. Over twenty-five have been saved. . . . [W]e closed the meeting February 18 with two at the altar, expecting to begin again there in the near future. . . . We came directly to Jackson Center, and I am holding my fifteenth week of continued meetings. God gives me strength in soul and body. Our hall here is full and we have a very attentive congregation.[127]

Concluding her Hume report, she exclaims, "We are looking for victory here in the strength of Israel's God. We are seeking for the lost."[128] Her ability to preach for fifteen weeks straight, her excited recollections of the number of converts, and her continual use of both Old and New Testament imagery provide a glimpse into Gage as an evangelist. While her faith and commitment to ministry did not need revivals to sustain it, she excelled when she could preach in the moment, using a fiery style that relied on simple phrasing and emotional appeal to reach her audience. In 1895, after her appointment to Hume, Gage held a series of revivals and meetings in Cridersville, Ohio. Enough money was raised to construct a simple church building there in that same year.[129]

The Strain of Ministry on Gage's Marriage

For a denomination divided about women's physical and emotional ability to travel as evangelists, Gage proved the stereotype was a fallacy. While Gage's husband drove her to some of her services, the amount of traveling she did implies she often traveled alone, just as Wetherald and Grant did in their ministries. Gage alludes to this in her 1894 address at the General Conference when she refers to traveling alone and preaching in Michigan where "there

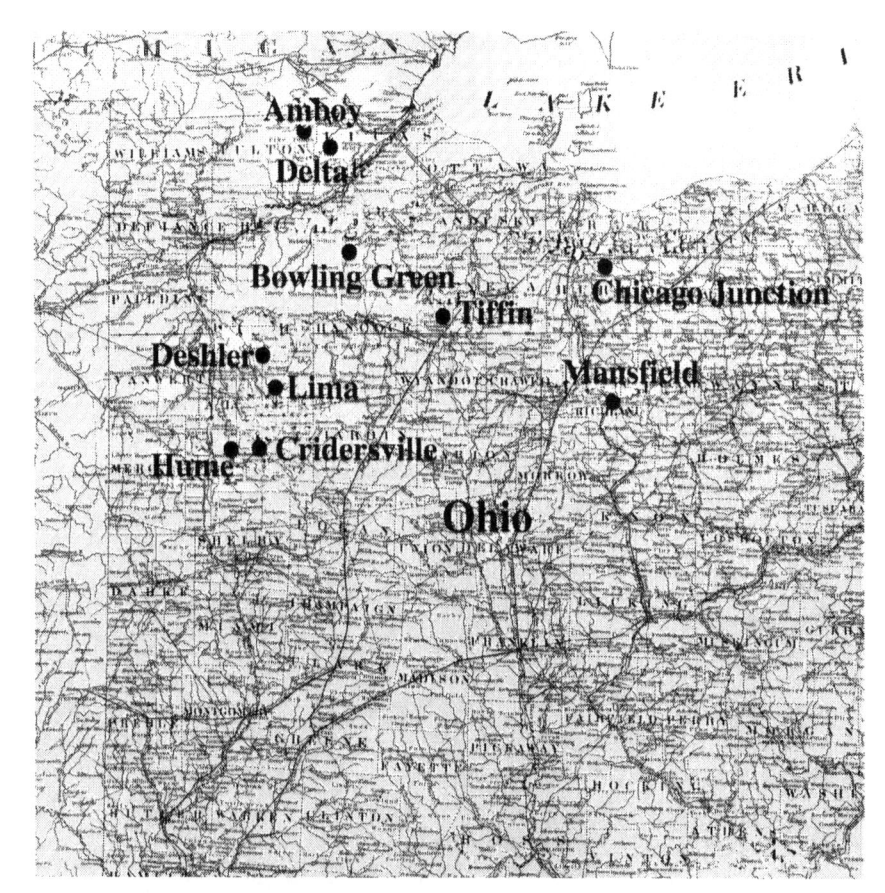

Fig. 2.9. Locations of Ida Gage's ministry in Ohio. Source: Library of Congress, Geography and Map Division; ministry illustrations by Alley Shaffer

were none of our people within twenty miles."[130] The job of an evangelist was both physically challenging and a strain on family relationships. The long hours on the road, transplanting their families every two years or less, and no guaranteed salary made the job extremely difficult. Some women had to teach during the day and hold church meetings on the nights and weekends to make enough money to live on.[131] Gage, Grant, and Wetherald all had the income of a spouse to supplement their salaries. Yet when evaluating their family life, only Sarah and John Grant's marriage held up under the strain of itinerant ministry.

At the beginning of their marriage, Charles Gage seemed supportive of his wife's ministry. Their daughter Edith remembers from the time the family moved to Bowling Green, Ohio, that Charles would drive Gage to her meetings, build the church building's fires, and keep the church clean.[132] However, while Edith never witnessed her parents' fighting,[133] there is evidence that Charles and Ida's marriage was struggling. When Edith was old enough to date, Gage adamantly refused to let her become involved with or engaged to her boyfriend Eugene Tingley until he converted to Christianity. As Edith recalled, at an annual camp meeting in Holland, Ohio, Gage approached her and told her if she wanted to correspond with Eugene, whom Edith was dating at the time, then have the letters sent directly to Edith. Gage told her daughter, "If you insist on writing to him, I want you to have your mail come to you in your own name, but I would rather see you laid in your grave than to see you marry that boy."[134] Gage's resistance to her daughter marrying an unbeliever very likely stemmed from her own experiences and troubled marriage.[135]

While this period in Gage's married life appears to have been difficult, none of this appears to have hindered her ministry. Gage was a master of maintaining a double consciousness—balancing both secrecy and disclosure to the denomination. Without her daughter's memoirs, the marital discord Gage hid from her congregations and the Ohio Free Methodist Conference could have remained hidden permanently. Gage did finally give permission for Edith to marry Eugene Tingley after he converted to Christianity, and the couple married in 1900. Shortly after her daughter's marriage, Gage was appointed to the Bennett Corner Circuit in the Cleveland, Ohio, area.[136] After returning from the Ohio Annual Conference, where she received her appointment, Gage packed up the family home in Toledo, Ohio, and moved to Fields Corners, Ohio. Charles was visiting family in Michigan at the time. When Charles returned to Toledo to find no wife and no home, he went back to Michigan, and the couple permanently separated.[137]

During this time, a woman separated from her husband would not have been viewed favorably within the Free Methodist Church. Yet, for eight years, Gage was able to hide or avoid discussing her separation. She was partly able to still pass as a married woman because Edith's husband, Eugene, felt called into ministry and the couple lived with Ida and assisted in her ministry.[138] The appearance of a happy home with mother, daughter, and son-in-law working together could have shielded many questions about Charles' whereabouts. Gage was an expert at silencing one part of her persona and emphasizing another,[139] using silence as a constructive means to maintain social respectability. During this time, Gage even transferred her evangelist's license to the Michigan Conference where she was appointed to Spring Arbor in 1908 and to Jaspar and Seneca in 1909.[140] She also served as the matron for the female students at Spring Arbor Seminary during this period. There is no indication that she faced censorship in Michigan or Ohio for her separation and in 1909 she left the Midwest, moving to Southern California with her daughter and son-in-law.

Family Secrets: "Forgetting" Gage's Contributions in California

It is here where family history diverges from denominational history. According to Edith's memoirs, her mother never again worked in active ministry after moving to California. Edith implies this was God's judgment because she had separated from Charles and officially divorced him once she was in California.[141] Even her grandson, Glenn Tingley, recounts in his autobiography that by the early 1900s, Gage was actively engaged in helping Glenn's mother raise her children and, at times, was the sole caretaker for him. Glenn Tingley would go on to be a successful evangelist in his own right and is credited as one of the first to realize the potential for radio evangelism.[142]

While the family narrative implies she stepped down from active ministry when she moved to California, the Southern California Annual Conference Minutes note this was not the case. She is listed in 1912 as an evangelist and then again in 1913, but this time under a new name: Ida Gage Wood. Between 1912 and 1913, Gage met a retired Methodist minister, Jesse Wood. Edith notes her mother primarily made money as a home care nurse during this period and met Wood through that job. Wood proposed, and with the help of Wood's son, who was a public defender in Los Angeles County, Gage divorced Charles and remarried.[143] Her marriage was against Edith's wishes and is perhaps the reason Tingley does not recount her mother's ministry during this time. What is interesting is, that after years of separation, Gage was willing to risk her ministry to divorce and remarry. Unlike Wetherald, there is no indication Charles was unfaithful so there would not have been a clear biblical precedent to support divorce.[144] Yet, the Free Methodist Church in Southern California does not seem to mind as is evidenced by her continuing to keep her evangelist license and the conference listing her under her new married name.[145] Gage's marriage to Wood was brief. Just a few years after her marriage, she was diagnosed with stomach cancer and died at age fifty-three on March 23, 1915. In recounting her mother's death, Edith says:

> About midnight, she lay there with her eyes closed and said, "Get me a paper and pencil." I didn't know where to get anything and thought she was delirious and didn't know what she was saying, so I said, "What do you want me to write?" Then she began on the 13th Chapter of 1 Corinthians, the Charity Chapter, and she preached a sermon.[146]

Edith interpreted her mother's final sermon as asking forgiveness for divorcing her father and marrying Wood, but when read in full, 1 Corinthians 13 is a chapter about loving others without envy, malice, or through self-serving means. Instead of asking forgiveness, perhaps Gage's final sermon summarized how she viewed her life and ministry. It was a message attempting to convey to her daughter how years of self-sacrifice and the physical and emotional strain of itinerant ministry had affected her. Perhaps, as well, as Edith noted, it was also asking for understanding from a daughter who disapproved of her decision to divorce and remarry. As Edith said in her memoir:

> I know she [Gage] was begging that we have charity for her. It was worrying about her. Soon after this, her breath began coming shorter and shorter. I ran and called for the rest of the folks, but before they got there, she was gone. . . . God bless her memory![147]

Interestingly, her divorce is not included in her *Free Methodist* obituary. The obituary, written by W.B. Olmstead, who had recruited her to move to the Ohio Conference, noted her conversion, her ministry in the Ohio Conference, service as a matron at Spring Arbor Seminary, and then her marriage in California to Wood. Her divorce was an open secret since the Southern California Conference had listed her under her new name, but unlike Grant and Wetherald, whose narratives began to be rewritten as soon as they died, Gage managed to maintain her dual persona posthumously.[148]

CONCLUSION

All three women in this chapter were remarkable for their ability to rhetorically navigate social and denominational norms by downplaying their domestic identities. This balancing act extended into their ability to maintain multiple roles simultaneously. Grant, Gage, and Wetherald all, at times, held revivals that lasted for days and weeks, leaving primary childcare responsibilities in the hands of family members. Their ministries also earned the respect of their colleagues as all three were often sent out to the frontiers of Free Methodism to help build new churches and make converts. In Gage's case, the Ohio Conference would often appoint her to a community without a Free Methodist society for a year or two to build a congregation, then move her to a new area of ministry to start more churches.[149] The success of their ministries proved to be a double-edged sword as both Wetherald and Gage ultimately divorced their spouses and continued their ministries on their own. Only Grant's marriage survived the stress of ministry and this could be in part because Grant often chose to conduct revivals on her own time, outside of official appointments by the Free Methodist Church. The flexibility of ministering at a time and location of her choosing perhaps helped keep her marriage intact as there seems to have been a concerted effort by both John and Anna Grant to balance and support their individual professional interests and family obligations.[150] Something that was not present in either Gage or Wetherald's marriages. Despite Gage's and Wetherald's domestic issues, there is little doubt all three women were exceptional, but by no means unique. By the time of Gage's death in 1916, there were four hundred and thirty-five licensed female evangelists serving in the Free Methodist Church. Where all three women stand out is in their appointments. Despite the hundreds of licensed women evangelists, by 1916 there were still less than half appointed to a circuit, making them stand out for their professional accomplishments and the respect they were held in by their male colleagues.[151]

NOTES

1. Christy Mesaros-Winckles, *Data on Free Methodist Women Evangelists 1876–1920* (March 2022), distributed by Christy Mesaros-Winckles.

2. Clara Wetherald had four different last names during her life. Her maiden name was Miller, her first marriage was to John Wetherald. Her second marriage to LeGrand Buell and her third marriage to Edward Harbridge. For the sake of consistency, she will only be referred to as Clara Wetherald in *Silenced* since it was her last name during her time as a Free Methodist.

3. Ida L. Gage, "Sixth Sitting—Monday Morning," *General Conference Daily*, October 17, 1894, 80–81; and Clara Wetherald, "Sixth Sitting," *General Conference Daily*, October 13,1890, 61.

4. Anna Grant continued to serve in the Free Methodist Church until her death in 1916. Ida Gage also served until her death in 1915. Vincent Burton, "Ida L. Wood," *The Free Methodist*, May 25, 1915; F.F. Grant, "Mrs. S. Anne Grant," *The Free Methodist*, July 11, 1916, 14; and Lucy Stone, ed., *The Woman's Column* 5, no. 46, November 12, 1892, 4.

5. Charles Morris III, "Pink Herring and the Fourth Persona: J. Edger Hoover's Sex Crimes Panic," *Quarterly Journal of Speech* 88, no. 2 (2002): 230.

6. Barbara Tuchman, *Practicing History* (New York: Ballantine Books, 1981), 20.

7. Michigan Congregational Conference, "Clara Harbridge Necrology Report," *Minutes of the Eighteenth Annual Meeting of the Michigan Congregational Conference* (Ann Arbor, Michigan, 1922), 50.

8. Ibid.

9. Gertrude Evangeline Miller, *Adam Miller Known Progenitor of the Branch of the Miller Family* (Miller Family Genealogy Collection, Evanston, IL, 1961), 42.

10. Family stories say Sarah Miller was an evangelist in the Free Methodist Church. However, I was not able to confirm this through annual conference minutes.

11. Dale Woods, *East Michigan's Great Adventure: A History of the East Michigan Conference of The Free Methodist Church 1884–1894* (Winona Lake, IN: Light and Life Press, 1984), 280.

12. The timing of Harvey Miller's second marriage and divorce from Esther implies that he remarried before the divorce was finalized. Franklin Ellis, *History of Genesee County Michigan* (Philadelphia, PA: Everts & Abbott, 1879), 444; Norm Luppino, "Harvey Miller Land Purchases" (Miller family history, unpublished manuscript); Norm Luppino (Miller family descendant) in discussion with author January 2012; *Miller Family Genealogy: Miller Family Bible* (owned by the Miller family)—the births of all of Harvey Miller's children, beginning with Perry Miller, are recorded in the front of the family Bible. Harvey's second marriage and birth of children begin in 1861 with Cirus Miller.

13. James Birney, *Divorce Petition: Esther A. Miller vs. Harvey Miller*, Saginaw County, Michigan, March 1862, accessed via personal email correspondence with Norm Luppino, April 5, 2012.

14. Frank Miller, "Rev. Clara L. Harbridge," *The Free Methodist*, December 13, 1921, 10–11.

15. Clara Harbridge, "Obituary: Esther Smith," 1903.

16. Gertrude Miller, *Adam Miller*, 43b.

17. A letter sent on behalf of her brother Perry Miller, asking for his military pension for his service in the Civil War. Clara Harbridge, "To the Commission on Pensions" (January 17, 1916), with Norm Luppino (Miller family descendant), in discussion with author, August 2011.

18. Frank Miller, personal letter testifying to his account of Harvey Miller's death. Notarized in Los Angeles County, California, n.d.

19. This was Clara's testimony about witnessing her mother's marriage to Wm. H. Smith in 1862. They only had a religious ceremony at a Methodist Episcopal Church in Maplegrove, Saginaw County, Michigan. Because Clara was present at the wedding, it suggests that she stayed with her mother until her marriage to John Wetherald in 1866. Genesee County, MI. *General Affidavit: Original Widow's Claim No. 670760*, April 21, 1891.

20. Clara Harbridge, "Esther Smith," 1903.

21. Ibid.

22. Alison Clarke-Stewart & Cornelia Brentano, "The Social Context of Divorce," in *Divorce Consequence and History* (New Haven, CT: Yale University Press, 2006), 3–4.

23. It's unclear if Wetherald was raised in the Methodist Episcopal Church or if Esther Miller raised the children in the Methodist Protestant Church, which was also where John and Clara Wetherald first served together as a married couple. Family stories are vague on this point. Clara's brother Perry Miller would serve with her in the Free Methodist Church and her brother Frank would become a superintendent in the Children's Evangelistic Union. According to family accounts, Clara's sister, Sarah Miller, was also an evangelist. Norm Luppino, email correspondence with author, February 19, 2011. Frank Miller, ed., *Evangel: Children's Evangelistic Union*, October, November, and December 1910, 1; and Woods, *East Michigan's Great Adventure*, 317 and 449.

24. Miller, "Rev. Clara L. Harbridge," 10–11; Michigan Congregational Conference, "Clara Harbridge Necrology Report," *Minutes of the Eighteenth Annual Meeting of the Michigan Congregational Conference* (Ann Arbor, MI: 1922), 51.

25. Ibid.

26. Early sources on Clara's Methodist roots include a letter from her sister, Sarah Miller, which references her father's and mother's life-long connection to the Methodist Church and the family attending a small Methodist church when she was a child and her mother helping lead the choir. Clara also discusses her early ministry in her 1890 General Conference speech, noting she married John because, at the time, she thought the only way a woman could be in ministry was through her husband. Sarah Miller, "Letter about father Harvey Miller," Family Correspondence to Mr. Geo W.G. Smith, Genesee County, Michigan (n.d.), Luppino, discussion, 2011; & Clara Wetherald, "Sixth Sitting," *General Conference Daily*, October 13, 1890, 61.

27. Ibid.

28. Harbridge, "Esther Smith," 1903.

29. Miller, personal letter testifying to his account of Harvey Miller's death.

30. Ibid.

31. "Genesee County Marriage Index to 1934," Ancestry.com, last modified March 21, 2012, http://www.rootsweb.ancestry.com/~mifgs/marriages/index.html.

32. As Fisher explains, existing institutions, such as the church denomination, provide the "plots" that help tell the stories. However, the people are full participants in making and sharing the messages they create as Wetherald did with her self-identification as a "missionary." Walter Fisher, *Human Communication as Narration: Toward a Philosophy of Reason, Value, and Action* (Columbia: South Carolina Press, 1987), 18.

33. *C. Perry Miller vs. I.S. Ferguson and the Estate of H. Miller deceased*, Stockbridge, Ingham County, Michigan, July 15, 1867, Luppino, discussion, 2012.

34. The Methodist Protestant Church was formed in 1830 by members of the Methodist Episcopal Church who felt Methodist clergy and particularly the bishop held too much power to the exclusion of laity. At the time Clara and John were members, women were not allowed to become ordained elders. However, in 1879 women within the Methodist Protestant Church formed a Woman's Foreign Missionary Society (WFMS); the formation of that organization led to increasing leadership roles for women. By 1894, the WFMS had four women elected as delegates to the Methodist Protestant Annual Conference; at that same conference the denomination officially approved ordination for women. Janette Hassey, *No Time for Silence: Evangelical Women in Public Ministry Around the Turn of the Century* (Minneapolis, MN: Christians for Biblical Equality, 1986), 50; Gertrude Miller, *Adam Miller*, 54, and Michigan Conference Archives of the United Methodist Church, "Minutes of the Michigan Annual Conference of the Protestant Methodist Church," 1866, 9. "Minutes of the Michigan Annual Conference of the Protestant Methodist Church," 1866, 9; "Minutes of the Michigan Annual Conference of the Protestant Methodist Church" (Published by Order of Conference, 1867), 11; "Minutes of the Michigan Annual Conference of the Protestant Methodist Church" (Published by Order of Conference, 1869), 18; "Minutes of the Michigan Annual Conference of the Protestant Methodist

Church" (St. Clair, MI: Published by Order of Conference, 1870), 19; "Minutes of the Michigan Annual Conference of the Protestant Methodist Church" (Pontiac, MI: Gazette Power Press Print, 1871), 21; "Minutes of the Michigan Annual Conference of the Protestant Methodist Church" (Flint, MI: Wolverine Citizen Steam Power Press Print, 1872), 24; Minutes of the Michigan Annual Conference of the Protestant Methodist Church" (Port Huron, MI: Times Printing and Publishing Company,1873), 30; "Minutes of the Michigan Annual Conference of the Protestant Methodist Church" (Hudson, MI: Jas. M. Scarritt Printing, 1874), 29; Rebecca McNitt, email to author, January 7, 2023.

35. Woods, *East Michigan's Great Adventure*, 317 and 446.

36. M. De Voist, "Hadley Society," in *History of the Eastern Michigan Conference of The Free Methodist Church* (Owosso, Michigan: Times Printing Company, 1925), 355; *Hadley Circuit Meeting Minutes* (1875–1890).

37. In 1881 the Canadian Conference appointed Miss Hagle to the Florence Circuit as an evangelist, Nancy Schantz to the Bell Haven Circuit, and Miss Hoffman and Mrs. Warren to the Severn Bridge Circuit. Mesaros-Winckles, 2022.

38. Ibid.

39. Woods, *East Michigan's Great Adventure*, 84, 285, and 316.

40. Clara Wetherald, "Dedication at Royalton, Michigan," *The Free Methodist*, October 10, 1888, 5.

41. Ibid.

42. Morris, "Pink Herring," 230; Sarah Wells, *Out of the Dead House: Nineteenth-Century Women Physicians and the Writing of Medicine* (Madison, WI: University of Wisconsin Press, 2001), 192.

43. None of Clara's speeches at the 1890 General Conference address her dual role as a wife/mother and preacher. Instead, she chooses to focus on topics such as women's "supposed" inferiority to men and the financial hardship women evangelist faced because they could not get rail discounts. In her speeches, even when defending her personal ministry, she makes no reference to John or her daughters, focusing instead on her success and calling. Sister Wetherald, "Fourth Sitting," *General Conference Daily*, October 13, 1890, 61, and J.G. Terrill, ed., "Tuesday Night at May Street Church," *General Conference Daily*, October 22, 1890, 190.

44. "State Items," *The Detroit Free Press*, July 5, 1891, 17.

45. J.F Calkins, "John Wetherald," *The Free Methodist*, January 13, 1903, 7.

46. "The City."

47. Miller, "Rev. Clara L. Harbridge," 10–11.

48. Ibid.

49. "Ellington, Michigan—Tuscola County," *United States Census Records*, July 11, 1870.

50. Elizabeth Elkin Grammar, *Some Wild Visions: Autobiographies by Female Itinerant Evangelists in 19th-Century America* (New York: Oxford University Press, 2003), 43–45.

51. Mary Wetherald, "Mary Wetherald, South Lyon, Mich.," *The Free Methodist*, April 1888, 6

52. Ibid.

53. Hiram Montgomery, "Experience," *The Free Methodist*, March 2, 1887, 7.

54. Clara Wetherald, "Letter to Benjamin Titus Roberts—Biographical Sketch of Brother and Sister Lincoln," October 4, 1888.

55. Clara Wetherald, "From Sister Wetherald," *The Free Methodist*, February 17, 1892, 5.

56. "Fell from Grace: Result of Clio Pastor's Visit to Saginaw," *Saginaw News*, February 25, 1891; "Clarissa Wetherald," *Genesee Democrat*, February 28, 1891.

57. Le Grand Buell, "Holly & Germany," *The Free Methodist*, May 27, 1891, 12.

58. Clara and John Wetherald's divorce was finalized in July 1891. "State Items," 17; "He Sold Buckwheat," *The Democrat*, July 4, 1891.

59. Arnold, *General Conference Daily*, 1.

60. "Fell from Grace."

61. Wetherald, "From Sister Wetherald," 5.

62. Ibid.

63. Walter Baker, "Sweet Are the Uses of Adversity," *The Religious Telescope*, July 14, 1909, 9.

64. Michigan Department of Community Health, Division of Vital Records and Health Statistics, "Michigan, Marriage Records, 1867–1952: 1892 Manistee–1892 Washtenaw" (Lansing, MI), Film, 47.

65. Clara is ordained at the Gaylord Congregationalist Church under the name Clara Buell and served from 1892 to 1893. Myrtle De La Mater, ed., "Role of Ministers," in *The First Hundred Years—Gaylord Congregational Church (United Church of Christ)*. Self-published June 1974.

66. Howard Snyder, *Populist Saints: B.T. and Ellen Roberts and the First Free Methodist* (Grand Rapids, MI: Wm. B. Eerdmans Publishing Co., 2006), 885.

67. Lucy Stone, ed., *The Woman's Column* 5, no. 46, November 12, 1892, 4.

68. "The Widow Will Preach," *The News and Observer*, June 25, 1895, 1; "She Preached the Sermon," *Daily Town Talk*, June 27, 1895, 1; "State Items," *The Detroit Free Press*, June 29, 1895, 4; "Buell's Widow Will Preach," *The Atlanta Constitution*, June 25, 1895, 3.

69. De La Mater, *First Hundred Years*, 14.

70. Buell, "Holly & Germany," 12.

71. Michigan Legislature, *Journal of the House of Representatives of the State of Michigan*, December 31, 1864, 54.

72. "To Preach at Her Husband's Funeral," *New York Times*, June 25, 1895, 10; "Widow Will Preach," 1; "She Preached the Sermon," 1; "State Items," 4.

73. "Buell's Widow Will Preach," 3.

74. Ibid.

75. Ibid.

76. Miller, "Rev. Clara L. Harbridge," 50–52.

77. Michigan Congregational Conference, "Clara Harbridge," 51.

78. Ibid.

79. F.F. Grant, "Mrs. S. Anne Grant," *The Free Methodist*, July 11, 1916, 14.

80. Ibid.

81. Vanecia Davis, 2021, *Vivan Verne Grant's Reflections on Sarah Anne Brown Grant*, interview by Christy Mesaros-Winckles.

82. Tracing Sarah Anne Grant's medical training has proved incredibly difficult. In the late nineteenth century, there were more colleges accepting women into medical programs but in reviewing what records exist I have not found her listed in any enrollment records for midwestern colleges. That does not mean she was not a trained doctor; as Burton Meyers notes in his history of medical education in Indiana, many early medical colleges lasted only a few years, and if they did survive were absorbed into other schools. Using family stories as a starting point, I estimate she was most likely training as a doctor in the 1870s or 1880s, at the latest the 1890s. During this time, she was in living in northern Indiana, and in that part of the country the closest college accepting women was The Fort Wayne College of Medicine, but women were not accepted there until 1892. The Fort Wayne College of Medicine eventually was absorbed into Taylor University and all records are housed in the archives at Taylor University's Zondervan Library. Reading early histories of Taylor, Fort Wayne College of Medicine is included but records about those years are extremely limited. Much of what is known about the college is from trustee minutes and reports, not enrollment records. William Ringenberg, *Taylor University: The First 150 Years* (Upland, IN: Taylor University Press, 1996), xi–xv; and Burton Meyers, *The History of Medical Education in Indiana* (Bloomington: Indiana University Press, 1956), 1–2 and 73–75.

83. Davis, discussion.

84. Nan Johnson, "Reigning in the Court of Silence: Women and Rhetorical Space in Postbellum America," in *Walking and Talking Feminist Rhetorics*, ed. Linda Buchanan & Kathleen Ryan (West Lafayette, IN: West Parlor Press, 2010), 279.

85. "The First Female Medical College: 'Will You Accept or Reject Them?' Doctor or Doctress?" Drexel University Legacy Center College of Medicine, Accessed August 2, 2021, https://doctordoctress.org.

86. Olivia Campbell, *Women in White Coates: How the First Female Doctors Changed the World of Medicine* (Park Row, Toronto: 2021), 25.

87. In searching for information on Sarah Grant's medical training, I also contacted Case Western, Drexel University (Women's Medical College of Pennsylvania archives), and the Indiana state archive but could not find information on her.

88. "Cousin Nell: A Love Story," *Connersville Examiner*, July 17, 1877, 1.

89. "Pennsylvania Girl," *The Indianapolis Journal*, June 21, 1884, 4.

90. Ibid.

91. "Female Doctor," *The Sullivan Democrat*, March 17, 1885, 2.

92. Davis, discussion.

93. Grant, "Mrs. S. Anne Grant," 14.

94. Mesaros-Winckles, 2022.

95. Annie S. Grant, "Waterloo Indiana March 2," *The Free Methodist*, March 14, 1892, 11.

96. Annie S. Grant, "West Iowa," *The Free Methodist*, August 21, 1894, 3.

97. Annie S. Grant, "Aurelia, Cherokee County, Iowa," *The Free Methodist*, November 30, 1897, 4.

98. C.E. Harroun Jr., "Oklahoma Letter," *The Free Methodist*, October 9, 1900, 12.

99. "El Reno Homesteader Filings," Oklahoma Historical Society, accessed May 12, 2022, https://www.okhistory.org/research/elreno; and "Homestead Applications," Oklahoma Historical Society, accessed May 12, 2022, https://www.okhistory.org/research/applications.

100. W.G. Hanmer, "Granite Oklahoma," *The Free Methodist*, March 24, 1903, 5.

101. W.H. Anderson, "San Diego," *The Free Methodist*, January 7, 1913, 5.

102. Anna S. Grant, "San Diego California," *The Free Methodist*, March 11, 1912, 12.

103. *San Diego Sun*, "San Diego, California," *The Free Methodist*, March 12, 1912, 5.

104. Mesaros-Winckles, *Data on Free Methodist Women*.

105. Grant, "Mrs. S. Anne Grant," 14.

106. Grant, "West Iowa," 3. In this report on a Free Methodist camp meeting Grant notes that "we traveled" perhaps implying the entire family went to the meeting.

107. Davis, discussion.

108. Burton Vincent, "Ida L. Wood," *The Free Methodist*, May 25, 1915, 14.

109. Montcalm County, "State of Michigan Marriage Records," 1879.

110. Edith Gage Tingley, *Memoirs I*, unpublished manuscript, 38.

111. Ibid.

112. Ibid., 2.

113. Ibid.

114. The date of birth for both of Gage's daughters is calculated from family records regarding how old both Henrietta and Edith were when Gage converted and went into ministry.

115. Ibid.

116. Vincent, "Ida L. Wood," 14.

117. Ida Gage, "Six Sitting," 81.

118. Ibid., 80–81; Tingley, *Memoirs I*, 2.

119. Ida Gage, "Bowling Green, Ohio," *The Free Methodist*, February 1, 1893, 4; "Local Items," *Wood County News*, October 21, 1892, 3.

120. Ibid.

121. Tingley, *Memoirs I*, 38.

122. Payne, "Pants Don't Make Preachers," 93.

123. Tingley, *Memoirs I*, 38.

124. Ida Gage, "Experience," *The Free Methodist*, February 8, 1893, 6.

125. S.K. Wheatlake, "Hume, Ohio," *The Free Methodist*, October 3, 1894, 4.

126. W.B. Olmstead, "Hume, Ohio," *The Free Methodist*, February 6, 1895, 5.

127. Ida Gage, "Hume, Ohio," *The Free Methodist*, March 6, 1895, 4.

128. O.L. Spencer, "Dedication at Cridersville Ohio," *The Free Methodist*, February 9, 1897, 5.

129. Ibid.

130. Gage, "Six Sitting," 81.

131. Tingley, *Memoirs I*, 2.

132. Ibid., 38.

133. Ibid., 30.

134. Mesaros-Winckles, *Data on Free Methodist Women Evangelists*; and Tingley, *Memoirs I*, 38.

135. Ibid.

136. Ibid.

137. Tingley, *Memoirs I*, 55.

138. Morris, "Pink Herring," 230.

139. Tingley, *Memoirs I*, 63 and 79.

140. Mesaros-Winckles, *Data on Free Methodist Women Evangelists*.

141. Tingley, *Memoirs I*, 79.

142. Glenn Tingley's Radio Revival show was a daily radio show (twice on Sundays) that began in Birmingham, Alabama, in 1929. It set a record for the oldest daily religious radio program in the United States with the same host. Judith Adams, *Against the Gates of Hell: The Story of Glenn V. Tingley* (Harrisburg, PA: Christian Publications, 1977), 89–94.

143. Tingley, *Memoirs I*, 82.

144. Arnold, "The Fourth Session," 1.

145. Mesaros-Winckles, *Data on Free Methodist Women Evangelists*.

146. Vincent, "Ida L. Wood," 14.

147. Tingley, *Memoirs I*, 82.

148. Precious McKenzie-Stearns, "Venturesome Women: Nineteenth-century British Women Travel Writers and Sport" (PhD diss., University of South Florida, 2007), 8–9.

149. Walter Sellew notes in his biography of Free Methodist missionary Clara Leffingwell that Leffingwell served as a Free Methodist evangelist before going to the mission field. No salary was guaranteed to an evangelist. It was not uncommon for an evangelist to have a second occupation, such as teaching, to provide a stable income. Walter Sellew, *Clara Leffingwell: A Missionary* (Chicago: The Free Methodist Publishing House, 1913), 34.

150. Davis, discussion.

151. Mesaros-Winckles, 2022. During the years Gage, Grant and Wetherald served in the Free Methodist Church, 1909 was the year with the highest number of women appointed to a circuit with one hundred and eleven serving. Besides 1909, 1912 saw one hundred appointed to circuits and 1914 saw one hundred and five Even in these years the number of women appointed did not come close to half of those holding a license. In 1909, there were four hundred and three licensed and one hundred and eleven appointed; in 1911, four hundred and three licensed and one hundred appointed; and in 1914, four hundred and fourteen licensed and one hundred and five appointed.

Chapter 3

"The Woman Question" in *The Free Methodist* 1886–1891

Women evangelists' struggle for acceptance was often illustrated in the pages of *The Free Methodist*. Beginning in 1886,[1] when the Free Methodist General Conference allowed women the right to be elected as delegates at annual and general conferences, there was a noticeable increase in articles on women's role within the denomination, and it remained a popular topic until women were granted the right to be ordained as deacons in 1911.[2] At which point, the discussion largely faded. As a periodical, *The Free Methodist* was somewhat unique as it regularly featured articles written by women. Often Progressive Era periodicals only featured women writers on the missions or Sunday School pages.[3] Yet in *The Free Methodist*, women's contributions included ministry reports by female evangelists, original editorials about Christian living, and contributions to the missions section. Particularly during Benjamin Titus Roberts' tenure as editor, articles discussing women's issues were given prominent attention, and numerous original articles by women were published.[4] Roberts was appointed editor of *The Free Methodist* at the 1886 General Conference, a move that surprised him but set the stage for women to have a more visible presence in denominational publications. He continued serving as *The Free Methodist*'s editor until 1890, when he stepped down, and Burton Jones was appointed editor.[5]

In addition to his time as an editor of *The Free Methodist*, Roberts also was editor and publisher of his independent religious periodical *The Earnest Christian*, which he founded in 1859.[6] *The Earnest Christian* consistently featured regular women contributors who wrote on religious life, spiritual growth, and conversion experiences. Roberts was a cunning editor who used both publications to draw attention to social and spiritual issues he felt were important. When examining the content of early Free Methodist print culture, women were actively writing, preaching, and pushing for social reform. However, not all subscribers enthusiastically embraced Roberts' promotion of suffrage and women's ordination. As editor, Roberts also gave critics space to express their views. *The Free Methodist* served an important social role within Free Methodism, providing a community source for denominational, national, and international news, as well as theological debates and ministry updates.

Fig. 3.1. Benjamin Titus Roberts. Source: Marston Memorial Historical Center

THE FREE METHODIST ECCLESIASTICAL STRUCTURE AND WOMEN'S INVOLVEMENT IN PUBLIC MINISTRY

During this period, opponents of women's ordination often applauded women's work as missionaries or Sunday School teachers but gave little recognition to women evangelists.[7] However, without the efforts of women evangelists, the denomination would not have grown as quickly as it did during its early years. Between 1874, when women were first allowed to become evangelists, and 1890 the denomination grew by 178 percent.[8] While there is a clear connection between denominational growth and adding the ministry category of evangelists, the number of women in that role remained relatively small until after 1894. In 1876, the first year women appeared in annual conference records as evangelists, there were only four, and all were in the Susquehanna Conference. It was not until 1880 that licensed women evangelists were also appointed to conference ministry circuits,[9] and the Canadian Conference led the way by appointing three women.[10] By 1890, when the denomination began debating women's ordination at its general conferences, there were forty-one female evangelists. Twelve of those women were appointed to circuits. The relatively small number of women serving in ministry perhaps contributed to the defeat of women's ordination at the 1890 and 1894 General Conferences. Many conferences still did not have any women serving as evangelists. Not until after the defeat of women's ordination in 1894 did the number of women serving as licensed evangelists significantly increase from forty-eight licensed evangelists in 1894 to 174 six years later in 1900.[11]

To fully understand why women evangelists and their advocates were pushing for ordination, it is essential to define the ecclesiastical structure of the Free Methodist Church. Before 1874, the *Free Methodist Book of Discipline* outlined three ministerial roles, all restricted to men. Free Methodist men could become a deacon, local preacher, or elder. Defined as a "traveling deacon" and elected by the annual conference, the deacon position was meant to support the work of conference elders. Deacons could baptize and assist elders in serving communion and were expected to fulfill the same role as a traveling preacher. The quarterly conference licensed local preachers and, once licensed, could be ordained a deacon. The roles of local preachers and deacons were also meant to serve as stepping-stones to the position of elder. A local preacher who was licensed for four years had the opportunity to become a deacon and then, after a deacon had been ordained for four years, had the opportunity to become an elder. *The Book of Discipline*'s use of masculine pronouns in defining these roles indicated that they were not available to women. The only ministerial category that included reference to both genders was the category of evangelists, noting that "any brother or sister" in good standing was eligible. Additionally, unlike the sections outlining the roles of local preachers and elders, the section of *The Book of Discipline* defining the role of evangelists included no guidelines for promotion to more senior leadership positions. Thus limiting women to a single category of public ministry, whereas their male colleagues had three options, including ordination as an elder, which also opened access to denominational governance roles such as serving as a district chairman or a general superintendent.[12]

FREE METHODIST WOMEN EVANGELISTS IN *THE FREE METHODIST*

The few active women evangelists in the denomination were regular contributors to Free Methodist print culture, with many regularly publishing ministry accounts. Each issue of *The Free Methodist* featured numerous original writings by women, showing their involvement at various levels.[13] As historian David Hempton notes, women not only played an important role in Methodist culture, but women also *shaped* Methodist culture. They were often the "silent majority" influencing denominational policy and practice.[14] Thus, it was no surprise that as an offshoot of Methodism, Free Methodism would also be heavily influenced by women's involvement. However, while women were vital to early Free Methodism's success, the rise of anti-suffragist rhetoric in the 1890s began to permeate into denominational discussions on women's ordination.[15] As the cult of domesticity rhetoric flourished in American periodicals, more men began writing into *The Free Methodist* in opposition to women's ordination or any role outside the home.[16] Advocates of ordination began to realize that the fight for gender equality would be a long, uphill battle. Because the religious periodicals of the nineteenth century served to inform and unite members of the denomination, Roberts' tenure as editor was crucial in giving women a voice and allowing their denominational service to become visible. A weekly publication, *The Free Methodist* had approximately 3,000 subscribers in 1886 before Roberts became editor.[17] However, while there were only 3,000 individual subscribers, it was not uncommon for the readership to be much higher due to single issues being passed among various families within communities.[18] In addition to *The Free Methodist*, the denomination began the special periodical *General Conference Daily* in 1886. This periodical was published once every four years, and subscribers of *The Free Methodist* were encouraged to subscribe, as it informed members about the daily sessions at General Conference. As a periodical, *General Conference Daily* provides an exceptional glimpse into the denominational debate on gender roles.

The 1890 edition featured the first two elected women delegates to the General Conference, Clara Wetherald of the East Michigan Conference and Anna Grant of the North Indiana Conference. Wetherald and Grant were regular contributors to *The Free Methodist* during the 1880s and 1890s, writing ministry reports and original articles supporting women in ministry. While no speeches by Grant were reported in the 1890 *General Conference Daily*, Wertherald's speeches were published and further illustrate the strong connection between women's involvement in denominational ministry and Roberts' desire to draw awareness of their contributions through publications. Chapter five will examine those speeches in detail.

THE FREE METHODIST AS AN ACTIVIST PLATFORM

The denomination's connection to social reform efforts was evident in how its publications embraced the moral and social issues of the time. The Free Methodist Church strongly supported the temperance cause, publishing a weekly temperance section in *The Free Methodist* for decades. While men wrote many of the original temperance articles in the 1886–1890 issues, Roberts also regularly published calls to support the Woman's Christian Temperance Union (WCTU),[19] and the work of WCTU president Frances Willard.[20] Temperance publications and activism served as one of the early avenues for women to pursue publication during the nineteenth century.[21] The fight against alcohol was close to many Free Methodist women's hearts. It was also regularly addressed in the mission section of *The Free Methodist,* where women shared news about religious and moral reform on the mission field. As Gere and Robbins note in their study of early twentieth-century women's mission magazines, these publications provided opportunities not available elsewhere: "Women reading and writing for the publications of foreign mission movement acquired a gendered agency through their use in print—one that influenced the larger enterprise in which they were participating."[22] For Free Methodist women, writing provided a sense of spiritual agency, giving them the power to voice their opinions and demand denominational support. Their writings illustrate the social tension in 1880s American culture between ministry and family. The women wanted to share their faith and engage in active ministry, but, at the same time, their writings show the tension between their duties at home and their duties in ministry. Fighting against the cult of domesticity, Free Methodist women had to illustrate their spiritual calling and commitment to family life. In an era where women's roles were still primarily confined to the domestic sphere,[23] this was no easy task.[24] Writing in *The Free Methodist* was one of the most accessible rhetorical tools at their disposal.[25]

Despite the importance of Progressive Era religious periodicals to women's empowerment, there remains much to explore, as most scholarly attention has focused on the writings of WCTU president Frances Willard or noted Methodist revivalist Phoebe Palmer and her periodical *A Guide to Holiness*.[26] However, periodicals from smaller denominations, such as The Free Methodist Church, provide an exciting glimpse into nineteenth-century women evangelists' day-to-day lives and need scholars' further attention.

When Roberts took over in 1886 as editor of *The Free Methodist*, tension over women's role in the denomination was already brewing. Yet, while women evangelists regularly published ministry reports, in the late 1880s, articles discussing women's role in the denomination were mostly written by men. Roberts often wrote and published articles during his early years as editor, supporting women's right to ordination. More conservative Free Methodists, such as W. Gould, a Free Methodist minister in the Susquehanna Conference in New York, countered his views. In July 1886, Gould wrote a series of articles opposing women's involvement in church governance. In his fourth article, "Ought Women to Govern in the Church?," Gould interpreted the creation account as proof that Eve was created as a helpmate for Adam. Thus, she was subject to his will before the fall. The story of Eve taking the forbidden fruit illustrates not that woman is more fallible than man but, as Gould noted, "The woman had specifically sinned, not for the sake of earthly enjoyment, but in high flown aspiring, as though she would emancipate herself from man, get before him and take him under her guardianship."[27]

Gould's arguments relied not only on biblical interpretation but also on his personal experience. Because of Eve's willful desire to subject man to her will, Gould explained that women have always been put under man's authority for their well-being. In 1872 the Susquehanna Conference granted an evangelist license to Jane Dunning, two years before the denomination officially approved licensing women as evangelists. Although permitted a license, the license Susquehanna granted Dunning was of lower status than a local preacher's license. Thus, according to the arguments of opponents such as Gould, the lower status restricted women from participating in church governance and maintained a delicate balance of gender roles in the denomination by allowing women to serve as they felt called but not in the same positions as their male counterparts.[28]

Roberts published a response to Gould's series a month later. His rebuttal drew heavily on English philosopher John Stuart Mills and his 1869 book *Subjection of Women*. As Roberts argued, anything but an egalitarian position allowed the enslavement of one gender to the other. Women's rights were greatly diminished because the law and religion relied on men to lead them. He stressed:

Let men be persuaded that women were created to live in "subjection" to them and be their servants, and it naturally follows that they will enact laws to secure this service for themselves on terms as favorable as possible. It took men a long time to find out that the Bible did not favor the enslavement of the colored race. But when they discovered that Paul laid down principles that would lose the bonds from every slave, then they saw that in his treatment of Onesimus he merely respected for the time the prejudices of the age. So in speaking of the "subjection" of women in those passages on which Brother Gould delights to dwell, the apostle simply paid a temporary deference to the prejudices of those but recently converted from heathenism; while, at the same time, he laid down principles which, if carried out, will emancipate from bondage every woman in Christendom, and allow her to take her place where she belongs side by side with man.[29]

Referencing his abolitionist roots, Roberts urged other Free Methodists to consider how gender equality fit within the denomination's firm stance on racial equality. The Free Methodist Church's social justice focus could not be selective. According to Roberts, social justice and equality require fighting for all oppressed groups' rights, regardless of gender or race. Looking at the Bible in a historical and cultural context would become one of Roberts' central tenets in his debates about gender equality.

The print debate between Roberts and Gould continued throughout 1886 and lead up to the 1886 Free Methodist General Conference, where *The General Conference Daily* noted that the "Woman Question" was fiercely debated. The 1886 General Conference granted licensed Free Methodist evangelists to be delegates for their conference. This was a relatively minor point of *The Free Methodist Book of Discipline*. However, since some licensed evangelists were women, a debate ensued. Gould had been elected a delegate from the Susquehanna Conference and used the position to continue his arguments against women in church governance. Other delegates weighed in, including A.F. Curry, another delegate from the Susquehanna Conference. Curry argued that the evangelist question was not about governance but was really about debating women's and men's equality. As Curry said:

Freedom is essential to responsibility. It's the same in heaven and earth. God has made men and women equal in this. I believe that in woman inheres [sic] the elements of supreme government. We ask her consent to be governed when she unites with the church in the same manner that we ask the consent of the man to be governed, and this recognizes her self-government. I well remember the struggle we had to get the recognition of the right of woman to preach, and this is a part of the same struggle; but that was gained. . . . We live in a time when the advance of thought is along this line. Women are being admitted to various occupations of men to the learned professions, etc. This amendment is being made at a time when they are filling chairs as professors in the seminaries of our land.[30]

Curry went on to note that the Congregationalist Church had recently ordained women as senior elders. For the Free Methodist Church to put off the debate on women's role in the denomination would be foolish. As Curry emphasized, "Hope was expressed that many other women might be called to the same work. But here comes up this opposition to this advanced movement. . . . The men who vote against this amendment will not dare to look a sensible woman in the face a few years from now."[31] Gould still vehemently opposed Curry's argument. Still, the delegates favoring the measure outnumbered those opposed and voted to give evangelists the right to serve as conference delegates. Only four delegates voted against it. Immediately following the vote, Gould promptly resigned from his position as a delegate in protest.[32]

IMPACT OF THE 1886 GENERAL CONFERENCE

The 1886 General Conference served as a trigger point for continued denominational discussion. As editor of *The Free Methodist*, Roberts was able to use the publication as a platform to promote women's equality, which is what he did from 1887 to 1890, giving women additional space in hopes of increasing

Fig. 3.2. The 1886 General Conference delegates. While women were not able to serve as lay delegates until the 1890 General Conference, this conference passed changes that paved the way for women's inclusion in church governance. Source: Marston Memorial Historical Center

support for their ministry by the 1890 General Conference. Under Roberts' leadership, *The Free Methodist* began to publish more ministry updates from women evangelists, such as Clara Wetherald. Accounts from women such as Wetherald provide a glimpse into these women's challenges as they pursued public ministry. For example, the October 10, 1888, *Free Methodist* included a report from Wetherald about a dedication she conducted at a church in Royalton, Michigan. Summarizing the dedication:

> I never saw such a scene before at a dedication. All seemed to feel the power of God and I had to go down into the congregation to get the names of the givers as I could not hear their names. It reminded me of the olden days when the glory of God filled the temple so that the priests could not minister at the altar.[33]

This experience occurred while Wetherald and her husband John were appointed to the South Lyon and Milford Circuit in Michigan. Throughout the 1870s and 1880s, Clara's joint appointments to ministry were more implicitly than explicitly recorded in conference records, John's name often was used, and Clara was referred to as "wife." However, when John and Clara were appointed to South Lyon, Michigan, they were both listed as appointed ministers—perhaps illustrating a growing acknowledgment of her work in the denomination.[34] In many of the ministry updates Wetherald sends to *The Free Methodist*, she and her husband traveled separately around the circuit to minister to the various churches. This joint appointment is further confirmed when Clara does not mention her husband in the Royalton article, implying that she traveled alone to perform the church dedication. Much of Wetherald's writing appears in the correspondences or testimony section of *The Free Methodist*. Though, during this period, Roberts also began to insert more original articles written by women on topics that reinforced the themes of equality he was fighting for within the denomination. Thus, *The Free Methodist* articles written by women served numerous purposes. Wetherald's articles illustrated the capability of women to serve in senior pastoral roles. Simultaneously, other women's writing drew attention to the larger question of gender roles always looming in the background during this time.

In the June 1, 1887, *Free Methodist*, a Mrs. Southworth from New York wrote an original article regarding women's submission entitled "Woman." Southworth ponders why only certain portions of Scripture are stressed by men and not others, particularly when that biblical passage seems to favor them over women:

> There seems to be a particular charm in the word *obey*, to some minds, when it refers to a wife. I heard a Christian young man say that he believed it was the duty of the wife to obey her husband, and if he ever got married, his wife would

have to *obey* him. Great importance is attached to some portions of Scripture while others just as important seem to be overlooked. Reference is often made to the wife being "the weaker vessel"; but why not give just as much importance to the other part of the verse "giving honor unto the wife." Please study the definition of honor and see where the wife will stand.[35]

Southworth emphasized that she was not speaking on the issue of women governing in the church but on the general welfare and status of women in society. Another article, published in the July 11, 1888, *Free Methodist*, featured a suffrage address by Mrs. A.G. Warne, who spoke on women's roles in both the church and the home. Towards the end of the speech, she notes biblical support for equality in ministry:

Upon examination of God's word, with what helps I could get, I find he has put no material difference between man and woman in dispensing his gifts. In Joel ii.28, we read a prophecy concerning the outpouring of the Spirit, and that women would prophesy or preach. To Mary was given the privilege of first preaching the resurrection. (John xx.17,18; Mark xxvi.7) That some women are called to this work I cannot doubt. That at proper times and in proper places they may do much good, I also believe.[36]

As the 1890 General Conference approached, more women writers filled the pages of *The Free Methodist*, urging conference delegates to vote in favor of women's ordination. Southworth's and Warne's articles illustrate that the issue of women's ordination was not just an issue of spiritual calling but also an issue of gender equality. A.F. Curry had also noted this at the 1886 General Conference, reminding his fellow Free Methodists that women were being admitted into roles as professors and other professional occupations. The question of equality in evangelical culture, and particularly in the Free Methodist Church, was fast becoming a question of whether Christians would follow larger social movements or remain entrenched in the past. Roberts and Free Methodist women realized they had an uphill battle to achieve ordination, let alone complete social equality. In the months leading up to the 1890 General Conference, Roberts began publishing articles favoring ordination. In the May 1890 issue, Wetherald wrote a two-page defense of her ministry and a woman's right to be part of the denomination's governing body entitled "Shall Women be Ordained?" She thought "the great difficulty is that man is not satisfied to be the head as God has designed him, but he seems to aspire to being neck and arms, and in fact the whole body, and monopolize the whole seat of authority."[37]

As Roberts did in his 1886 rebuttal to Gould, Wetherald invokes comparisons to racial equality. Subtly reminding fellow Free Methodists of their passion for social justice, she compares the plight of women restricted from full participation in denominational governance to the plight of the slave oppressed because of the color of their skin. Emphasizing the dual forms of oppression, she concludes with a quote from black suffragist Sojourner Truth: "In speaking on women's rights, she [Truth] said, 'Men need not make such a fuss about women having anything to do in the church, for it was God and a woman that produced for the world a Savior and man had nothing to do with it."[38]

The October 1, 8, and 22, 1890, editions of *The Free Methodist* also included articles from supportive male colleagues and women evangelists, urging fellow Free Methodists to vote in women's favor. W.B.M. Colt, a Free Methodist elder, published a historical defense of women in Christian leadership positions from the first-century church in the October 1 and 8 editions entitled "Why not?"[39] Colt had been a vocal supporter of women evangelists at the 1886 General Conference. Roberts' daughter-in-law Emma Sellew Roberts, who was serving as co-principal at Chili Seminary along with Roberts' son Benson, followed Colt's article in the October 22 edition with an article entitled "Help it On."[40] Her article shows that other denominations, such as the Congregationalist Church, already allowed women to be ordained. However, she notes that within the Free Methodist denomination, prejudices still ran high:

> Many women among us are filling the pulpits with acceptability, many more are living in less favorable quarters have a message on their soul, to proclaim which no opportunity is given. They still cling to the church whose principles they espouse. Every Sunday they are found at church listening, perhaps to an attempt at preaching, made by one not especially gifted or blessed. They attend camp meetings, speak words of power in exhortation and testimony, but their call to ministry and preaching ability are entirely ignored.[41]

Sellew Roberts' and Colt's articles were published in October as the General Conference was occurring and served as a conclusion to Roberts' months-long rhetorical offensive for women's ordination. Yet, despite the desire of Roberts and other supporters of gender equality, the denomination was a democracy, not an autocracy. Even Roberts, the founder of the denomination, did not have the power to demand ordination unilaterally, and because the 1890 Conference only had two voting women delegates (Wetherald, from the Eastern Michigan Conference, and Anna Grant, from the North Indiana Conference), the likelihood of a decision passing favoring women was slight. Additionally, Roberts was the only general superintendent wholeheartedly in favor of ordination. In 1890 the other superintendents, Edward Hart and George Coleman, were divided on the issue. Hart voted for ordination, while Coleman voted against it. After Roberts died in 1893, Hart switched his vote from "yea" and "nay" in 1894.[42] Even more so than in 1886, the 1890 debates on women's role in the denomination were long, intense, and sometimes vicious.[43]

Roberts would not live to see the debate on women's ordination conclude in 1894. He had suffered from poor health for several years and urged other Free Methodists to step up and replace him in crucial roles. In the February 1890 *Free Methodist*, he had published a rare plea for grace in his role of editor, noting "the editor is in great danger of giving out utterly from overwork,"[44] as he had numerous letters to respond to. Nevertheless, despite his exhaustion, he did not slow down after the 1890 General Conference. Instead, in 1891 he wrote and published *Ordaining Women*, his treatise on complete gender equality in the church, the home, and society.[45] His book was not universally accepted in the denomination and was even banned from certain annual conferences.[46] His fellow general superintendent, George Coleman, also published a lengthy and critical review of the book in *The Free Methodist* as a special supplement.[47] Roberts responded in his own special supplement to *The Free Methodist*, his response serving as the last substantial contribution he made to a denominational publication. Nevertheless, even without Roberts' presence at the 1894 General Conference and beyond, the debates continued as Free Methodists wrestled with women's role within the denomination.[48]

NOTES

1. An earlier version of this chapter was published in Christy Mesaros-Winckles, "Hear Our Plea: Voices of Early Free Methodist Women in Denominational Print Culture," *Westminster Papers in Communication and Culture* 8 no. 3 (2011): 25–46.

2. Walter Sellew, *Why Not? A Plea for the Ordination of Those Women Whom God Calls to Preach His Gospel*, 2nd edition (Chicago: Free Methodist Publishing House, 1914), 3.

3. Mary Kupiec Cayton, "Part 2: Harriet Newell's Story: Women, the Evangelical Press, and the Foreign Mission Movement," in *A History of the Book in America, vol. 2*, ed. Robert Gross and Mary Kelly (Chapel Hill: University of North Carolina Press, 2010), 408–15.

4. Howard Snyder, *Populist Saints: B.T. and Ellen Roberts and the First Free Methodist* (Grand Rapids, MI: Wm. B. Eerdmans Publishing Co., 2006), 835.

5. Burton Jones was the editor of *The Free Methodist* after Roberts retired in 1890. Richard Blews, *Master Workman: Biographies of Late Bishops of the Free Methodist Church During Her First Century 1860–1890* (Winona Lake, IN: Light and Life Press, 1960), 99.

6. Ibid., 512.

7. George M'Culloch, "Ordaining Women," *The Free Methodist*, September 12, 1894, 2–3; C.M. Damon, "The Woman Question," *The Free Methodist*, September

19, 1894; William Gould, "Ought Women to Govern in the Church? No. 4," *The Free Methodist*, July 7, 1886.

8. Blews, *Master Workman*, 671.

9. In examining annual conference minutes from the 1870s onward, women did not appear as licensed evangelists in annual conference minutes until 1880 in the Susquehanna Conference. Christy Mesaros-Winckles. *Data on Free Methodist Women Evangelists 1876–1920*, March 2022, distributed by Christy Mesaros-Winckles.

10. A Miss Hagle was appointed to the Florence Circuit, and Miss Hoffman and Mrs. Warren to the Severn Bridge Circuit in the Canadian Conferences. Susquehanna Conference in New York was the only other conference in 1881 with licensed women evangelists. It would not be until 1883 that two other conferences would include women evangelists in their rolls—Michigan, with Clara Wetherald listed, and Pittsburgh, with Marietta Barnhart. Mesaros-Winckes, *Data on Free Methodist Women Evangelists 1876–1920*.

11. Sellew, *Why Not*, 3.

12. Free Methodist Church, *The Doctrine and Disciplines of The Free Methodist Church* (Rochester, NY: General Conference, 1866), 51–53 and 80–81; Free Methodist Church, *The Doctrine and Disciplines of The Free Methodist Church*,(Rochester, NY: B.T. Roberts, 1875), 84–85.

13. In reviewing *The Free Methodist* from 1880 through 1920, there were contributions from women in the Experience, Editorial, and Ministry Updates sections of every issue. This is a topic that should be explored further to categorize the types of articles and contributions of women writers in Free Methodist print culture.

14. David Hempton, *Methodism: Empire of the Spirit* (New Haven, CT: Yale University Press, 2006), 149.

15. Susan Marshall, *Splintered Sisterhood: Gender and Class in the Campaign against Woman Suffrage* (Madison, Wisconsin: University of Wisconsin Press, 1997), 125–130.

16. A.D. Yocum, "The Crown of Womanhood," *The Free Methodist*, June 17, 1891, 1; George M'Culloch, "Ordaining Women," *The Free Methodist*, September 12, 1894, 2–3; Wilson Hogg, "Educate Women for Higher Womanhood," *The Free Methodist*, August 22, 1899, 1; and R.B.S., "Women in the Pulpit," *The Free Methodist*, April 24, 1900, 2.

17. Synder, *Populist Saints*, 672.

18. Richard Altick, *The English Common Reader: A Social History of the Mass Reading Public 1800–1900* (Columbus, OH: Ohio State University Press, 1998), 323.

19. M. Taylor, "Woman's Christian Temperance Union," *The Free Methodist*, July 27, 1887, 3.

20. C.F. Hawley, "Miss Willard and the Minor Secret Orders," *The Free Methodist*, February 25, 1888, 2.

21. Mary Kelly, "Introduction," in *A History of the Book in America vol. 2*, ed. Robert Gross and Mary Kelly (Chapel Hill: University of North Carolina Press, 2010), 53–57.

22. Anne Ruggles Gere and Sarah Robbins, "Gendered Literacy in Black and White: Turn of the Century African-American and European American Club Printed Texts," *Signs* 21, no. 3 (1996): 643–78.

23. Historian Catherine Berkus argues that religion was among the few places to transcend the domestic sphere. Both men and women were needed to promote the gospel and their denomination. Thus, creating space for women to step into the role of preacher. Catherine Berkus, *Strangers and Pilgrims: Female Preaching in America 1740–1845* (Chapel Hill: University of North Carolina Press, 1998), 13–14.

24. Barbara Epstein, *The Politics of Domesticity* (Middletown, CT: Wesleyan University Press, 1986), 67.

25. Susan Cruea, "Changing Ideals of Womanhood in the 19th-Century Women's Movement," *American Transcendental Quarterly* 19, no. 3 (2005): 187–204.

26. Patricia Bizzell, "Frances Willard, Phoebe Palmer and the Ethos of the Methodist Woman Preacher," *Rhetoric Society Quarterly* 36 (2006): 377–98.

27. In the original article, the quote regarding Eve's sin reads as follows, "The woman had specifically sinned, not for the sake of earthly enjoyment merely (*delitzsch*), but in high flown aspiring." The word *delitzsch* only appears as a surname in German dictionaries, implying that this is perhaps an editorial error in the article. William Gould, "Ought Women to Govern in the Church? No. 4," *The Free Methodist*, July 7, 1886, 2.

28. Jack Richardson, *B.T. Roberts and the Role of Women in Ministry in Nineteenth Century Free Methodism* (M.Div. thesis, Colgate Rochester Divinity School, 1984), 80–81.

29. Benjamin Titus Roberts, "Ought Women to Govern in the Church? Reply to W. Gould's Fourth Article," *The Free Methodist*, August 11, 1886, 5.

30. T.B. Arnold, ed., "Fifth Session," *General Conference Daily*, October 19, 1886, 3.

31. Ibid.

32. T.B. Arnold, ed., "A Card," *General Conference Daily*, October 27, 1886.

33. Clara Wetherald, "Dedication at Royalton, Michigan," *The Free Methodist*, October 10, 1888, 5.

34. Mesaros-Winckles, *Data on Free Methodist Women Evangelists*.

35. C.F. Southworth, "Woman," *The Free Methodist*, June 1, 1887, 2.

36. A.G. Warne, "Woman's Work in the Church," *The Free Methodist*, July 11, 1888, 2.

37. Clara Wetherald, "Shall Women be Ordained?" *The Free Methodist*, May 14, 1890, 2–3.

38. Ibid.

39. W.B.M. Colt, "Why Not?," *The Free Methodist*, October 1 and 8, 1890, 2.

40. Emma Sellew Roberts, "Help It On!" *The Free Methodist*, October 22, 1890, 2.

41. Ibid,

42. "Women May Not Preach," *Decatur Daily Republican,* October 18, 1894, 3; "Women May Not Preach," *The Commercial Appeal*, October 17, 1894, 8; "Women Preachers," *Great Falls Tribune*, October 20, 1894, 1; "Free Methodists Oppose Ordination of Women as Ministers," *Arkansas City Daily Traveler*, October 16,

1894, 8; "Free Methodists Oppose Ordination of Women as Ministers," *Weekly Republican-Traveler*, October 18, 1894, 1; "Against Women as Preachers," *Iowa City Press-Citizen*, October 17, 1894, 1; "The News Condensed," *Crestline Advocate*, October 18, 1894, 6; "Morning News: Eastern," *Los Angeles Evening Express*, October 17, 1894, 2; and Free Methodist Church, *Minutes of the 1890 General Conference* (unpublished meeting minutes, 1890), transcript.

43. The defeat of women's ordination at the 1890 General Conference made regional newspapers but was initially incorrectly reported as the resolution passing. Perhaps another indication of the chaotic nature of debates and the vote at the 1890 Conference. "The Free Methodists," *The Dubuque Daily Herald*, October 11, 1890, 1, and "Of General Interest," *Ames Intelligencer*, October 16, 1890, 6.

44. Snyder, *Populist Saints*, 854.

45. Benjamin Titus Roberts, *Ordaining Women* (Chili, NY: Earnest Christian Publishing House, 1891).

46. In his address at the 1894 General Conference, A.F. Norrington, a delegate from Canada, cited lack of education as the main reason the annual conferences voted against women's ordination. As he stated, "Had our own people been informed on the subject and had not discussion at some of the annual conferences been suppressed by vote, and had not so much button-holing and electioneering been done with uninformed persons to induce them to vote against the measure [it would have passed.]" He went on to note that at one camp meeting he attended, he heard the general superintendent, chairman, and ordained elders mention they had forbidden the sale of *Ordaining Women* at that camp meeting. According to Norrington, the ordained elder "said sneeringly, 'Oh! I wouldn't waste time with such a book.'" A.F. Norrington, "Third Sitting," *General Conference Daily*, October 16, 1894, 68.

47. G.W. Coleman, "Ordination of Women," supplement to *The Free Methodist*, June 17, 1891.

48. Benjamin Titus Roberts, "Ordination of Women: A Review of an Article by Rev. G.W. Coleman," in supplement to *The Free Methodist*, August 12, 1891.

Chapter 4

The 1890 and 1894 General Conference Debates on Women's Ordination

In the lead-up to the quadrennial Free Methodist General Conference in 1890, the debate about women's ordination filled the pages of *The Free Methodist*.[1] *The Free Methodist* had been edited since 1886 by Benjamin Titus Roberts, and as discussed in chapter three, Roberts was a vocal advocate of ordaining women and used the publication to promote testimonies of women such as Clara Wetherald, whose success Roberts saw as proof of women's suitability for pastoral ministry. On the other hand, opponents of women's ordination frequently wrote to refute Roberts' perspective. Tensions carried over from the pages of *The Free Methodist* onto the floor of the 1890 and then 1894 General Conferences. These debates occurred during a crucial moment in American religious history and are connected to more significant questions about the role of women in the public sphere.

Depending on the Protestant tradition, the ordination question was dealt with differently in the United States. The Methodist Episcopal Church North[2] granted women licenses to preach in 1869, only to rescind all of them at the 1880 General Conference. It was not until 1919 that women were again allowed to hold preaching licenses, and full ordination did not occur until 1924. Congregationalists had ordained women at the individual church level since Antoinette Brown Blackwell in 1853 and the Unitarian and Universalist Church since Olympia Brown in 1863. Additionally, other offshoots of the Methodist Episcopal Church allowed women's ordination from their denomination's founding. The Church of the Nazarene wrote women's ordination into its original constitution in 1895, and the Wesleyan Methodist Church allowed conferences the freedom to license and ordain women.[3] While the Free Methodist Church did not ordain women, since 1874, it had granted them the right to hold an evangelist's license,[4] and in 1886, women were permitted to become delegates to quarterly, annual, and general conferences,[5] which at least gave them a seat at the table for denominational decisions. Still, much of nineteenth-century Protestant culture restricted women's quest for equality. They began to gain entrance to colleges, entered the medical profession, started law careers, and pursued a life outside the domestic sphere in numerous areas. However, the profession of ordained church elder was still mostly outside their reach.

However, the job of a preacher was more than just another occupation; it was a spiritual calling bound up in biblical interpretation regarding gender and leadership roles. Thus, women preachers were seen by some Free Methodists as a threat to women's God-ordained role as a wife and a mother. Before the 1890 General Conference, the pro-ordination articles published served as one of the few times women and men spoke out forcefully for ordination. As the 1890s progressed, the debate slowly shifted away from favoring ordination to increased opposition. By 1894 the debate over women's roles in the church was a debate among men, with women largely silenced on the matter.

Within Free Methodism, two opposing ideological camps emerged in the years prior to the 1890 General Conference. Roberts and his supporters forwarded a vision of biblical equality for the denomination. At the same time, fellow general superintendent George Coleman strongly opposed women's ordination, relying on the cult of domesticity rhetoric for his position. The third general superintendent, Edward Hart, waffled on the topic, first voting for women's ordination at the 1890 General Conference and then voting against it at the 1894 General Conference.[6] Thus, beyond Roberts, Free Methodists had few vocal supports of gender equality at the highest level of denominational leadership.

Furthermore, many late nineteenth-century American publications extolled the virtues of women remaining in the domestic sphere, helping perpetuate a rhetorical culture that supported gendered divisions of labor.[7] In reality, gendered labor existed more as a rhetorical construct than a reality in the Progressive Era. As historian Amanda Vickery notes, in both the United Kingdom and the United States, only the wealthiest families could afford to truly practice separate gender roles within the home. Nevertheless, because popular culture embraced the notion of domestic virtue, it was difficult for advocates of gender equality to gain rhetorical traction.[8] These larger debates ultimately resulted in two competing rhetorical visions for women's biblical and social roles within Free Methodism—visions that frequently came into conflict on the pages of *The Free Methodist* and the floor of the general conference.

As this tense rhetorical climate developed, female evangelists such as Wetherald, Gage, and Grant found it increasingly difficult to authoritatively construct their rhetorical identity—an identity that was intimately bound up with gender, discourse, and power. While women's ordination was being discussed in the abstract on the pages of *The Free Methodist*, the embodiedness of women evangelists' lives and experiences was easier to forget, as the primary focus was on the success of their ministries. However, when the women appeared in person to debate ordination, their gender was physically present, pushing their ministerial accomplishments to the background. During the 1890 and 1894 debates, Wetherald and Gage used distinct verbal performative styles to destabilize the discursive construction of gender and push for women's ordination. They could no longer rely on language and logical persuasion to gain acceptance. Instead, they engaged in a type of performativity to interrogate established gender roles through both their words and actions.

In response to their efforts, opponents evoked biblical passages out of context. They issued warnings predicting ordination would lead to an increasingly progressive theology that was counter to the Free Methodist mission of upholding "the gospel standard of Christianity." In other words, they accused proponents of ordination of radicalism disguised as piety. Opponents were threatened by what they saw as a fundamental re-interpretation of gender roles, and to many undecided Free Methodists, their arguments were compelling. Despite the best efforts of men like Roberts and women like Wetherald and Gage, the organizational pressures of Free Methodism ultimately created a culture of silence, pushing dissenting voices to the margins. Ironically, by displaying their gender at the General Conferences and rhetorically linking it to their authority to preach, Wetherald and Gage were ultimately silenced—forced to either conform to the new dominant discourse of Free Methodism or leave the denomination altogether.

THE 1890 GENERAL CONFERENCE

As seen in *The Free Methodist* and annual conference minutes from 1890, the role of women in both the denomination and society was being fiercely debated. As the 1890 General Conference began in Chicago, it became clear early on that the "woman issue," as it was referred to in the *General Conference Daily*, would not be put to rest. The 1890 Annual Conference Minutes show forty-one women held evangelist's licenses that year, and by 1890 some conferences, such as West Kansas and Missouri, included women in their conference rolls alongside men as "preachers," a category that generally included only ordained elders in many conferences.[9] Nevertheless, despite the inclusion of women in ministry, few conferences were appointing women to circuits. In 1888 and 1889, the denomination saw a small spike in women's appointments, with an average of sixteen women serving on preaching circuits. However, by the time of the 1890 General Conference, that number had dropped to twelve.[10] The difference between the number of women with evangelistic licenses versus appointments indicated divisions within the denomination.[11] While opponents hoped the question would disappear, that was not to happen. As the 1890 General Conference began, sixty-seven-year-old B.T. Roberts was suffering from exhaustion and poor health, but was determined to continue his push for women's ordination, opening the conference with a proposed resolution affirming women's right to ordination:[12]

> Resolved, That the Gospel of Jesus Christ, in the provision which it makes, and in the agencies which it employs for the salvation of mankind, knows no distinction of nationality, condition or sex: therefore, no person who is called of God, and who is duly qualified should be refused ordination on account of sex, or race, or condition.[13]

The resolution, named "The Roberts' Resolution," sparked a debate over policy, governance, and scriptural interpretation that continued for days. As Wilson Hogue notes in his 1916 history of the denomination, "Few questions if any have evoked greater interest and called out so fully the debating talent of a General Conference among Free Methodists, as did this."[14] Hogue describes the debate about women's ordination as "testing the law of 'perfect love'" and being incredibly long and very heated.[15] The competing rhetorical visions of the pro-ordination and anti-ordination Free Methodists would continually repeat the same points in 1890 Conference debates and debates at the 1894, 1907, and 1911 General Conferences. Little "persuasion" occurred; it was simply a repetition of both opposing ideologies with little discussion engendered and even less compromise accomplished.[16] Delegates came to the conference with firmly established beliefs on women's roles and were rarely persuaded to change their minds.[17]

It was primarily because Roberts held considerable sway as both a general superintendent and founder of the denomination that the issue even came to the floor in 1890. Additionally, Roberts' influence helped propel Wetherald to center stage as the conference poster child of a successful women evangelist. She was asked to preach at one of the conference's evening services and spoke on the record twice in defense of her ministry. It is doubtful her example would have been as influential if Roberts did not also argue for women's ordination. His frustration regarding opposition to the measure is evident in his opening remarks:

> It is hard to speak to men's stomachs for they have no ears to hear. It is a very hard thing to speak to men's prejudices. They are stronger than the sense of justice. They are stronger than the love of truth, even in many good men. We

can hardly estimate the power of prejudice, and yet I think as Christian men we ought to conquer our prejudices and adhere to truth however it may be in conflict with our training. Prejudices on this subject are the growth of centuries. Truth may be in conflict with our training and prejudice on this subject. We have been brought up to regard woman as inferior to man, and are not willing the same rights to be given to her. . . . Some of men's prejudices are one way and others are another. My prejudices are one way and those of many of you are another; and I think I can make it clear from the Bible, if you will listen candidly to me, that the resolution before us ought to receive a unanimous vote.[18]

Like Wetherald, Roberts' plea to move beyond prejudice and consider women's social and spiritual rights fell on deaf ears as other delegates opposed women's ordination. Roberts' address did not seem to draw much support for women's ordination, even though the speech pushed him to the verge of collapse.[19] As with the debates in other denominations during this time, opponents based their arguments not on the nature of God and what the Bible said regarding women's roles but on the nature of women and their "natural" inferiority.[20]

For example, O.M. Owen, a delegate from Susquehanna, New York, acknowledged the right of women to own property and have social equality with men. Although, biblical equality and denominational leadership were another matter:

We would acknowledge her to be the equal of man in intellect, equal in ability, but not equal in authority. She has her sphere of labor, and in that sphere she may equal and sometimes excel over man in this sphere. That God never intended woman to be the leader in the church, nation, or family may be seen from the law and the testimony.[21]

Owen based his argument on a literal interpretation of the Bible using only the English translation, whereas Roberts and Wetherald took a historical/cultural approach to biblical interpretation. Roberts also referred to original Greek texts to justify why women should be ordained. Opponents felt no need to explore the Greek texts. As Wilson Hogue, a delegate to the Genesee Conference in New York, explained, they were not learned men, and "a discussion about Greek roots and verbs and nouns is an inexcusable waste of time. Five words of plain English on this subject are worth ten thousand words in an unknown tongue."[22]

Relying on the same rhetoric as anti-suffragists,[23] the opponents justified their position, citing the numerous rights women were already gaining in other areas of American culture. Superintendent Edward Hart appealed to the delegates' patriotism and knowledge that women were not as oppressed as the pro-ordination advocates made it appear:

We are not in England or in Germany, but in republican America—in the land where the question of human rights and equality is being solved on a basis of right and equity as it is no other land. The women of America may in their sphere weld [sic] an influence for good that can be equaled under no other condition. It is the soft hand of woman that rocks the cradle of the nation. This question stripped of all that is foreign to it should be discussed on the basis of New Testament teaching.[24]

Hart's appeal to strip the debate of "all that is foreign" was a subtle stab at Roberts' attempt to refer to the original Greek of the New Testament. Buried deep in the anti-ordination rhetoric was an underlying fear by the male delegates of having their influence within the denomination diminished.

While there were two female delegates to the 1890 General Conference, Anna Grant and Clara Wetherald, only Wetherald spoke on the record in defense of her ministry. Some other male delegates also spoke in defense of their female colleagues. Since opponents based their arguments on a literal scriptural interpretation and cultural norms, Wetherald flipped the debate to focus not on biblical interpretation but on the physical and financial hardship women evangelists faced:

For twenty-four years I have preached the gospel and have never been laid aside from the ministry but six months. I have had people come many miles to have me marry them, and I would not do it. I have labored many years for $100 a year. The railways refuse to grant permits to women who are not ordained, no matter if they are licensed. I do not stand here because I want to be honored. That is all taken out of my heart. There are those who have been saved under my labors who have desired to receive the Lord's Supper from my hands, but I could not administer it. God has given us this right, but the conference refuses it.[25]

Wetherald traveled extensively, preaching around the country, but her role as a preacher was limited by church rules prohibiting her from performing all the duties of an ordained elder. While she alluded to the financial gender disparity, she was also subtly critiquing the belief that ordaining women will upset the "natural" order. Wetherald was given a second opportunity to promote women's ordination when she preached the Tuesday, October 14, evening sermon. Her sermon was scheduled for the night before the debate on women's ordination. Appropriately, she chose to preach on 1 Corinthians 14:34–35—one of the most contested passages in the Bible on women's role in the church. "Let your women keep silence in the church: for it is not permitted unto them to speak."[26] Wetherald noted that while only two verses in the Bible refer to women remaining silent, those two verses were continually being used to repress women's ability to preach. Pointing out the hypocrisy:

I once spoke to a woman on the subject of pride, and she told me that she had searched the Bible and had only found 144 passages speaking on that subject, and yet with all this said against pride the church will hardly conform to the plainness in dress; yet one or two passages are sufficient in the minds of many upon this subject. But I was not going to preach on the subject of pride. Paul was the best educated of all the apostles, and he was well versed in Scripture and knew these facts, and he would not present a doctrine or standard contrary to these passages quoted, and that would make him contradict himself. I pity any woman who is down on her own sex. I suppose there are some; God help them![27]

Wetherald framed the right to ordination from a historical and cultural reading of the Bible. Wetherald continued her sermon by explaining that the Apostle Paul knew that when the Holy Spirit descended from heaven at Pentecost, it did not distinguish between genders. The single passage asking women to remain silent must be taken in the historical context of the early church and at Corinth, to whom the letter was written. Roberts continued this line of argument in opening remarks the next day. However, due to sloppy reporting or purposely delaying publication, Wetherald's sermon on women's role in the church was not published in the *General Conference Daily* until October 22, 1890, at the end of the general conference. This date was well after the denomination would have read other remarks for and against ordination. While the publication of Wetherald's sermon was delayed, her attempt to challenge opponents' beliefs was impressive. She stood alone in her defense. As the only woman to preach at the general conference and the only woman to defend women's rights in the denomination, she attempted to bridge the divide through her words and example.

Wetherald's speech and the speeches of the other delegates published in the *General Conference Daily* provided Free Methodists who could not attend valuable information about proceedings. However, coverage was not without editorializing, as J.G. Terrill, the editor of the *General Conference Daily*, included numerous editorial comments, attempting to provide an interpretation of events. In his commentary about Wetherald's speech, Terrill noted:

> We call particular attention to the speeches of Rev'ds B.T. Roberts . . . and Rev. Mrs. Clara Wetherald . . . we speak of the above speeches, not from any special favoritism to the parties, or to either side of the question, but because of their being more elaborate and more fully discussing the question.[28]

Rhetorically, his reference to Wetherald as "Rev." is intriguing, illustrating her prominence in the denomination. She was not an ordained elder like Roberts, but the same title referred to her. At the conference, other women, including women missionaries, are called "Miss" or "Mrs." in the *General Conference Daily.*[29] As the most vocal advocate of women's right to

ordination at the 1890 General Conference, Wetherald is an example of someone who intentionally chose to live at the margins of social and theological
acceptance in the denomination. She had succeeded in rhetorically passing,
crafting a professional identity that had gained her respect and attention, but
when it came to the issue of ordination, she was not willing to disguise her
strong support for continued social acceptance. Her addresses at the conference focused on women's "God-given right" to preach, which subverted the
language of "natural" roles for women to argue for "naturally equal" roles
instead of a "naturally inferior" role.

Indeed, as the debate unfolded in 1890, it became increasingly clear that
Wetherald had to switch her rhetorical strategy. Before 1890 her rhetoric
focused on her identity as an evangelist. However, now with the debate
focusing on women's inability to be both a wife, mother, *and* evangelist,
she reframed her identity to identify first as a woman and secondly as an
evangelist. In her conference address, Wetherald used the story of a female
sheepdog who left her pups to find the sheep and returned home to care for
her puppies. As she said, "Let women be considered in the matter. They say
woman is not adapted to the regular ministry. I think she is peculiarly fitted
to care for souls."[30] Wetherald attempted to construct both a performative
and rhetorical identity that would help persuade other delegates that women
were capable of public ministry. Despite her best efforts, language and performativity were bound to work against her. In an organizational culture that
did not fully recognize her gifts, language was bound to silence her. In many
ways, the women's ordination proponents faced an insurmountable battle
against a long-established hierarchy of language and biblical interpretation.
As debates continued, the 1890 debates on women's ordination dissolved in
chaos, with delegates unsure how to vote or even what they were voting on.
As it was called, the Roberts' Resolution failed by two votes—forty opposed,
thirty-eight in favor of women's ordination. Terrill, in his editorial notes on
the conference, described the scene:

> It is not for those who favor the ordination of women to be discouraged, nor
> for any who are opposed to it, if there be such, to glory in its defeat. The vote
> Wednesday evening was not decisive on that question. There were involved with
> it other questions that distracted the minds of some and caused others to vote
> contrary to their pronounced positions. There are some among us who believe
> there is nothing natural or scriptural in the way of the ordination of women. But
> they hold that we are not prepared for it until the church as a body has expressed
> its opinion on the subject; and they, therefore, favor it being submitted to the
> annual conferences; and because the ordination of women is such a wide depar-
> ture from the custom of the church universal, they think it best that more than a
> majority should decide it.[31]

However, the issue was not dead. Instead, the "woman issue" was put on hold for four years so annual conferences could voice their opinion, sending delegates back in 1894 to vote on the issue. Interestingly, several Midwest newspapers reported that Roberts' Resolution had passed. The incorrect news accounts perhaps indicate how chaotic the debates and votes on the resolution were.[32] As the 1890 General Conference concluded, Wetherald took another chance to persuade her fellow Free Methodists to support women's ordination. On Thursday, October 16, the day after the Roberts' Resolution was voted down, she spoke about the issue of women's natural duties and the arguments raised in opposition to women preaching:

> I know we have responsibilities that others do not have, and I think of all others, we should have the support of the church. I do not see why the heavens should fall and everything be turned bottom side up if five elders should lay their hands on my head and say, "Take thou authority to preach the word of God and to administer the holy sacraments in the congregation." I know that the Lord has laid his hand upon my head, and he will carry me through. You say that the financial question should not come into this discussion. Why not, if it comes in with the men? I say it is a question of equality. If it is said that it means males only when it says "he," then we must all sit down without hope of salvation. But I deny that it has that meaning. A man said to me, "There is no salvation for woman in the Bible. There is no place in the Bible where it says she has a soul."[33]

Directly attacking her opponents, Wetherald boldly claimed that if ministry is not open to women because the Bible prohibits it, what was to prevent salvation from only being open to men? No response to Wetherald's address is recorded in the *General Conference Daily*.

After 1890 Wetherald was no longer trying to subvert the discourse or pass within the denomination. On a larger societal scale, she still was attempting to place her role as an evangelist ahead of her gender, but within the Free Methodist Church, such a distinction was not possible. By 1892 she had left the Free Methodist Church and become a ministerial candidate in the Congregationalist Church, leaving the defense of women's ordination in the hands of Ida Gage, a rising evangelist in the Ohio Conference, whose revivals and success at church planting were attracting attention across the region.[34]

ROBERTS' *ORDAINING WOMEN*

In 1891, after women's ordination narrow defeat, Roberts turned his arguments into a self-published book, *Ordaining Women*. The book received mixed reactions within the denomination, and Free Methodist general superintendent George Coleman published a lengthy review in a special June 17, 1891, *Free Methodist* supplement, arguing against Roberts' premise that women were morally, intellectually, and socially equal to men. In the same issue, an unidentified woman also wrote a rebuttal of Roberts' arguments. The unnamed woman, who identifies as a woman evangelist with a husband who is an ordained Free Methodist elder, rejects the claim that other women evangelists desire ordination. Directly attacking Mariet Hardy Freeland's earlier review of *Ordaining Women*, in which Freeland hoped the book would deliver women in the same way *Uncle Tom's Cabin* delivered African-Americans, she wrote:[35]

> [G]reat deliverance implies clearly as great an oppression? . . . She [Freeland] says, *"especially in the* Free Methodist Church." This surprises me still more. Are the sisters of our loved Zion really oppressed in any degree like unto the bondage of the colored race? Are they under whip and lash deprived of their liberty, and waiting for the "ordination of women" to set them free? I cannot "accept the situation."[36]

The author's comment illustrated the deepening opposition to ordination within the denomination and increasing confusion over biblical interpretation by both men and women.

After 1890 Roberts was no longer the editor of *The Free Methodist*. As each editor had the license to highlight topics they felt relevant,[37] Roberts' book *Ordaining Women* received little attention in the publication, except for two special supplements with book reviews. In the June 17, 1891, supplement, Coleman's three-page critique exemplified cult of domesticity rhetoric and simultaneously elevated and degraded women. On the first page of his review, Coleman includes a poem outlining gender roles. While not an exceptional example of poetry, it does show how language was twisted to both appear to honor yet devalue women at the same time:

> Woman completes what man begins;
> 'tis hers to polish and refine;
> But if she builds *alone* she sins
> Against her art and God's design.[38]

Coleman's review of *Ordaining Women* was based on the belief that there was a scriptural, historical, providential, and practical argument against women's ordination. Citing various biblical passages, Coleman gave the leadership example from Numbers 12:2, where Moses and Aaron were given leadership positions over Israel's tribes, but their sister Mariam was not. Furthermore, Coleman argued that when the twelve patriarchs of Israel were called from Jacob's thirteen children, no mention of Jacob's daughter Dinah was included.[39] According to Coleman, it was not just the Old Testament that indicated women were not called to the same roles as men; it was the New Testament as well. For example, Coleman reasoned that when Jesus called his disciples to organize the early church, no women were included among the numbers, nor were women mentioned during the Great Commission in Matthew 28:16–20 and Mark 16:14–15.[40]

Furthermore, historical examples of church leadership illustrated that women were not to lead the church or be ordained. They "were wonderfully endowed with Holy Ghost power and efficiency, but they lived and died without suspecting that the Scriptures taught any such thing as the ordination of women." Citing historical church leaders such as John Wesley, John Knox, Frances Asbury, and Thomas Coke, Coleman argued that none of these men ever found this "new doctrine" of women's ordination.[41] Coleman's providential argument primarily focused on the different social roles of men and women. As he noted:

> Though the "equality of the sexes" is freely granted, or rather, that men are not superior to women, is freely granted, or rather that men are not superior to women, if even their equal, it does not follow that the lines of labor designed by God for them to follow are always the same. Men are clearly fitted by nature to grapple with the rough elements and occupations of life; while women are better adapted to keep house, train the children and guide the household than men. It would be worse than useless to try and subvert this order. God designed men and women to marry and raise a family, and "if the salvation of the world is the principal object for which we labor, there has never been committed to a human being a more honorable, glorious, and fruitful field than God has placed in the hands of the mother. Give one generation the proper training and instruction, and the problem of the world's salvation is solved."[42]

Coleman's providential argument was the same argument used by anti-ordination advocates at the 1890 General Conference. As Coleman's critique concluded, he expressed concern that women would be unfairly favored for ministerial roles over eligible men and that women would only serve short appointments, leaving the ministry when they married and had children. Coleman insisted there was no need to ordain women when eligible men sought ministerial appointments. For women to pursue ministry was to deny their God-ordained role in the home.

As Coleman explained, "Women cannot balance both a professional life with family life—her children will be 'robbed of the grand inheritance' they were gifted from God."[43]

There was nothing original in Coleman's critique of women's ordination. However, his article's timing most likely contributed to many Free Methodists not picking up Roberts' book. Roberts notes this concern in his rebuttal to

Coleman and goes so far as to accuse Coleman of critiquing his book without even reading it. Roberts wrote a defense of his book in a special supplement in the August 12, 1891, *Free Methodist*. Like Coleman's, Roberts' supplement included additional articles. In Roberts' case, this included a section, "What Is Said About This Book," which included excerpts from positive reviews from other periodicals such as *The Pentecost, The Union Signal, The Wesleyan Methodist*, and the *Evangelical Messenger*.[44] Roberts' critique is just as lengthy as Coleman's, and his rebuttal is pointed, as he directly attacks Coleman's lack of scholarship at the start of his editorial. Calling Coleman's review mainly his interpretation of Scripture and societal views, he berated Coleman for having only one outside citation to the biblical commentator Adam Clarke.[45] Charging that Coleman was acting like a sophist, he point by point went through the fallacies in Coleman's article.[46]

According to Roberts, the first fallacy is that Coleman assumes the question of women's ordination needs to be proved. It would result in radical changes to church polity. However, women already served as evangelists, members of a church's official board, and conference delegates with the Free Methodist Church. Women's approval as ordained elders would only change what women already preaching were allowed to do. As Roberts explained:

> Suppose a woman who is a local preacher among us, be ordained. This gives her the right to baptize her converts, to marry and to administer the Lord's Supper. But as far as church government is concerned she has not a particle more authority than she had before.[47]

Roberts then protested how the ordination question had been sent back to annual conferences after 1890 and would ultimately be decided by a three-fourths vote of approval or disapproval at annual conferences and then a two-thirds approval by the 1894 General Conference. Roberts argued that no church policy required the issue to be decided in this manner.[48] He contended that Coleman ultimately changed the question of the ordination of women to whether women could be equally called to ministry roles as men. One of Roberts' defenses throughout his article focused on Coleman's lack of research and historical understanding of early church leaders. Critiquing Coleman's interpretation of early Methodism, Roberts agreed that Wesley, Asbury, and others could not conceive of women in the same role as them, but the reason they could not conceive of such an idea was that, in the time of Wesley, the laws of England put married women's condition as no better than slaves.[49] Citing John Wesley's idea of some women having an "extraordinary call" to ministry, Roberts argued that within the Free Methodist Church, there already was a precedent for women serving as ministers. Canada had been appointing women to circuits since 1881.[50] Thus, Roberts explains that

Coleman's providential argument that women are not suited to full-time ministry is invalid within the denomination.[51]

Roberts' book was not universally well-received within the denomination, as some annual conferences banned its sale at their conventions.[52] The lack of denominational support, especially from the denomination's superintendents, pointed to continued organizational silencing of gender equality rhetoric. Fortunately, the conversation about women's ordination did not end completely, as in the months before the 1894 General Conference, *The Free Methodist* was once again filled with articles for and against ordination. However, unlike the 1890 articles published during Roberts' tenure as editor, the 1894 articles featured few women contributors, being written mostly by men.[53] The rhetorical climate was shifting leading up to the 1894 General Conference. Roberts died suddenly in 1893, and after his death, opponents of ordination took the opportunity to oppose women's full enfranchisement. Only a few men and women were still openly supportive, and all three Free Methodist general superintendents were opposed.[54] Additionally, during the four-year interim, the annual conferences had voted on women's ordination, and the denomination was split almost equally on the issue. Yet women's involvement did not dimmish because of the opposition. In fact, women were becoming licensed evangelists in greater numbers.[55] While annual conference delegates had a vote, delegates to the 1894 General Conference were not required to vote as their annual conference had voted. For instance, some annual conferences, such as Pittsburgh, voted forty-two to eighteen in favor of women's ordination but sent General Conference delegates who voted against women's ordination.[56]

THE 1894 GENERAL CONFERENCE

Unlike the lead-up to the 1890 General Conference, the lack of articles by women in *The Free Methodist* did not necessarily mean Free Methodist women no longer cared about the topic but likely indicated that many of the women evangelists were too busy with their own ministry circuits to engage in editorial debate. For instance, Ida Gage, a General Conference delegate from Ohio, was relatively silent on women's ordination. Her grueling travel schedule likely was a factor. Nevertheless, as a delegate, she was ready to defend her ministry. Representing Ohio, which had voted eighteen to fourteen to approve ordaining women,[57] Gage was a natural spokesperson. With the death of Roberts in 1893, voices such as Gage's were vital. While there were four female delegates to the General Conference in 1894—Marietta Barnhart of the Pittsburgh Conference, Ida Gage of Ohio, Clara Sage of Wabash, and Jane Coleman of Wisconsin—the delegates were still overwhelmingly male, and the debate had shifted to focus on whether the denomination was going to follow the larger social trend of granting women equality in the public sphere. As C.M. Damon said in a September 1894 issue of *The Free Methodist*, "the woman question":

> Will not down; and unless we are prepared to roll back the march of progress by closing the doors of the institutions of higher learning, which have lately been opened to woman, we may as well adjust ourselves to the trend of events in all civilized nations, and prepare to meet the oncoming participation and influence of women in public affairs. That this trend is toward her emancipation, elevation and enfranchisement, needs no proof to the thoughtful student of the times.[58]

Damon's defense was partially influenced by the ministry of his wife, Grace Damon, who regularly held an evangelist's license in the Minnesota and Northern Iowa Conference. Damon stressed that the lack of legal and spiritual equality was grossly under-acknowledged and understood. According to Damon, the denomination could no longer stand by and allow inequality to continue.[59]

Still, for every advocate, there were just as many detractors. In September 1894, George M'Culloch wrote an article in *The Free Methodist* arguing, "The advocates of woman's ordination are working for a state of things which is entirely unknown to Methodism (as a body) or to any other truly evangelical church; but which is mainly found in the practice of the Universalists, the Unitarians, and the Adventists. Do we wish to pattern after them?"[60] Arguments like M'Culloch's were common, as some Free Methodists worried ordaining women would lead to increased secularization within the denomination. More so than in 1890, the 1894 debates illustrated that the rhetorical power rested in the hands of men. Women had little control over the debate language, and only when they were willing to use the language of the dominant hierarchy were they granted attention.

Indeed, as the debate over women's ordination officially began at the 1894 General Conference, D.J. Santmier from New York stood up to denounce women's preaching as contrary to the natural order. Referring to a story "a woman at the last general conference" told, he told the story of a sheepdog and her puppies, noting, "In this illustration the dog represents the woman and the puppies her children. Now I want to say if that dog is to represent my wife and the puppies my children she shall stay at home and take care of the puppies."[61] Using the same illustration Wetherald used in 1890, Santmeir twisted the narrative to focus not on women's ability to balance numerous tasks but on the need for women to stay home and nurture the family. Because Wetherald's address was published in the 1890 *General Conference Daily*, Santmier likely read it there. His refusal to name Wetherald illustrates

Fig. 4.1. The 1894 General Conference delegates. There were four women delegates at the 1894 Conference—Jane Coleman, Ida Gage, Clara Sage, and Mariette Barnhart. Jane Coleman is #89 in the second row directly to the right of the B.T. Roberts photo; Clara Sage is in the second row to the left (#61). Ida Gage is next to her (#62), and Marietta Barnhart (#64) is in the second row to the right of Ida Gage. Source: Marston Memorial Historical Center

how some Free Methodists were already silencing her ministry after she left the denomination. After the sheepdog illustration, Santmier concluded his address with a passionate cult of domesticity argument:

> God's word declares, "I will therefore that the young women marry, bear children, guide the house, give no occasion to the adversary to speak reproachfully." These to be ordained, it declares, should be men. If this be not so, our opposers must show that women have wives and are commanded to rule over their households.[62]

While delegates had been vocal in their opposition at the 1890 General Conference, with Roberts gone opponents in 1894 were even more pointed in their remarks. O.M. Owen, who also spoke in opposition to ordination at the 1890 General Conference, contended that women's ordination was not in-line with biblically mandated roles:

> My contention is that God designed that man should be the leader and ruler, and just as the word says, "woman shall be a helpmeet unto him." We have a president of the United States and a vice president, and no one would contend

that the vice president was equal in authority to the president. He is simply a helper in official matters.[63]

Drawing similar conclusions as Santmier, Owen emphasized that women were "helpers," not "leaders." Only Gage spoke to defend her ministry in response to the intense hostility. She addressed Owen's comments directly, along with Santmier's use of Wetherald's story indirectly, in her remarks:

> Referring to what my brother from the Susquehanna conference [Owen] said with regard to the president and vice president of the United States, if I have a proper understanding, the vice president has the authority to perform all the duties of the president in his absence. I come to you as a vice president, and I wish that this question could be settled. I am not an enthusiast on this subject. I am in sympathy with the brother who is in the canoe with the sisters, because, of course, their situation seems to be perilous at times. My brother who spake on my left favorably referred to a certain illustration, which to my mind, was out of place [Santmier] and yet, looking at it in the light that when our sisters leave their children with their neighbors to go berrying, or help their husbands dig potatoes, no one criticizes it at all. But when they go out to rescue the lost and unsaved, there is a great deal of comment made. I feel very much like the colored man when he thanked God for the "sperience."[64]

Gage drew comparisons between racial and gender equality, just as other Free Methodists had been doing in the denominational publication. As she continued her speech, Gage gave her testimony, concluding with a critique of those who claimed women were physically unable to handle itinerant ministry, remarking that the Lord made her strong enough to "stand as much as an iron woman." Like Wetherald in 1890, Gage's remarks appear to go unaddressed by her male colleagues. Although, unlike Wetherald, she did not attempt to appeal to history and biblical interpretation, instead directly ignoring the suggestion to only speak about ordination and not personal experience, commenting, "My brother says this is not a testimony meeting, but I want to say just a few words. I have 'sperience' on this line."[65] Gage insisted her personal experience was valuable and necessary to understand why her ministry was important and why her critics' arguments were flawed.[66] Blatantly shunning conference speech conventions, Gage would not be silenced or conform, something post-1894 she continued to do.

Towards the end of the debate, Freeborn Brooke, a delegate from the Illinois Conference, summarized the long-standing debate on women's roles in the church. Brooke would become one of the most outspoken defenders of women's ordination in the Free Methodist Church, publishing articles in *The Free Methodist* and defending women's right to ordination as elders at the 1907 and 1911 General Conferences.[67] Brooke noted that a delegate left in protest at the 1882 General Conference when women were first granted evangelists' licenses. As Brooke put it:

> Now the question is one of consistency. We must go ahead or go back. Go back? Never. But here we find the same old spirit that was defeated at Burlington and buried at Coopersville. Now it cries, "We let woman preach and we let her in office, what more does she want?" Her friends contend for all her rights, and sooner or later all her rights she shall have. But let it be remembered that it was not through the clemency of her opposers that she gained the rights now possessed; but she, with her friends, fought her way in the teeth of the bitterest opposition and took the field by force. Now her dearest friend, her most able defender, lies in habiliments of death [B.T. Roberts], but be ye assured that "he being dead, yet speaketh," and that this battle will never cease until the minister of the gospel in the Free Methodist church, who meets the requirements of the Discipline, shall be ordained without distinction of sex.[68]

Brook's quote, "he being dead, yet speaketh," became a common expression by supporters during conference debates. The quote reminded their opponents that while Roberts' was no longer present, his vision for the church was still alive. However, despite efforts of advocates to remind their fellow delegates of Roberts vision, only thirty-five delegates voted for women's ordination and sixty-five against it when the final vote was taken.[69] Once again, the outcome of the vote made headlines as newspapers around the country published the results.[70]

The news coverage of the 1890 and 1894 General Conferences illustrates that while the Free Methodist Church was not a large denomination, the debates regarding women's ordination and roles reflected broader social and theological tensions emerging during that period. This was also the same decade noted anti-suffragists Rev. Charles Parkhurst and Edward Bok were rising to prominence,[71] and the Free Methodist defeat of women's ordination resulted in headlines such as "Women Preach Only in the Home" or "Women May Not Preach," illustrating how the press connected the denomination's decision to larger social tensions.[72] The denomination was at a crucial turning point. Support for premillennialism was on the rise. With the general superintendents opposed to furthering women's rights within the denomination, it seemed the progressive social gospel of Roberts was losing favor among Free Methodist leaders. The influence of premillennial theology was already present in 1890 and 1894 at the General Conferences, strongly favoring a literal interpretation of Scripture and the belief that Christ would establish his kingdom on earth sooner rather than later. Premillennialism also emphasized a literal interpretation of biblical passages regarding gender roles.[73]

As the century concluded, Wilson Hogue, an outspoken premillennialist, became editor of *The Free Methodist*.[74] The political landscape for Free

Methodist women was changing rapidly post-1894. Hogue, a vocal critic of women's ordination at the 1890 and 1894 General Conferences, regularly highlighted news articles by prominent anti-suffragists and tended to favor editorial content from other like-minded Free Methodists. While their accomplishments were still regularly included in *The Free Methodist*'s correspondence section, the other pages featured articles favoring the cult of domesticity and emerging fundamentalist theology.

AFTER 1894: CHANGING CONCERNS

The tension in Free Methodism between Wesleyan theology, particularly the concept of Christian perfection, and premillennialism is apparent in *The Free Methodist* during Wilson Hogue's tenure as editor and beyond. Premillennialism appealed to Free Methodists opposed to women's ordination because it provided an ordered, seemingly rational approach to biblical interpretation. An interpretation that provided hope for the rapid social changes and subsequent "sin" those new freedoms brought. Premillennialists did not herald the rise of women in the pulpit. Instead, it was seen as an indication of society's continued spiritual decline.

Historian Margaret Bendroth notes that premillennialism offered men a very appealing theological interpretation of their own self-worth. While the rise of twentieth-century fundamentalism is complex and cannot be traced to a single theological interpretation, many historians believe premillennialism strongly influenced the movement.[75] It was somewhat ironic for Free Methodist leaders to embrace premillennialism and the cult of domesticity rhetoric that anti-suffragists promoted. The anti-suffragist movement was not a populist movement. It emerged from the wealthy Puritan elite of Massachusetts and New York, who worried that women's increasing participation in the public sphere directly threatened their way of life.[76] At its founding, Free Methodism had shunned the Methodist Episcopal Church's favoritism towards the upper middle class and wealthy and had intentionally emphasized freedom and universal access to the gospel among its founding principles.[77] Anti-suffrage was in direct contrast to those principles. In many ways, early twentieth-century Free Methodism reverted to the upper-middle-class norms it had tried to escape in the Methodist Episcopal Church.[78] Free Methodists like Hogue recognized women's legal inequality and favored increased legal protections for women, but the progress stopped there. Women were still viewed as spiritually inferior and incapable of serving in church governance, especially in the upper levels as conference superintendents or bishops. The debates in the 1890s had begun with the question, "are women as capable of preaching as men?," but by 1900, the debate was quickly shifting into a debate about church governance, as some Free Methodist men desired to keep top positions of influence exclusive to men.

NOTES

1. An earlier version of this chapter was published in *Wesley and Methodist Studies* and is used with permission from Penn State University Press. Christy Mesaros-Winckles, "Why Not Now? The 1890 and 1894 Free Methodist Debates on Ordaining Women," *Wesley and Methodist Studies* (Winter 2021): 45–68, https://doi .org/10.5325/weslmethstud.13.1.0045.

2. The granting of preaching licenses in 1869 and the rescinding of those licenses in 1880 all occurred with the Northern Methodist Episcopal Church. United Methodist Church, "Timeline of Women in Ministry," last modified February 22, 2019, https:// www.umc.org/en/content/timeline-of-women-in-methodism.

3. The 1895 date refers to the formation of the first Church of the Nazarene in Los Angeles, California, under Dr. Phineas Bresee. Janette Hassey, *No Time for Silence* (Minneapolis, Minnesota: Christians for Biblical Equality, 1986), 52.

4. The ministerial category of evangelist was added to *The Free Methodist Discipline* in 1874. "Evangelists are a class of preachers called to God to do this work, to labor and promote revivals of religion and to spread the cause of Christ in the land; but are not called to a pastoral charge or to government within the church." B.T. Roberts, ed., *Doctrines and Discipline of the Free Methodist Church* (North Chili, NY: 1874), 84.

5. Douglas Cullum, "Fanatical Women," in *Earnest: Interdisciplinary Work Inspired by the Life and Teachings of B. T. Roberts*, ed. Andrew C. Koehl and David Basinger (Eugene, OR: Pickwick Publications, 2017), 24.

6. Free Methodist Church, *Minutes of the 1890 General Conference* (unpublished meeting minutes 1890), transcript, and "Free Methodists Oppose Ordination of Women as Ministers," *Arkansas City Daily Traveler*, October 16, 1894, 8.

7. Sue Morgan and Jacqueline deVries, "Introduction," in *Women, Gender and Religious Cultures in Britain, 1800–1940*, ed. Sue Morgan and Jacqueline deVries (London: Routledge, 2010), 8.

8. Amanda Vickery, "Golden Age to Separate Spheres? A Review of the Categories and Chronology of English Women's History," *The Historical Journal* 36, no. 2 (1993): 384.

9. Christy Mesaros-Winckles, *Data on Free Methodist Women Evangelists 1876–1920* (March 2022), distributed by Christy Mesaros-Winckles.

10. Ibid.

11. Ibid.

12. Jack D. Richardson, *B. T. Roberts and the Role of Women in Ministry in Nineteenth-Century Free Methodism* (M.Div. thesis, Colgate Rochester Divinity School, 1984), 101; Wilson T. Hogue, *History of the Free Methodist Church*, vol. 2 (Chicago: Free Methodist Publishing House, 1915), 201; and J.G. Terrill, ed., "An Important Resolution," *General Conference Daily*, October 11, 1890, 43.

13. Hogue, *History of the Free Methodist Church of North America*, 192.

14. Ibid.

15. Ibid.

16. Once a group has accepted a specific worldview, getting individuals to change their perspective is challenging because they have bought into a narrative that is not only what they believe but is often a part of their identity. Specific beliefs tied to religion are especially difficult to change. See Earnest G. Bormann, "Fantasy and Rhetorical Vision: The Rhetorical Criticism of Social Reality," *Quarterly Journal of Speech* 58, no. 4 (1972): 396.

17. Howard Snyder, *Populist Saints: B.T. and Ellen Roberts and the First Free Methodist* (Grand Rapids, Michigan: Wm. B. Eerdmans Publishing Co., 2006), 864.

18. J.G. Terrill, ed., "Seventh Sitting," *General Conference Daily*, October 18, 1890, 106–7.

19. Hogue, *History of the Free Methodist Church*, 192.

20. Hassey, *No Time for Silence*, 7.

21. O.M. Owen, "Seventh Sitting," *General Conference Daily*, October 17, 1890, 117.

22. Wilson Hogue, "Seventh Sitting," *1890 General Conference Daily*, October 17, 1890, 119–22.

23. The contradictory rhetoric within Free Methodism put women on a pedestal as the spiritual guide for the family while at the same time blaming her for the fall in the book of Genesis. Because of Eve's choice, the argument went, women were incapable of leading the church. This same contradictory rhetoric was present in the anti-suffrage movement at the turn of the twentieth century. Anti-suffragists decried the suffragette's negligence of her family as she traveled to promote suffrage. Nevertheless, to fight suffrage, the people opposed to the suffragist's travel had to make exceptions allowing anti-suffrage women to travel to promote their political agenda. Both Free Methodists opposed to women's ordination and anti-suffragists took the approach of "some" roles outside the home for women but not "all" roles outside the home. Anne Benjamin, *Women Against Equality: The Anti-Suffrage Movement in the United States 1895 to 1920* (Piedmont, NC: Lulu Publishing, 2014), 214–15.

24. Edward Hart, "Seventh Sitting," *1890 General Conference Daily*, October 17, 1890, 122.

25. Sister Wetherald, "Fourth Sitting," *General Conference Daily*, October 13, 1890, 61.

26. 1 Cor.14:34–35 NIV.

27. Wetherald "Fourth Sitting," 61.

28. J.G. Terrill, ed., "Tuesday Night at May Street Church," *General Conference Daily*, October 22, 1890, 190.

29. J.G. Terrill, ed., "Notes," *General Conference Daily*, October 13, 1890, 63.

30. Sister Wetherald, "Fourth Sitting," *General Conference Daily*, October 13, 1890, 61.

31. J.G. Terrill, ed., "Notes: The Meaning of the Vote," *General Conference Daily*, October 17, 1890, 125.

32. "The Free Methodists," *The Dubuque Daily Herald*, October 11, 1890, 1; and "Of General Interest," *Ames Intelligencer*, October 16, 1890, 6.

33. Wetherald, "Fourth Sitting," 61.

34. W.B. Olmstead, "Hume, Ohio," *The Free Methodist*, February 6, 1895, 5.

35. Freeland's book review was republished numerous times in 1891 as the quoted expert was part of an advertisement for *Ordaining Women* in *The Free Methodist*. W.M.B. Colt was also quoted in the advertisement. "Ordaining Women," *The Free Methodist*, June 3, 1891, 9.

36. A Woman, "The Other Side of the Question," *The Free Methodist*, June 17, 1891, 4.

37. Richard Blews, *Master Workman: Biographies of Late Bishops of the Free Methodist Church During Her First Century 1860–1960* (Winona Lake, IN: Light and Life Press, 1960), 99.

38. G.W. Coleman, "Ordination of Women," supplement to *The Free Methodist*, June 17, 1891, 1.

39. Ibid., 2.

40. Ibid.

41. Ibid., 3.

42. Ibid.

43. Ibid.

44. "What Is Said About This Book," supplement to *The Free Methodist*, August 12, 1891, 3–4.

45. Benjamin Titus Roberts, "Ordination of Women: A Review of an Article by Rev. G.W. Coleman," supplement to *The Free Methodist*, August 12, 1891, 1.

46. Ibid.

47. Ibid.

48. Ibid.

49. Ibid., 3.

50. Mesaros-Winckles, 2022.

51. Roberts, "Ordination of Women," 3.

52. A.F. Norrington, "Third Sitting," *General Conference Daily*, October 16, 1894, 68. *The Free Methodist* 1891 supplement with B.T. Roberts' response to General Superintendent Coleman's review of *Ordaining Women* also featured positive comments from *The Pentecost, The Union Signal, The Wesleyan Methodist*, and the *Evangelical Messenger* about the book. "What Is Said About This Book," 3–4.

53. In examining *The Free Methodist* between 1891 and 1894, ten articles were published on women's ordination. Eight of those articles were written by men. Richards notes in his master's thesis that issues of the 1886 *Free Methodist* featured the most articles on the subject (approximately 40), whereas, in 1890, there were less than 10. Richards, "B. T. Roberts and the Role of Women in Ministry," 141.

54. J.G. Terrill, ed., "Delegates to General Conference & Vote on Ordination of Women," *General Conference Daily*, October 11, 1894), 8. See appendix one for a breakdown of the vote by the annual conference.

55. After the 1890 General Conference, the number of female evangelists increased from around 40 women in 1890 to approximately 60 women by 1893. Women

were still not appointed in high numbers to preaching circuits, but even those numbers saw an increase from 12 appointments in 1890 to 23 appointments in 1893. Mesaros-Winckles, 2022.

56. Terrill, "Delegates to General Conference," 8.

57. Ibid.

58. C.M. Damon, "The Woman Question," *The Free Methodist*, September 19, 1894, 2–3.

59. In the early 1900s, the couple was also appointed together for ministry circuits. Mesaros-Winckles, 2022.

60. George M'Culloch, "Ordaining Women," *The Free Methodist*, September 12, 1894, 2–3.

61. D.J. Santmier, "Sixth Sitting," *General Conference Daily*, October 15, 1894, 59–62.

62. Ibid.

63. O.M. Owen, "Sixth Sitting," *General Conference Daily*, October 15, 1894, 67.

64. Mrs. Ida L. Gage, "Sixth Sitting," *General Conference Daily*, October 17, 1894, 80–81.

65. Ibid.

66. Ibid.

67. Freeborn Brooke, "Do Women Preachers Ever Wear Out?," *The Free Methodist*, May 30, 1911, 3; Lynn Webb, ed., *1907 General Conference Daily*; and W.B. Olmstead, ed., *1911 General Conference Daily*.

68. Freeborn Brooke, "Monday—Ordination Speeches," *General Conference Daily*, October 18, 1894, 94.

69. Terrill, "Delegates to General Conference," 8.

70. "Women May Not Preach," *Decatur Daily Republican*, October 18, 1894, 3; "Women May Not Preach," *The Commercial Appeal*, October 17, 1894, 8; "Women Preachers," *Great Falls Tribune*, October 20, 1894, 1; "Free Methodists Oppose Ordination of Women as Ministers," *Arkansas City Daily Traveler*, October 16, 1894, 8; "Free Methodists Oppose Ordination of Women as Ministers," *Weekly Republican-Traveler*, October 18, 1894, 1; "Against Women as Preachers," *Iowa City Press-Citizen*, October 17, 1894, 1; "The News Condensed," *Crestline Advocate*, October 18, 1894, 6; and "Morning News: Eastern," *Los Angeles Evening Express*, October 17, 1894, 2.

71. Susan Marshall, *Splintered Sisterhood: Gender and Class in the Campaign against Women's Suffrage* (Madison, WI: University of Wisconsin Press, 1997), 85.

72. "Women May Not Preach," 3; "Women May Not Preach," 8; "Women Preachers," 1; "Free Methodists Oppose Ordination of Women as Ministers," 8; "Free Methodists Oppose Ordination of Women as Ministers," 1; "Against Women as Preachers," 1; "The News Condensed," 6; and "Morning News: Eastern," 2.

73. Snyder, *Populist Saints*, 809.

74. Zenas Osborne, "Model Woman," *The Free Methodist*, November 21, 1899, 2; & G. Leonard Coughron, "Woman in Her Place," *The Free Methodist*, May 6, 1902, 2.

75. Margaret Bendroth, *Fundamentalism and Gender 1875 to Present* (New Haven, CT: Yale University Press, 1993), 100 & 112.

76. Historian Susan Marshall explains that in the United States, class relations hardened in the 1880s as urban problems increased with the arrival of foreign-born industrial workers. Wealthy Boston families fearful of all-out class warfare formalized the Boston Anti-Suffrage Association in the early 1890s. By the early 1900s, the organization's officers came from the Boston upper class. Many of the husbands were associated with Harvard or worked in the legal profession. Both the Boston Association and the New York Association intentionally recruited only women of "high social standing" for membership in their chapters. Marshall, *Splintered Sisterhood*, 35–55.

77. Theologian Kevin Watson also notes this tension in the Methodist Episcopal Church. In his book *Old or New School Methodism? The Fragmentation of Theological Traditions*, he argues that the expulsion of B.T. Roberts from the Methodist Episcopal Church was a wake-up call for the denomination. Three decades later, Methodist Episcopal leaders, such as Matthew Simpson, argued that the "New School Methodism" principles that got Roberts expelled were actually what unified all Methodists across numerous denominations. Ironically, while the Methodist Episcopal Church was beginning to re-embrace these tenants in the 1880s, the Free Methodist Church was slowly going away from them as they shifted towards the support of premillennialism, reformed eugenics, and race suicide (see chapter seven for a detailed overview). Kevin Watson, *Old or New School Methodism? The Fragmentation of Theological Traditions* (Oxford University Press, 2019); Edward Hart, Burton Jones, Walter Sellew & Wilson Hogue, "Pastoral Address Cont.," *The Free Methodist*, July 23, 1907, 9; and J.T. Logan, "Eugenics," *The Free Methodist*, December 31, 1912, 9.

78. Snyder, *Populist Saints*, 505.

Chapter 5

Shifting Narratives on Women's Role in *The Free Methodist* 1894–1915

Narratives constantly evolve and change, especially within organizations, as leadership shifts. At the turn of the twentieth century, the Free Methodist Church is a prime example of shifting organizational narratives. Until the early 1890s, under Roberts' leadership, the denomination embodied a progressive interpretation of the gospel, embracing women's contributions and allowing them to become licensed evangelists and elected lay delegates at quarterly, annual, and general conferences.[1] However, by the 1890s, Free Methodism was much more a religious *institution* than a religious *movement*. *The Free Methodist Book of Discipline* formalized church policy and paths to ministry. As sociologist Richard Niebuhr explains in *The Kingdom of God in America*, there is an immense difference between a religious institution guided by formal policy and procedure and the prophetic nature of a religious movement. The religious organization is conservative and cautious, yielding to various outside social factors affecting the lives of its members. Whereas the religious movement pushes the boundaries of social conventions or, as Niebuhr explains, "influencing rather than being influenced."[2]

After Roberts died in 1893 and the subsequent defeat of women's ordination at the 1894 General Conference, there was a noticeable shift in the denomination's narrative, particularly in how Free Methodist leaders viewed women's contributions as preachers, delegates, and their ministry capabilities. From 1894 to 1906, no action was taken on women's ordination.[3] However, the 1907 General Conference revisited the issue and established a deaconess order for women and allowed women evangelists to be elected as ministerial delegates to quarterly and annual conferences if they were appointed for a minimum of two years to a circuit.[4] The 1911 General Conference took things a step further and allowed women to be ordained as deacons, with the same responsibilities and privileges as their male colleagues.[5] The shifting organizational view on women's involvement was also seen in *The Free Methodist* as Wilson Hogue, a vocal opponent to women's ordination, became editor from 1894 until 1902. Hogue had been a General Conference delegate for the Genesee Conference at the 1890 and 1894 General Conferences where he voted against women's ordination.[6] During this period, *The Free Methodist* also regularly featured commentary on women's role within the church, society, and the home, but as editorial leadership shifted, so did the publication's tone.[7] The most powerful narrative tool in the denomination was now under the leadership of someone who did not share the progressive views of Roberts. Hogue would go on to become a general superintendent in the denomination from 1903 to 1919 and write one of the earliest comprehensive histories of Free Methodism,[8] thus ensuring that early denominational history was preserved from his perspective.

As rhetorical scholar Walter Fisher explains, organizational narratives compete until one dominant narrative emerges, capturing the audience's attention.[9] During Hogue's tenure as editor, the narrative regarding women evangelists gradually shifted from outright questioning of women's physical and intellectual capabilities to reluctant acknowledgment that they had limited biblical justification to serve, but not at the level of elder. Instead, the new narrative argued that women's strengths naturally led them into ministries favoring teaching, nurturing, and caring responsibilities such as the established 1907 deaconess order. However, despite the support of denominational leaders, Free Methodist women did not rush to join the deaconess order. By 1912 there were only eleven women with a deaconess license compared to four hundred and thirty-five women with an evangelist's license.[10]

Among the first deaconesses was Rebecca Sellew in 1910.[11] Sellew was the wife of general superintendent Walter Sellew. Sellew supported women's ordination as deacons and had written a short book, *Why Not? A Plea for the Ordination of Those Women Whom God Calls to Preach His Gospel*. In it, Sellew argued there was biblical justification for their ordination, but only at the level of deacon. The Free Methodist Publishing House published the pamphlet twice, first in 1894 and again in 1914, after the denomination had approved ordaining women as deacons at the 1911 General Conference.[12] The creation of specifically female categories of ministry at the 1907 and 1911 General Conferences seemed to satisfy most supporters of women's ordination. Many Free Methodist leaders no longer saw the need to ordain women as elders once they became ordained deacons. Thus, women evangelists were once again thrust into the rhetorical position of finding ways to gain respect and acceptance in ministry without the designation of "elder."

Fig. 5.1. Wilson Hogue served as a Free Methodist general superintendent from 1903 to 1919 and as the editor of *The Free Methodist* from 1894 to 1903. Source: Marston Memorial Historical Center

THE SHIFTING TITLES FOR WOMEN EVANGELISTS

A noticeable rhetorical shift occurred in women evangelist reports during the first two decades of the twentieth century. More self-identified as "pastor" or "evangelist," whereas in the 1890s, more women signed their names at the end of the ministry reports.[13] After women could be ordained deacons in 1911, the first female deacons also began using "Rev.," a title usually used only for ordained elders. Local newspapers as well began referring to women deacons as "Rev.," but the denominational appointments republished in local newspapers continued to call women deacons "Miss" or "Mrs.," implying that perhaps the title "Rev." was self-styled as a way for women deacons to be accepted in their local communities.[14] After all, ordination as a deacon was still ordination, and as a deacon, women could now serve communion, marry, and baptize members of their congregations.[15] The only roles not open to women were conference superintendent or bishop,[16] as only ordained elders could serve in those roles.[17]

In addition to choosing authoritative titles for their reports, women evangelists emphasized spiritual sanctification in their testimonies. However, this emphasis on personal vice and subsequent sanctification should not be viewed as an attempt by women to fit within the rhetoric of their "naturally weaker state."[18] Instead, it should be seen as another rhetorical tool women evangelists used to illustrate that men and women experienced the same challenges and sanctification. At a time when the editorial, reforms, and family circle sections of *The Free Methodist* often highlighted gender differences and designated gender roles, these ministry reports were the most powerful rhetorical tool available to women.

Competing rhetorical visions within Free Methodism became even more pronounced during this period. One narrative favored the Methodist theology of sanctification, where everyone, regardless of class, race, or gender, was equally forgiven, saved, and capable of serving in ministry. The other favored the premillennial interpretation of Scripture, which was very literal and emphasized man's fall from grace because of woman's sin. The premillennial narrative paradoxically condemned women as less capable of ministering because of original sin while also elevating them as the spiritual nurturer of the home.[19] Depending on who was the editor of *The Free Methodist,* one of these narratives was favored more than the other. Hogue favored the premillennialist narrative, whereas Charles Ebey, who replaced him as editor in 1904, condemned it.[20]

WILSON HOGUE AS EDITOR OF *THE FREE METHODIST* 1898–1903

The "different but capable narrative" was one Hogue embraced as it also neatly fit within his premillennial theology. This frame of argument had been present in the 1890 debates on women's ordination and within *The Free Methodist*, particularly in the 1892 special supplement where General Superintendent George Coleman's presented theological arguments against Roberts' book *Ordaining Women*.[21] Under Hogue's editorial leadership, it became even more common to see front-page snippets of current news or editorials favoring the "different but capable" narrative.[22] The simplicity of gender definitions appealed to individuals resistant to immense social changes in the Progressive Era. As historian Margret Bendroth notes in her history of American fundamentalism, this premillennial theology neatly defined both masculine and feminine roles:

> Dispensationalism allowed women the relief of being sinners, with full access to divine grace. It affirmed their desire to serve and invested it with new meaning, for in premillennial thought, missionary service was more than a cultural imperative—it heralded the triumphant return of Christ himself. Men, in turn, found their masculinity both affirmed and challenged; even endless toil could be a form of spiritual obedience. Furthermore, dispensationalism offered a more nuanced expression of manliness than the tireless virility demanded by the secular world. It opposed feminizing forces in religion and society yet allowed men a romantic, passionate outlet.[23]

Premillennialism was in direct opposition to the egalitarian theology laid out by Roberts in his book *Ordaining Women*.[24] Decidedly anti-suffrage, premillennialism views on gender were always sharpest during times of stress and transition, such as the early twentieth century. Some of the most famous anti-suffrage advocates would emerge during this time. One such advocate was Edward Bok, who Hogue favorably highlighted on the periodical's front page in 1899. The first page of *The Free Methodist* usually contained the editor's summaries of important current events and opinions of interest to readers. Hogue summarized Bok in a section entitled "Educate Women for Higher Womanhood," where he lambasted women pursuing a college education, quoting Bok's: "If the instinct of daughter, sister or wife dies out in the college-bred woman, even in the course of the most brilliant career, the world will forget to love her; it will scorn her justly." Hogue suggested the solution was for women to be cheery and tidy wherever they went, making their environment always "home-like" lest she forget her role as the primary nurturer.[25] Bok's writings regularly touted women's "natural moral superiority" as justification for maintaining separate spheres for the sexes.

A favorite rhetorical tactic of Hogue's was suggesting limitations on women's leadership roles in the church instead of outright banning them from public ministry. In the February 20, 1900, *Free Methodist*, Hogue published an article entitled "Women's Work" written by an author identified only as J.S. The author quotes Episcopalian Bishop Potter,[26] an advocate for women serving in deaconess or other mission-oriented organizations, several times throughout the article:

> Bishop Potter, when he considered a woman's highest sphere, replied, "Wifehood, motherhood, sisterhood, the ministry of sympathy and love. This being the case, the woman who is looking for work in service of the Lord but who is kept at home by family duties, if she fulfils [sic] her God-appointed ministry, will find the noblest and most enduring work in training her children for the Lord."[27]

J.S. noted that women who minister outside the home were best suited for the "ministry of sympathy and love" or teaching or home mission work such as visiting the sick. The article concluded with a critique of the relatively new ministry role of preaching. The author applauds women for "trying" but encourages them to pursue more effective forms of ministry, such as acts of kindness and training children in the home.[28]

"Woman's Work" garnered enough attention from readers that a rebuttal was published in March 1900 by an R.B.S. However, even the rebuttal still acknowledged women's highest sphere as motherhood. It applauded women who fulfilled that role successfully, noting they would do more for God as a mother than any woman working outside the home. Women's advancement was lauded but always with a caveat that their highest calling was still in the home. This was a common theme in *The Free Methodist* during this period.

Hogue's Views on Suffrage

Another common rhetorical tactic by anti-suffragists was acknowledging women's need for increased legal protection while at the same time insisting that they did not need to vote to gain those protections.[29] Hogue's philosophy on suffrage was very much in line with this view. For example, in the August 22, 1901, *Free Methodist*, Hogue wrote an editorial entitled "Women's Rights," in which he addressed women's lack of legal control over their own property, wages, and guardianship of their children. The article was favorable toward increased legal protection for women, but the article in no way fully endorsed women entering the public sphere.[30]

Another instance of Hogue's philosophy can be seen in the November 17, 1903, article by A.J. M'Kinney. In the article M'Kinney attacked suffrage as ineffective, using Colorado as an example. Colorado had given women the vote in 1893, and anti-suffragists loved to cite immorality in the state as an example of how giving women the vote had limited societal impact.[31] M'Kinney's argument was based on his experience as a resident of Colorado. Hogue included an interview with him at the end of the editorial, asking M'Kinney questions on the merits of suffrage. While his responses were decidedly anti-suffrage, Hogue did acknowledge in his interview introduction that "Women should not be denied the right of suffrage simply because they are so unfortunate as to have been born women."[32] As an editor, Hogue recognized women's legal inequality, but, as evidenced by his comments in M'Kinney's interview, women were still viewed as spiritually inferior.

Hogue's Perspective on Women in Ministry

Even articles Hogue included that defended women's ministry did so from a limited perspective. In the January 8, 1901, issue, a J.H. Collins wrote an editorial, "Bible Defense of Woman's Ministry," outlining examples of women as prophetesses. Citing Deborah in Judges and the Samaritan woman in John and Pentecost in Acts, where the Holy Spirit was given to both men and women, Collins argued that women were equally qualified as spiritual prophets or deaconesses. However, Collins' defense of women in ministry continually referred to women's unique abilities. "With womanly intuition and motherly love she makes direct to the citadel of the heart, and, conquering there she soon conquers all for Jesus."[33] The "unique nature" of women was also a common argument by anti-suffragists who used this rhetoric to discourage political enfranchisement. The same arguments were often used by Free Methodists who opposed women being ordained as elders. The conflict was not that women should serve in ministry; instead, it was about what type of ministry was socially acceptable and biblically justified.

Unlike Collins' veiled critique, many *Free Methodist* articles during this period were not even subtle in their anti-suffrage rhetoric. For example, in the May 6, 1902, issue, an article by G. Leonard Coughron entitled "Woman in Her Place" blamed women working outside the home as the cause of all social evils that, unless corrected, would "subvert the whole social and business part of life":

> It is a foregone conclusion that women are crowding men out of employment. All careful observers are aware of this. And why is it? Is it because she is competent to fill many positions in the business world? I think all, or nearly all, will

agree that is not the case. It is because they, not feeling the care or responsibility of anyone depending upon them for support, can work and do work for less than a man with a family or one who expects to be under these responsibilities. All intelligent people acknowledge the propriety of the man in supporting the family, his children, and the companion whom God has given him for a helpmeet. He is the one to go forth and battle against the world's fierce blasts of disappointment, hunger, and woe. He is whom God has made the stronger to buffet the world's cold frowns, and shield and shelter her that is the weaker vessel.[34]

Coughron's article was refuted by an author only going by E.M. in the June 17, 1902, issue. However, even the rebuttal was not a defense but a critique of men not rising to their responsibilities.[35] E.M. wrote about attending a missionary work meeting and noting several unaccompanied single women in attendance. When the author inquired why they did not have male escorts, the response was the local men were "loafers plenty, but no companions for self-respecting girls."[36] The editorial concluded with a plea to hold men accountable: "Yes, we agree that people are going too fast, and in the wrong direction, but when we set about making provision for good fatherhood the motherhood will fail into line again."[37] In addition to emphasizing separate spheres, Hogue often remained neutral, if not slightly opposed, to women's suffrage. Although detractors favored separate roles for each gender, within *The Free Methodist* correspondence section, women evangelists painted a very different narrative as they sent in ministry accounts from around the country. Thus, while most of the publication emphasized gender differences, women's ability to publish their accomplishments in the correspondence section ensured their contributions were still visible. Reflecting the increasingly conservative nature of the denomination, fewer women were appointed to ministry circuits during this time. For example, in 1903, there were 295 licensed women evangelists, but only seventy-eight (or fifteen percent) were appointed to a circuit. This disconnect between licensing and appointment was a regular topic in *The Free Methodist*, particularly under the editorial leadership of Hogue's replacement Charles Ebey.[38]

CHARLES EBEY AS EDITOR OF *THE FREE METHODIST* 1903–1907

The editorial tone of *The Free Methodist* shifted under Hogue's sucessor, Charles Ebey. Unlike Hogue, Ebey's front-page editorial content supported suffrage and women's involvement in ministry.[39] However, while Ebey's editorials were largely pro-equality, like Hogue, women's voices were primarily relegated to the correspondence section. As the 1907 General Conference approached, it was clear delegates would be asked to make crucial decisions regarding women's roles within their denomination.

For decades Free Methodists had been presented with both positions, making space for those who supported a progressive social gospel and those who supported premillennialism. In the coming decade, the decision on which narrative best fits Free Methodism would be decided by its members. While many women wrote ministry reports during this period, there are a few who stand out as prolific writers: Blanche Stamp, an evangelist who traveled the country preaching with her husband, Christopher Stamp; Eliza Witherspoon, an evangelist in southern Missouri and Arkansas; Laura Lamb, an evangelist in Pennsylvania and Ada Hall, an evangelist in northern Iowa and Minnesota. Lamb and Hall were also among the first women to be ordained deacons.[40]

ELIZA WITHERSPOON, TRAILBLAZING EVANGELIST IN SOUTHERN MISSOURI

Witherspoon had been preaching in southern Missouri since the 1880s. At first, she ministered alongside her mother and sister but later as a solo evangelist. In her 1895 *Free Methodist* report, she told readers her family was "advocating the principles of Free Methodism" in that part of the country for the past seventeen years and were the lone Free Methodists in the region. The 1895 report highlighted a three-week series of revival meetings Witherspoon, her mother, and sister had recently concluded where "God sent us help and souls were converted to God—more than twenty souls." After 1895 Witherspoon's ministry reports focus on solo work as a Free Methodist evangelist in Arkansas, southern Missouri, and eventually Kansas, and depending on the year, she also had the special designation of conference evangelist, meaning her annual conference designated her as a traveling preacher with no set church appointment.[41] By 1900 the *Free Methodist Book of Discipline* outlined two distinct licensure paths for evangelists. The quarterly conference could license individuals, who would be reviewed for their license renewal four times a year. The annual conference could also license evangelists after successfully serving as quarterly conference evangelists for four years.[42] Witherspoon's designation as a conference evangelist indicated she had achieved an annual conference license and demonstrated the trust her conference had in her ministry abilities. In addition to serving as an evangelist, Witherspoon was also an annual conference delegate in 1895 and 1900 serving on conference committees discussing education and raising money to publish the minutes. She was also appointed a lay delegate to the 1911 General Conference.[43]

Fig. 5.2.   Locations of Eliza Witherspoon's ministry in southern Missouri and Arkansas.
Ministry illustrations by Alley Shaffer

Witherspoon devoted her life to ministry, never marrying and living with
her mother in Bates, Missouri, well into her forties. Like other Free Methodist
women evangelists of the time, by 1900, Witherspoon self-identified as an
"evangelist" for census reports.[44] She had a passion for Sunday school work,
and her reports in *The Free Methodist* regularly emphasized this, as well
as her work preaching and assisting in revival services. Her early reports
also often emphasized the communal nature of her ministry by regularly
using "us" and "we" when referencing ministry accomplishments. In her
July 8, 1895, *Free Methodist* report from Virginia, Missouri, she noted, "In
the month of April we held meetings for three weeks. God sent us help and
souls were converted to God—more than twenty in number. Five professed
experiences of holiness."[45] The report also mentions her work in organizing a
Sunday school in Virginia. Witherspoon ends the report with a prayer closely

resembling Psalm 77: "'God keep each one' is my sinner prayer. 'Thy way of God is in the sanctuary; who is so great a God as our God? Thou art be that doest wonders.'"[46] Just as Gage, Grant, and Wetherald used in their reports, Witherspoon interweaved biblical passages in her ministry accounts. The practice helped women evangelists rhetorically connect spiritual precedent to their ministry accomplishments so the reader could see the connection.[47] As Witherspoon's career progressed, her ministry reports began to emphasize her accomplishments. This change was perhaps partly due to her increased leadership roles within her annual conference and the need to illustrate her success.

After 1900 she continued to work alone in ministry and to self-identify as a minister even though she was not an ordained elder. In her October 15, 1905, update from Phelps, Missouri, she only uses "I," emphasizing her intensive work in the area. "I desire to state a few facts concerning the Lord's work in this place," and "I have been doing all that I could for the salvation of precious souls for nearly three years." She ended her report with personal testimony, using her experiences as a rhetorical tool to help illustrate her familiarity with biblical passages and her commitment to evangelism:

> Glory to God in the highest. I am pressing on my way upward. The Lord enables me to grow stronger every day. I am so glad I belong to the blood-washed company. I love the Lord. I love His people. I am devoting all I have to his cause—talent, time, voice, silver, and gold; not a mite do I withhold. I would gladly give more if I had more.[48]

Witherspoon's reference to silver and gold is perhaps a reference to I Corinthians 3:12–13, which notes that only works of silver and gold will withstand the fire of judgment and be judged as worthy.

In the 1910 U.S. Census, she listed her occupation as "minister" and the "wage earner" in her residence. The 1910 census also listed her as living with an Ollie and Bessie Dryer. Ollie Dryer was another women evangelist in Witherspoon's annual conference who was co-appointed with her to the Harrison County Circuit in 1908.[49] This type of co-appointment happened several times throughout her career. In 1910 she was co-appointed to Harrison with Grace Huntsinger.[50] Witherspoon was designated as a mentor to these new evangelists, indicating her success and respect within her annual conference. Witherspoon appears to spend most of her career in areas with relatively few other Free Methodists. This is evident in her 1911 General Conference testimony published in *The Free Methodist*. Witherspoon had been elected a General Conference delegate by the Southern Missouri and Arkansas Conference. In the article, she admitted that having the money to attend the conference was a surprise and that she was grateful other Free

Methodists stepped up to assist her. Her lack of financial resources is another example of the financial hardships many women evangelists faced as they were given immense responsibility, but not granted the benefits, such as rail fare discounts, that the title of "elder" brought.[51] In her testimony about the conference, Witherspoon recalled she had never seen so many "Saved people before."[52] In fact, the 1911 *General Conference Daily* note that she gave the opening prayer for the nineteenth session. That session was significant, and having a woman evangelist give the opening prayer was most likely intentional as Bishop Walter Sellew brought forth a motion asking delegates to grant women the right to be ordained deacons.[53] After serving as a conference evangelist and filling several circuits in rural Arkansas and Missouri for seventeen years, Eliza moved to Kansas around 1912. She continued her work with the Free Methodist Church in Kansas until she died in 1932.[54]

BLANCHE STAMP, TRAVELING REVIVAL LEADER

Like Witherspoon, Blanche Stamp did not fit the emerging denominational rhetoric of separate ministry spheres for women. A licensed evangelist and spouse of Christopher Stamp, a prominent Free Methodist minister, she spent much of her life traveling the United States and co-preaching revival services alongside her husband.[55] In 1903 Christopher Stamp was elected a general conference evangelist and held that position until 1913. While Christopher was the ordained elder and elected evangelist, he was intentional in his reports of including Blanche's work.[56] However, despite Christopher's intent to fully recognize Blanche's ministry, her contributions were mainly forgotten by Blanche's death in 1945. Her obituary in *The Free Methodist* noted her only as a devoted spouse who supported her husband's ministry. No indication of her solo ministry or co-ministry with Christopher is mentioned. This rewriting is another indication of rhetorical tensions within the denomination. Obituaries in *The Free Methodist* were written by clergy or family who knew the deceased. Depending on the writer's views, women evangelists and deacons were either lauded for their contributions or had their work downplayed, if it was mentioned at all.[57]

Even during her lifetime, Blanche's contributions were somewhat out of the ordinary. Most of the Stamps' ministry updates were published in *The Free Methodist* under Charles Ebey's editorial leadership. A vocal supporter of women's suffrage and ordination, Ebey regularly wrote editorials and highlighted news stories featuring advancements for women's suffrage. Because the debate on women's ordination and role within the church was still intense during his term as editor, Ebey was known for adding editorial comments when reporting on denominational news. For example, in an update on the

Fig. 5.3.   Blanche Stamp circa 1912. Source: Marston Memorial Historical Center

1907 General Conference and Christopher Stamp's re-election on the first ballot as a general conference evangelist, Ebey commented, "We venture to say, however, that in our opinion no small part of the generous praise accorded our friend and brother is to the fact of his having had so able an assistant and helpmeet in the person of his talented wife, who, by the way, is a woman."[58] Ebey's aside illustrated the continued rhetorical tension regarding women's place. As the ministry partner to a well-known evangelist, Blanche's ministry was front and center in the denominational debate on gender roles.

Blanche had been a licensed evangelist in the Pittsburgh Free Methodist Conference since 1894. By 1902 she was traveling widely with Christopher and holding revival services nationwide.[59] After Tennessee, the Stamps held revivals in Louisiana and Mississippi for two months. In an August 30, 1902, *Free Methodist* report from Gallatin, Tennessee, she provided a glimpse into their revivals. Assisting J.M. Keen and W. Mayfield, who were district elders, they pitched a large tabernacle in the center of Gallatin, where Blanche noted, "the Lord began to send the crowds." Blanche said the location was "the most needy field I ever was in, and I believe God will come and answer the prayer in the salvation of many people."[60]

Reports to *The Free Methodist* often noted both "C.W. and Mrs. B.E. Stamp" or "our revival." Local newspaper accounts also speak of a couple who were both extremely powerful preachers. A March 29, 1912, front-page announcement in the *LeMars Semi-Weekly Sentinel* called Christopher and Blanche speakers who were "highly recommended by the pulpit and press" and invited community members to come to hear them preach during a series of revival meetings at the local Free Methodist Church.[61] Blanche is also called a "speaker of rare ability" in a December 14, 1912, article in the *Rock Island Argus*.[62] In describing Christopher, a 1921 article in the Kittanning, Pennsylvania, *Simpsons Daily Leader Times* described him as a preacher and orator who had "few equals and no superiors." The newspaper also noted that Christopher had preached not only in the United States but also in Europe.[63]

In addition to these secondhand reports, Stamp wrote vivid accounts of their ministry experiences. In an April 16, 1911, *Free Methodist* report, Blanche recalled a visit to Manhattan, Kansas, where she was "preaching the gospel of peace." A sixty-seven-year-old Catholic woman came to hear her, and while she was "very deaf" and had not been in a church for forty years, she seemed keen on listening to Blanche preach:

The Spirit applied the truth and touched her hearing. She was seized with old-time conviction. She heard every word of the sermon and came with a broken heart to the altar and prayed earnestly though all was dark and the manner of the altar service new and strange to her.[64]

Blanche and Christopher visited the woman after the service, and Blanche recalled this visit in her report:

> It was truly sad to look upon her face. She would frequently stop and say, "Sister Stamp, I hope I am forgiven, but oh I want to know it." Again and again she would repeat the words, "I hope I am saved, but I want to know it." At last she exclaimed, "O Sister Stamp, I know it! I know it! Think of a woman sixty-seven years of age, and never happy in her life. O wonderful gospel!" Having now a thirst for the word of life, she bought a Bible and is now daily drinking at the foundation of the stream that maketh glad the city of God.[65]

While Blanche usually wrote their reports, Christopher did send in several as the general conference evangelist in 1913. In an August 5, 1911, report, his support of Blanche as his equal in ministry is quite clear when he outlined reasons why he would not publish his travel schedule. "After considering it carefully, we concluded it would not be in the best interests," he said. Christopher explained that it was impossible to predict how long a revival would take, and they did not want to be held to a schedule that might be impossible to keep. The Stamps' refusal to publish their schedule was unique, as all the other appointed general conference evangelists' published their preaching itineraries. Christopher even noted that the editor of *The Free Methodist* had been hounding him for their schedule. In concluding the report, Christopher again used "we," noting, "we may regard the question differently in the future, but in the meantime, we shall follow our first thought." As general conference evangelist, he continued to refer to his appointment as an unofficial co-appointment with Blanche, noting this again in his June 15, 1915, resignation announcement:

> When first elected twelve years ago, Mrs. Stamp joined in the determination to spare no effort to make our department a success. Our three young daughters, having been converted while they were children, had the work of God at heart, and decided that it would be best for Mrs. Stamp to travel with me as much as possible and that they would continue their school work at the A.M. Chesbrough Seminary at Chili, New York. Their summer vacations were spent with us in our meetings, and these were seasons of great joy to us all.[66]

The Stamps' ministry illustrates an egalitarian marriage and ministry partnership. It draws attention to a common difficulty many female evangelists faced when choosing between raising their children or preaching the gospel.[67] In the Stamps' case, their daughters' support is remarkable. Their rigorous travel schedule appears not to have had a determinantal effect on family life, as their daughter Ada also became a licensed evangelist, regularly assisting her parents in services.[68]

Fig. 5.4.   Christopher Stamp circa 1912. Source: Spring Arbor University White Library Archive

Blanche's continual co-billing as a revivalist did not fit neatly into the emerging denominational narrative of women serving in secondary ministry roles such as deaconess or deacon.[69] The Stamps continued ministering together even after Christopher stepped down as general conference evangelist. While Blanche was still a licensed evangelist when women were granted ordination as deacons in 1911, there is no indication she chose to become one. However, other female evangelists did take the opportunity to become ordained and to change their status from "evangelist" to "reverend."

WOMEN DEACONS—EARLY "REVERENDS" IN REGIONAL PERIODICALS

When the 1911 General Conference gave annual conferences the authority to ordain women as deacons, they did so with the caveat that "this ordination of women shall not be considered a step towards ordination as an elder."[70] Indeed, women were not allowed to be ordained elders until 1974.[71] Supporters of women's ordination as elders seemed to realize that the quest for ordination beyond deacon was a losing battle. So, instead of continuing the fight, they embraced the decision and rhetorically used it to provide legitimacy to women in ministry. When the first women were ordained as deacons in 1913, Bishop Burton Jones, a supporter of women preachers, wrote a front-page editorial in *The Free Methodist* applauding the accomplishments of the first five ordained women. Jones chose to identify Laura Lamb, Ada Hall, Bersha Green, Anna Bright, and Minnie Beers as "Reverend." However, there is no indication this was an official title used by the denomination, as annual conference appointments continued to use the terms "Miss" or "Mrs." for women appointed to circuits, regardless of whether they were evangelists or deacons. The title "Rev." only appears by ordained elders in annual conference minutes.[72] Women and men who used the title "Rev." were making a clear rhetorical move to grant women increased credibility in their ministries.

Laura Lamb and Ada Hall, two of the early female deacons, readily embraced the usage of "Rev." Both women were long-serving evangelists in the denomination. Lamb had been appointed to circuits in the Pittsburgh Conference for nineteen years before her 1913 ordination, and Hall had been appointed to circuits in the Minnesota and Northern Iowa Conference for ten years.[73] Hall had aggressively campaigned for ordination, publishing an article entitled "Forward, Backward, Which?" in the April 25, 1911, *Free Methodist*. In the article, she outlined the frustrations of female evangelists who continually had to defend the denomination's position on women's ordination to outsiders:

ORDAINED WOMEN

REV. LAURA LAMB

REV. S. ADA HALL

REV. ANNA L. BRIGHT

Fig. 5.5. The first Free Methodist women deacons. Bersha Green is on bottom left, Minnie Beers is on bottom right. Note that the author Bishop Burton Jones refers to the deacons with the title "Rev." both in the captions and in the article. This is the only *Free Methodist* article that uses this title for the women deacons. Source: Spring Arbor University White Library Archive

We have been humiliated and ashamed when we have to explain to outside people the position of our church on this question. They always go away disappointed, for they expect better things of us because of our high spiritual standard. As laborers together with God and with one another in the great harvest field, seeing the night so soon cometh, is it not wise that you rather help those women who labor among you, and save them from laboring under the present humiliating hindrances?[74]

Hall explained that women did not desire to excel above their male brethren but to have recognition and a title that reflected their contributions:

> We came from the position of an evangelist-pastor one hour to that of a conference preacher . . . [t]he next we know not what we are nor to what class we belong. Is not this a subject of more importance than deciding names? If we had but one name and knew what it stood for, we would be thankful. This question will not never [die] down or be settled until the right is reached.[75]

Hall's article pinpointed an ongoing rhetorical trend within the denomination—changing the title of women's roles to give the appearance of more ministerial authority without giving them any authority. When women were first licensed as evangelists in 1874, they were simply called "evangelists." However, as Hall noted later, the designation became more complex as evangelists could be licensed by quarterly or annual conferences. The annual conference minutes became littered with evangelists called "quarterly conference evangelists," "annual conference evangelists," and the former title of "evangelist." Further complicating things was the 1907 General Conference ruling allowing female evangelists to be elected ministerial delegates to quarterly and annual conferences if they had been appointed as a local pastor for two consecutive years.[76] Hall's frustration over titles is perhaps one of the reasons she embraced ordination in any form, as it provided her a way to finally legitimize her role as a local pastor and gave her the authority to finally baptize, marry, and serve communion. Hall flipped the script and used whatever title was available to elevate herself to the position she was already filling.

ADA HALL, ADVOCATE FOR WOMEN IN MINISTRY

Even before becoming an ordained deacon, Hall was a well-known preacher in MInnesota and northern Iowa, appointed to several circuits before her 1913 ordination.[77] When she was ordained deacon, the *Palo Alto Reporter* published her photo and a front-page story about her ministry and appointment in Mason City, Iowa. Mason City was one of her most prolonged appointments, serving there from 1908 through 1909.[78] Hall herself writes about Mason

City in the April 25, 1911, *Free Methodist*. In the report, Hall noted that the church had a full house for Easter Sunday.[79] She also chose to identify herself as "pastor" in the report. Local papers regularly referred to her as Rev. Ada Hall when announcing services or special events she was participating in. Ordination as deacon provided a solution to Hall's frustration regarding titles for women evangelists. As noted in her April 1911 *Free Methodist* article, it also was a relief from social embarrassment as more denominations were ordaining women and the Free Methodist Church was not. In addition to self-identifying as a pastor and being called a "Rev.," Hall also identified as a "home missionary" in certain reports.[80]

According to the 1915 annual conference minutes, Hall was appointed as the conference missionary for northern Iowa and Minnesota. The role involved travel and church planting, which Hall reported on in a July 27, 1915, *Free Methodist* update. At the time, she was working with fellow Free Methodists to establish a society in Spring Valley, Minnesota, and was experiencing numerous roadblocks:

> The battle has been hard and long. Opposition from preachers and old professors has been kept up throughout. We have enjoyed the marks that Jesus said should attend His people, being defamed, misrepresented, called liars, deceivers, trouble-makers, crazy, holy-rollers, and have even been distinguished by the Norwegian's most emphatic expression of contempt: "Rodden Pok!"[81]

Despite the incredible opposition, Hall established a Free Methodist class of nine new members. She would continue to serve in this role for several years before marrying C.E. Marsh in 1923. The couple moved to the Arizona and Southern California Free Methodist Conferences, where they were often co-appointed.[82] Like Stamp, Hall was a gifted evangelist who drew crowds. A 1925 article in the *Modesto Evening News* noted a week-long revival service led by Hall-Marsh where an "immense crowd" was present. Her obituary in the June 24, 1938, *Free Methodist* also illustrated the impact of her ministry. It was rare for women to not only have an obituary but also tributes of their ministry published, and Hall had an entire column of tributes published in addition to her obituary.[83] Minnie Beers, also one of the first women deacons, wrote a tribute to Hall, reminiscing how she was "fearless in her stand for things she believed vital to the spirituality of the church she loved." Beers also noted that Hall was a vocal champion for women in ministry and had requested that her funeral service be conducted entirely by women preachers. Another tribute by E. Merle McCoid described Hall's concern for current and future generations of Free Methodists. Quoting Hall, McCoid said she often noted "the old paths are still the best paths. Let's contend for the faith,"[84] McCoid also wrote Hall's obituary and chose to refer to her as "Rev."[85] Not every female deacon was given that honor, as both Minnie Beers' and Bersha Green's obituaries only briefly mentioned their ordinations, and Beers is not even called "Rev." in her 1958 *Free Methodist* obituary.[86] Among the first five women deacons, only two seem to have been able to reshape their ministerial role post-ordination. Like Hall, Laura Lamb also identified as "Rev." numerous times and was referred to by that title in local publications. The other three women deacons—Beers, Bright, and Green, were not consistently identified by their titles.

LAURA LAMB, INSTITUTION BUILDING IN PENNSYLVANIA AND FLORIDA

Lamb's ministry was one of institution building for the denomination. Converted as a teen, Lamb first began ministry at the Free Methodist Olive Branch Mission in Chicago. By 1911 she was a licensed evangelist in the Pittsburgh Conference and, by 1913, an ordained deacon. Her reports to *The Free Methodist* were accounts of church plants she was active in establishing.[87] In March 1915 she sent two reports of revivals in Greensburg, Pennsylvania, where she was helping establish a new Free Methodist society. Lamb reported:

> Meetings are increasing interest. House full. Twenty-five at altar last Sunday. In all, forty-five have been forward. Some are praying through in the old-fashioned way. Tobacco and Worldliness are being given up. Our hearts are encouraged. We are just getting started.[88]

She concluded with her name and self-identified as "pastor." In addition to establishing a Free Methodist society in Greensburg, Lamb is also credited with establishing the Free Methodist work in East Pittsburg, where she was appointed from 1901 to 1904.[89] Her obituary in *The Free Methodist* noted that she built the church and the parsonage and paid off all debt. In 1925 she transferred to the Georgia and Florida Conference, where her obituary credited her with establishing the church in St. Petersburg, Florida, and building the church and the parsonage.[90]

Lamb's and even Hall's work in establishing new churches exemplify what many Progressive Era women evangelists were doing. Instead of accepting parallel forms of ministry, such as the Free Methodist deaconess order, they took leadership opportunities that put them in charge of both men and women. Religious historian Priscilla Pope Levinson labels women evangelists such as Lamb and Hall as "pioneering leaders in America who held supreme power and authority over their institution, even over men."[91] The 1907 General

Conference decision to allow women evangelists serving as local pastors to be elected ministerial delegates at quarterly and annual conferences had been highly controversial. Critics saw the 1907 governance change as a threat to men's God-given spiritual authority in the church. In contrast, the subsequent decisions to create a deaconess order and ordain women as both critics and supporters widely applauded deacons. Nevertheless, despite successful examples of women in senior leadership positions at the local level, the Free Methodist Church continued to resist allowing women access to the highest positions of church leadership.[92] Supporters of women's ordination saw the decision as evidence that women were finally getting the recognition they deserved.[93] In reality, the decision still limited women's role within the church. The subsequent creation of the Free Methodist Deaconess Order in 1907 and women's ordination as deacons in 1911 were steps towards cementing the rhetoric of separate spheres as the dominant narrative within the denomination.

NOTES

1. Women had been granted the right to be delegates at the 1886 General Conference when the role was opened to evangelists. They had been able to be licensed evangelists since 1874. See T.B. Arnold, ed., "Fourth Session," *General Conference Dailies*, October 18, 1886; B.T. Roberts, ed., *The Doctrines and Disciplines of The Free Methodist Church 1874* (North Chili, NY: 1875), 84; and B.T. Roberts, ed., *The Doctrines and Disciplines of The Free Methodist Church 1886* (North Chili, NY: 1887), 84.

2. Richard Niebuhr, *The Kingdom of God in America* (Middletown, CT: Wesleyan University Press, 1988), 13.

3. Benson Roberts, ed., *1898 General Conference Dailies*; and W.B. Olmstead, ed., *1903 General Conference Dailies*.

4. Free Methodist Church, *The Doctrines and Disciplines of The Free Methodist Church* (Chicago: Free Methodist Publishing House, 1908), 100–101.

5. Free Methodist Church, *The Doctrine and Disciplines of The Free Methodist Church* (Chicago: Free Methodist Publishing House, 1912), 49.

6. Wilson Hogue, "Seventh Sitting," *1890 General Conference Daily*, October 17, 1890, 119–22; and G. Terrill, ed., "Delegates to General Conference & Vote on Ordination of Women," *General Conference Daily*, October 11, 1894, 8.

7. Ibid.

8. Wilson Hogue, "Was It Wise? No. 1," *The Free Methodist*, February 7, 1911, 2; Wilson Hogue, "Was It Wise? No. 2," *The Free Methodist*, February 14, 1911, 2; and Wilson Hogue, *History of Free Methodism Volume 2* (Chicago: Free Methodist Publishing House, 1915), 242.

9. Walter Fisher, *Human Communication as Narration: Toward a Philosophy of Reason, Value, and Action* (Columbia: South Carolina Press, 1987), 18.

10. Christy Mesaros-Winckles, *Data on Free Methodist Women Evangelists 1876–1920* (March 2022), distributed by Christy Mesaros-Winckles.

11. Ibid.

12. Walter Sellew, *Why Not? A Plea for the Ordination of Those Women Whom God Calls to Preach His Gospel*, 2nd edition (Chicago: Free Methodist Publishing House, 1914), 3; and William Olmstead, ed., "Nineteenth Setting," *General Conference Daily*, June 30, 1911, 4.

13. For examples of women self-identifying as pastors, see Laura Lamb, "Greensburg, Pennsylvania," *The Free Methodist*, December 14, 1915, 7; and Ada Hall, "Gleanings: Mason City, Iowa," *The Free Methodist*, April 25, 1911, 5.

14. Local newspapers regularly refer to Laura Lamb, Ada Hall, and Anna Bright with the designation "Rev." after their ordination as deacons. Minnie Beers appears in local papers with the title "pastor." However, in annual conference appointments published in local newspapers, none of the women are given these titles. Instead, they are listed as "Miss" or "Mrs." for appointments, whereas ordained male elders are referred to as "Rev." It seems to imply that the Free Methodist Church was not using the term "Rev." for women deacons. See "Free Methodist Church," *The Corvina Argus*, May 22, 1925, 8; "The Week's Doings," *Palo Alto Reporter*, December 9, 1915, 5; "First Meeting of District," *South Haven Daily Tribune*, October 2, 1914, 9; "Double Funeral," *The Goshen Democrat*, March 21, 1913, 1; "Free Methodist Pastors Named," *Centralia Evening Sentinel*, August 31, 1925, 6; "Apollo PA Is Chosen for 1923 Meeting," *East Liverpool Evening Review*, October 9, 1922, 4; "Church Announcements," *Charleroi Mail*, June 30, 1919, 6; and "Free Methodists," *The Covina Argus*, October 15, 1926, 1.

15. *The Free Methodist Book of Discipline* outlined two different deacon positions. A traveling deacon was a ministerial role open to men and allowed an individual to perform the duties of a traveling preacher, to marry, baptize, and assist with communion. It was an elected position within an annual conference, and traveling deacons were required to complete a course of study. The deacon position for women was included in the "Annual Conference" section and noted that women would have the same rights and responsibilities as male deacons with one caveat—the position was not to be seen as a step towards ordination as an elder. Free Methodist Church, *Doctrines and Disciplines of the Free Methodist Church* (Chicago: Free Methodist Publishing House, 1911), 49 and 82.

16. The 1907 General Conference also approved changing the general superintendent title to bishop. The move was controversial; some saw it as returning to a Methodist Episcopal governance structure. Hence, why the title changes in this chapter. Wilson Hogue wrote two editorials on the decisions before the 1911 General Conference. Hogue, "Was It Wise or Otherwise No.1"; Hogue, "Was It Wise or Otherwise No. 2."

17. The duties of a bishop include serving as chairperson at annual and general conferences, helping establish new societies and conferences, upholding and promoting church policy, helping ministers transfer to other conferences, and traveling throughout the entire denomination. Free Methodist Church, *Doctrines and Disciplines 1911*, 85–89.

18. Catherine Berkus, "Writing Religious Experience: Women's Authorship in Early America," *The Journal of Religion* 92, no. 4 (October 2012): 172.

19. In 1905 Charles Ebey published an editorial, "The Millennium," in which he argued that the Free Methodist Church did not embrace premillennialism, despite its rising popularity. Quoting from Benjamin Field's *Hand Book of Christian Theology*, which was required reading for the local preacher course of study, Ebey notes several issues with premillennialism, including the strict literal interpretation of the Bible and not allowing individuals and organizations free will. However, by 1915 the denomination had taken a different path, and some leaders were advocating for books favorable to premillennialism to be included in its course of study curriculum. Charles Ebey, "The Millennium," *The Free Methodist*, June 26, 1906, 8; and Freeborn Brooke, "Shall We Commit the Church to Premillennialism?," *The Free Methodist*, March 9, 1915, 2.

20. As editor of *The Free Methodist*, Charles Ebey regularly used the front page and editorial page to highlight suffrage and women's ordination. In my research, I counted thirteen articles positively discussing the topics during his tenure as editor. Charles Ebey, "Woman's Suffrage," *The Free Methodist*, March 8, 1904, 8. Ebey opposed premillennialism and wrote an editorial pointing out theological errors. Ebey, "The Millennium," 8.

21. G.W. Coleman, "Ordination of Women," supplement to *The Free Methodist*, June 17, 1891.

22. The premillennial view on gender roles was the forerunner to the early twentieth-century fundamentalist movement, which continued emphasizing the "different but capable" narrative. Margaret Bendroth, *Fundamentalism and Gender 1875 to Present* (New Haven, CT: Yale University Press, 1993), 50–53.

23. Ibid., 52.

24. Benjamin Titus Roberts, *Ordaining Women* (Chili, NY: Earnest Christian Publishing House, 1891).

25. Wilson T. Hogg, "Educate Women for Higher Womanhood," *The Free Methodist*, August 22, 1899, 1.

26. Free Methodists saw other examples of deaconess orders in Protestant America. Bishop Henry Potter was an American Episcopalian bishop who was a vocal temperance advocate and reformer. He served on the Episcopal Committee on Organized Services of Women in 1871, which outlined various roles for women in the Episcopal Church, including deaconess orders, lay women support of foreign and domestic missions, and "Sisterhood Auxiliaries" in local congregations. Michael Bourgeous, "The Work and Well-Being of Woman in American Social Christianity: The Case of Henry Codman Potter (1895–1908)," in *All Things Human: Henry Codman Potter and The Social Gospel in the Episcopal Church* (Champaign: University of Illinois Press, 2004), 133.

27. J.S. "Women's Work," *The Free Methodist*, February 20, 1900, 10.

28. Ibid. The article was featured in the "Family Circle" section. This section commonly featured reprints from national publications. However, there is no indication that "Women's Work" was such an article as it does not end with the typical note citing its original publication. Hogue perhaps solicited it for that section.

29. Artour Aslanian, "The Use of Rhetoric in Anti-Suffrage and Anti-Feminist Publications," *The Journal of Transdisciplinary Writing and Research from Claremont Graduate University* 2, no. 1 (2013): 3.

30. Wilson Hogue, "Women's Legal Rights," *The Free Methodist*, August 27, 1901, 8.

31. Jane Apostol, "Why Women Should Not Have the Vote: Anti-Suffrage Views in the Southland in 1911," *Southern California Quarterly* 70, no. 1 (1988): 31.

32. A.J. M'Kinney, "Woman's Suffrage," *The Free Methodist*, November 17, 1903, 3.

33. J.H. Collins, "Bible Defense of Woman's Ministry," *The Free Methodist*, January 8, 1901, 2.

34. G. Leonard Coughron, "Woman in Her Place," *The Free Methodist*, May 6, 1902, 2.

35. E.M. "More About Women in Her Place," *The Free Methodist*, June 17, 1901, 2.

36. Ibid.

37. Ibid.

38. Hogue, *History of Free Methodism*, 244.

39. Charles Ebey, "Lay Preachers," *The Free Methodist*, May 21, 1902, 1.

40. Burton Jones, "Women Ordained to Office of Deacon," *The Free Methodist*, November 25, 1913, 1.

41. Mesaros-Winckles, 2022.

42. Ibid.

43. Ibid., and J.T. Logan, ed., "General Conference Proceedings," *The Free Methodist*, June 27, 1911, 1.

44. "Bates, Missouri," U.S. Census 1900.

45. Eliza Witherspoon, "Virginia Missouri," *The Free Methodist*, July 8, 1895, 3.

46. Ibid.

47. Brekus, "Writing Religious Experience," 172.

48. Eliza Witherspoon, "Phelps Missouri," *The Free Methodist*, August 15, 1905, 14.

49. Ibid.

50. Ibid.

51. Clara Wetherald had referred to women evangelists' lack of rail fare discounts as one of many financial hardships they faced in her 1890 General Conference address—something that could easily be remedied if the denomination granted them the title "elder." Clara Wetherald, "Sixth Sitting," *General Conference Daily*, October 13, 1890.

52. Eliza Witherspoon, "Experience," *The Free Methodist*, October 17, 1911, 14.

53. W.B. Olmstead, ed., "Nineteenth Sitting 1:30 p.m. Thursday, June 29," *General Conference Daily*, June 30, 1911, 4.

54. Judy Mayfield, ed., "Riverview Cemetery, Arkansas City, Kansas: Eliza C. Witherspoon (1855–1932)," accessed August 20, 2021, from https://www.findagrave.com/memorial/47339038/eliza-c-witherspoon.

55. C.W. Stamp, "A Statement," *The Free Methodist*, June 15, 1915, 4; and Wilson Hogue, *History of Free Methodism*, 244.

56. J.T. Killon, "Blanche Stamp," *The Free Methodist*, April 20, 1945, 14; V.H. Mottweiler, "Minnie Beers," *The Free Methodist*, February 4, 1958, 13; E. Merle McCold, "Ada Hall Marsh," *The Free Methodist*, June 24, 1938, 14; M.C. Ballew, "Price-Laura Lamb," *The Free Methodist*, August 26, 1938, 14; and James Thompson, "Bersha Green," *The Free Methodist*, March 8, 1955, 14.

57. Charles Ebey, ed., "Free Methodist Deaconesses," *The Free Methodist*, July 9, 1907, 1.

58. Mesaros-Winckles, 2022.

59. Blanche Stamp, "Gallatin, Tennessee," *The Free Methodist*, August 30, 1904, 12.

60. "Revival Meetings," *LeMars Semi-Weekly Sentinel*, March 29, 1912, 1.

61. "Bits of Scripture," *Rock Island Argus*, December 14, 1912, 7.

62. "Church Notices," *Simpson Daily Leader*, December 24, 1921, 3.

63. Blanche Stamp, "A Remarkable Conversion," *The Free Methodist*, May 16, 1911, 5.

64. Ibid.

65. Stamp, "A Statement," 4.

66. Priscilla Pope-Levison, *Turn the Pulpit Loose* (New York: Palgrave McMillan, 2004), 13–16.

67. Emphasizing their sacrifice as evangelists, Stamp respectfully asked the 1916 General Conference not to reappoint him.

In *Turn the Pulpit Loose*, Priscilla Pope-Levison notes that family responsibilities, pregnancy, and recovery often delayed women's ministry careers in the nineteenth century. Those with children often agonized over leaving them with family or other caretakers but felt their call from God superseded any other role. Pope-Levison, *Turn the Pulpit Loose*, 13–16.

68. "The Churches," *Emporia Gazette*, April 15, 1911, 2; "Begin Revival Services at Free Methodist Church," *Daily Inter Lake*, October 9, 1916, 3; "Sunday Services," *The Bradford Era*, February 24, 1917, 7; "At the Free Methodist Church," *Cedar Rapids Evening Gazette*, June 6, 1913, 2; and Stamp, "A Statement," 4.

69. In reviewing the *Annual Conference Minutes of the Free Methodist Church of North America* from 1911 to 1920, Blanche Stamp is listed as an evangelist with the Pittsburgh Conference and living in Chicago. However, she is never listed under the conference deacons. The 1911 *Doctrine and Disciplines of The Free Methodist Church* also clearly outlines the deaconess role as a non-preaching role. Free Methodist Church, *Doctrine and Disciplines of the Free Methodist Church* (Chicago: Free Methodist Publishing House, 1914), 102–3.

70. Ibid., 49.

71. R.L. Page, ed., "First Lady Elder in Free Methodism," *Pittsburg Conference Herald* 35, no. 1, September 1974, 1.

72. In the *Annual Conference Minutes of the Free Methodist Church of North America*, the standard reporting practice was to call women evangelists and women deacons "Mrs." or "Miss" and ordained male elders by "Rev."

73. Jones, "Women Ordained to Office of Deacon," 1.

74. Ada Hall, "Forward, Backward, Which?," *The Free Methodist*, April 25, 1911, 6.

75. Ibid. The original wording is slightly awkward, so the inserted words are my clarifications. The exact wording of Ada Hall's quote is as follows: "We came from the position of an evangelist-pastor one hour to that of a conference preacher (?) The next we know not what we are nor to what class we belong. Is not this a subject of more importance than deciding names? If we had but one name and knew what it stood for, we would be thankful. This question will not never down or be settled until the right is reached."

76. Charles Ebey, ed., "General Conference Proceedings," *The Free Methodist*, July 2, 1907, 8–9.

77. Mesaros-Winckles, 2022.

78. Ibid.

79. Ada Hall, "Mason City, Iowa," *The Free Methodist*, April 25, 1911, 5.

80. Ada Hall, "Spring Valley, Minnesota," *The Free Methodist*, July 27, 1915, 4.

81. Ibid.

82. McCold, "Ada Hall Marsh," 14.

83. "Tributes to Ada Hall Marsh," *The Free Methodist*, June 24, 1938, 13; and McCold, "Ada Hall Marsh," 14.

84. Ibid.

85. Ibid.

86. Mottweller, "Beers," 13; and Thompson, "Green," 14.

87. Jones, "Women Ordained to Office of Deacon," 1.

88. Laura Lamb, "Greenburg, Pennsylvania," *The Free Methodist*, March 23, 1915, 5.

89. Mesaros-Winckles, 2022.

90. M.C. Ballew, "Price-Laura Lamb," *The Free Methodist*, August 26, 1938, 14.

91. Pope Levinson, *Turn the Pulpit Loose*, 17.

92. Before the 1911 General Conference, *The Free Methodist* featured articles critical of the 1907 General Conference decision to allow women appointed to a circuit for two years to be ministerial delegates in their annual conference. The writer was only identified as "Manetho." Wilson Hogue denied being "Manetho," but before the 1911 General Conference, he published several articles on the same topic with similar points. Manetho, "General Conference—A Review," *The Free Methodist*, September 17, 1907, 2; Manetho, "General Conference—A Review V," *The Free Methodist*, September 24, 1907, 2; Wilson Hogue, "Admission of Women to Annual Conferences no. 1," *The Free Methodist*, April 4, 1911, 2; and Wilson Hogue, "Admission of Women to Annual Conferences no. 2," *The Free Methodist*, April 11, 1911, 2. Those opposed to the 1907 decision had hoped to revisit it at the 1911 General Conference, but no movement was made to backtrack on the decision in 1911.

93. The governance debates before the 1911 General Conference included several articles in favor of women's ordination. Supporters had been encouraged by the decisions of the 1907 General Conference and hoped to use that momentum to finally gain ordination for women. See Freeborn Brooke, "Do Women Preachers Ever Wear

Out?," *The Free Methodist*, May 30, 1911, 3; Lynn Webb, "Women's Ordination," *The Free Methodist*, May 30, 1911, 2; and W.M. Adams, "The Woman Question," *The Free Methodist*, May 9, 1911, 2.

Chapter 6

Cementing Women's Roles

The Deaconess Order and Ordination as Deacons

In October 1913, Rev. S.V. Coe sent *The Free Methodist* an update about Life Line Mission's new home, which had just been purchased for $9,000. Detailing the purchase, Coe reported the new location included a large yard, brick barn, and a small grocery store, that would help subsidize the mission's work. Located in Kansas City, Coe and his wife, Kate, served as superintendents at Life Line, overseeing the day-to-day operations. In the 1913 report on Life Line's outreach efforts, Coe noted the mission had cared for twenty-six "erring girls" and eighty-two babies, provided fifty baskets of food and one hundred and thirty-eight Christmas dinners, given out over 2,000 articles of clothing, and held over fifty jail meetings.[1] One of just several Free Methodist philanthropic endeavors, missions such as Life Line helped fuel the establishment of the Free Methodist Deaconess Order in 1907.[2] By the turn of the twentieth century, Free Methodist leaders were becoming increasingly concerned about maintaining denominational stability as industrialization and immigration were quickly changing American society.

The internal arguments for and against women's ordination were divisive. Free Methodist leadership, particularly the bishops, saw cementing specific ministry roles for women as essential for preserving Free Methodist values. Women-led ministries such as the deaconess order were highly appealing to Free Methodists who wanted to encourage women to serve but did not want them to venture too far from their primary duties in the home. As historian Lori Ginzberg explains in her research on nineteenth-century women and benevolence organizations:

> Benevolent women—and men—were quite prepared to use the ideology of femininity as a weapon against female organizing that served interests thought

too radical. The language of gender spheres, with its charge of "straying," was often used less to describe the boundaries of women's benevolent activity than to assert the unpopularity of a cause, less to police oneself than to question other women's "femininity."[3]

The work of benevolence was seen as biblically acceptable by Free Methodists. Once the deaconess order was established in 1907, *The Free Methodist Book of Discipline* was very clear in defining the deaconess role as separate from that of evangelist or pastor, and once the 1911 General Conference allowed women to become ordained deacons, the *Book of Discipline* advised annual conferences that ordination as a deacon would not be a path to ordination as an elder.[4] The two decisions illustrated ongoing tensions between supporters of women's complete enfranchisement in church ministry and governance and opponents who favored specific spheres of influence for women. Opponents argued that women were best suited for ministries using their natural gifts of caring, protecting, and nurturing. If a woman was to leave her family for ministry, she should still be in a maternal role. A February 26, 1916, *Free Methodist* article by Janette Osmun best summarizes this view:

> Women's sphere is found in the schools, in church work, in hospitals, in the sick room, in orphanages, in mission work, at home and abroad, on battle-fields, spending her life in loving service, anywhere that she may minister comfort and relief to the souls and bodies of suffering humanity.[5]

Narrowly defining women's sphere of ministry was not a uniquely Free Methodist decision. Indeed, as religious historian Betty DeBerg explains, many Protestant denominations saw maintaining control over the role of ordained elder as crucial to maintaining God's natural order. Placing women in authority over men at a time when American Protestants felt increasingly threatened by waves of Catholic immigrants seemed far too radical. As DeBerg explains, "None of the religious leaders declared a desire to remove women from church work altogether. These ministers and their churches were far too dependent on the skill, dedication, time, and money women gave readily to the church."[6] By 1911 Free Methodist women had seen advancements in governance and ministry, but progress slowed after the 1911 decision allowing women to be ordained deacons. No further movement would occur until 1974, when women were granted the right to be ordained elders.[7]

Among the new roles open to women by 1911 was the opportunity to become a ministerial delegate in their quarterly and annual conferences. Additionally, ordination as a deacon allowed women to baptize and marry individuals within the Free Methodist Church. However, a deacon could not serve communion without an elder present,[8] and only elders could serve as district elder or bishop.[9] Denominational leadership saw these expanded roles as a solution to "the woman issue." As Bishop Walter Sellew noted in his booklet *Why Not? A Plea for Those Women God Has Called to Preach the Gospel*, women now could belong to every official body within the denomination and fill every official position, except district elder and bishop. "The reason women are not allowed by our discipline to fill these positions is not that these positions carry special authority with them, as they do not," Sellew explained. "The reason women are not allowed these positions is that we have thought best to restrict these positions to those whom we have ordained elders."[10] Furthermore, Sellew argued that even if women were granted the right to become ordained elders, denominational leadership could still restrict them from those roles if it was thought prudent. As Sellew saw it, by 1911 women already had the same rights to preach and govern, and what was left was the question of administrative ability, for which he firmly believed men were the most qualified.[11]

SEDIMENTING WOMEN'S MINISTRY IN
THE FREE METHODIST CHURCH

The desire to maintain the status quo in denominational governance and leadership reflected Free Methodism's growing preoccupation with external "threats." Preserving traditional women's roles was just one tactic to ensure Free Methodist culture survived the growing Catholic menace. As historian Donald Dayton notes, the turn of the century shift towards fundamentalism by Free Methodist leaders was not surprising. Roberts' progressive vision of *inclusion* was morphing into a policy of *exclusion* as an emphasis was placed on following specific denominational policies and Christian living guidelines.[12] As Dayton explains, this shift in organizational vision often occurs as subsequent generations fail to buy into the original message at the same level of intensity as the denomination's founders. As time passes, that original vision becomes convoluted, reflecting the concerns of current leaders. Ironically, many things that led to the Free Methodists' separation from the Methodist Episcopal Church in 1860 would become part of Free Methodist culture by the early twentieth century.[13]

The Free Methodist bishops were becoming increasingly preoccupied with the decline of Anglo-Saxon Protestant values.[14] Additionally, the denomination would follow the same path regarding women's public ministry as the Methodist Council of 100 after John Wesley's death.[15] The 1911 deacon decision was seen as resolving any ongoing concerns about women's ministry. However, what occurred was what Judith Butler would call a "sedimentation" of gender norms, essentially institutionalizing gender norms for ministry in the coming decades. So, rather than outright refusing to ordain women, the rhetorical evidence points to active dismissal of the topic and a rhetorical shift to other concerns.[16] From 1911 to 1974 Free Methodist women who entered ministry had three approved tracks: evangelist, deaconess, or deacon. While these ministry paths opened numerous doors at the local level, decisions at the denominational level still largely excluded women as they could only be elected as lay delegates to the General Conference. The result was that decisions affecting the entire denomination were still mainly made by men. Since men could be elected as lay and ministerial delegates to the General Conference, it was almost guaranteed that more men would secure delegate spots and maintain the majority vote for denominational decisions. Leaders such as Sellew argued that male dominance in church governance was what women wanted. In *Why Not? A Plea for Those Women God Has Called to Preach the Gospel*, Sellew acknowledged that women were the majority of members in local societies but contended that women "willingly delegate her power" to men. Sellew explained that women would step up as annual or general conference delegates only when a suitable man could not be found.[17]

Consequently, the denominational decisions from 1907 to 1911 were fueled partly by outside social factors, partially by emerging fundamentalism within the denomination, and partly by the rhetoric of leaders such as Sellew and Hogue, who were intentionally crafting a narrative that stability rather than change was essential for the preservation of Free Methodism. One of the best documents explaining Free Methodist concerns for this period is the 1907 pastoral address from Bishops Edward Hart, Burton Jones, Walter Sellew, and Wilson Hogue.[18] In their address, the bishops urge their fellow Free Methodists not to be "visionaries, vainly occupied with the hidden things of the future and the impracticable things of the present," but to instead be practical and deal with a host of pressing problems facing the denomination including intemperance, increased worldliness (preoccupation with fashion and entertainment), an increase in divorce and the subsequent decline of family life, along with "race suicide," which was also contributing to declining morals and families in the United States.[19] The rhetoric of the Free Methodists bishops was also supported through the editorials of *The Free Methodist* editor J.T. Logan, who served as editor starting in 1907. Logan regularly published editorial content that supported the concerns of the bishops, ensuring Free Methodists were regularly receiving advice and summaries of national news stories illustrating those fears.[20] To understand the motivations and rhetoric behind the establishment of the Free Methodist Deaconess Order and the 1911 deacon decision, this chapter will primarily focus on the 1907 and 1911 General Conference speeches in the *General Conference Daily* and Ebey and Logan's use of *The Free Methodist* to support first the deaconess order and then the increasingly insular vision of denominational leaders.

FRAMING THE NEED FOR A FREE
METHODIST DEACONESS ORDER

Between 1865 and 1900, at least 13.5 million immigrants arrived in the United States. About nine million of those immigrants arrived between 1900 and 1910.[21] American society was changing quickly, and the United States was becoming increasingly Catholic as many new immigrants came from Ireland, Italy, and Eastern Europe.[22] The Free Methodist bishops were concerned that America was on the verge of being controlled by the Vatican and that the Anglo-Saxon majority would soon be out-populated.[23] Their 1907 pastoral address cited Theodore Roosevelt and the term "race suicide" as one of the most pressing concerns of the denomination. Popularized by Roosevelt in his 1905 speech "American Motherhood," the term "race suicide" referred to immigration fears of Anglo-Saxon America.[24] In his address, Roosevelt outlined the importance of family life, particularly the role of the mother, in maintaining American morality:

> The nation is in a bad way if there is no real home, if the family is not of the right kind; if the man is not a good husband and father, if he is brutal or cowardly or selfish, if the woman has lost her sense of duty, if she is sunk in vapid self-indulgence or has let her nature be twisted so that she prefers a sterile pseudo-intellectuality to that great and beautiful development of character which comes only to those whose lives know the fullness of duty done, or effort made and self-sacrifice undergone.[25]

This emerging concern dovetailed with already present premillennialist concerns about gender roles. For decades Free Methodist women evangelists had fought rhetoric accusing them of pursuing a path outside biblically defined gender roles. Detractors saw women evangelists as part of the emerging "Modern Woman," more concerned with a career than with having a family.

Arguments against women preaching complemented race suicide arguments which also defined the "Modern Woman" as "unnatural" and "detrimental to her race." More than ever, women were needed in the home to ensure that educated, middle- and upper-class Protestant culture survived. As reproductive historian Simone Caron explains, "Pushing white middle- and upper-class women into the home as mothers preserved male hegemony over higher education and professional opportunities. Women with young children could not realistically compete with men for respected career opportunities.[26] While these rising concerns surrounding moral and family decline may seem uniquely a twentieth-century concern, it was not. Protestant leaders have issued race suicide warnings since the late nineteenth century. As early as 1867, Congregationalist minister John Todd warned fellow Protestants that immigrant families were becoming larger and would soon replace them as the dominant group in the United States. Because many of these immigrants came from predominantly Catholic countries, it was alarming that denominations, such as the Free Methodist Church, worried about Catholic control of American social and political life. The 1910 U.S. Census helped fuel these concerns, as immigrant women had a significantly higher birth rate than native-born women.[27] Additionally alarming to Protestants was the social activism of early twentieth-century American Catholics.[28] As Catholic hospitals, rescue missions, and orphans became fixtures in major metropolitan areas, Free Methodist leaders worried about the lack of Methodist impact in social services. This concern is best expressed in a December 10, 1907, article republished from *The Methodist Protestant* in *The Free Methodist*. In the article, the author Rev. C.E. Redeker outlined the history and importance of deaconess orders to the spread of Protestantism:

> In the United States, there is scarcely a city of more than 30,000 inhabitants that does not possess a Catholic hospital managed by nuns or Sisters of Charity. The Catholic Churches have thereby gained the favor of the general public, and their Sisters of Charity have not only become servants but also pioneers of the church.[29]

Establishing a deaconess order offered Free Methodists a route to promote organized social services. Supporters also noted that other Protestant traditions had already established such orders, such as the Methodist Episcopal Church, which established the office of deaconess in 1888.[30]

Part of these social services would include work with unwed mothers and orphans. Evangelism was also one motivating factor for Free Methodists already working at rescue missions. However, an underlying and largely unspoken motivation was race suicide concerns which were likewise tied to reformed eugenics philosophy. As the 1910 Census illustrated, the immigrant population—the poor and the uneducated—were reproducing in far greater numbers than middle- and upper-middle-class Protestant families. Reformed eugenics argued that left to their own devices, children from these groups would fuel a continued decline in morality and traditional family life—concerns cited in the 1907 bishops' address.[31] Free Methodist rescue homes practiced this philosophy by making every attempt to place children in the care of well-meaning Protestant families.[32] By 1912 *The Free Methodist* even featured pro-eugenic editorials, as seen in an article Logan republished from *The Methodist Protestant* praising eugenics researchers for finding ways to isolate detrimental hereditary factors and encourage "defective" descendants not to reproduce.[33] Consequently, the motivations behind establishing the Free Methodist deaconess order were not straightforward and went beyond providing acceptable ministry outlets for women. The exclusionary philosophies of reformed eugenics and race suicide were also highly influential in the order's founding.[34]

THE 1907 GENERAL CONFERENCE DISCUSSION
ON THE DEACONESS ORDER

When the resolution to approve a deaconess order came to the floor at the 1907 General Conference, it was met with enthusiastic support. It passed through a committee with thirty-five votes in favor and only seven opposed.[35] Very few concerns were raised, but among the topics discussed were governance, mission, and uniforms for the order. Speaking in favor of the order, Charles Ebey reminded delegates that there were already churches with such orders and that the need for a Free Methodist order was great. Reflecting on his personal experiences with deaconesses, Ebey recalled:

> I have noted for years the labors of the deaconesses of other churches and have always felt a feeling of satisfaction and gratification on entering a depot in our larger cities and see [sic] one of these plain looking ladies dressed in black with white cuffs and white ribbons attached to their bonnets and I feel like going up

Fig. 6.1. A photo from the 1907 *Free Methodist* showing what a day of work looked like at the 1907 General Conference. Source: Spring Arbor University White Library Archive

to them and saying, God bless you and your noble work. Their work is to meet the incoming trains and get acquainted with young girls that come into the cities and who do not know anything about the cities and see that they are taken care of and placed in good environment and kept out of the hands of designing, malicious and wicked men.[36]

As Ebey saw it, one of the primary motivations for the Free Methodist Deaconess Order was increased engagement in social service ministry. Even before establishing a deaconess order, the Free Methodist Church had begun rescue missions to address the need for safe housing for single, young women.[37] While there were not scores of Free Methodist women waiting to join the order, delegate Lynn Webb noted rescue workers in St. Louis were eagerly awaiting its approval, and Evansville Junior College, under the leadership of Grace Webb, was ready to offer deaconess training.[38] General Conference discussions on the order were largely positive. However, the issue of a uniform for a deaconess was the one point of contention in discussions, as some Free Methodists worried a uniform would be perceived by the public as a pro-Catholic endorsement, being too similar to the habit worn by nuns.[39] On July 9, 1907, in one of his final front-page editorials in *The Free Methodist*, Ebey announced that the General Conference had approved establishing the order and encouraged his fellow Free Methodists not to be "squeamish about adopting the deaconess garb," as the uniform was a way for women to connect with the people they were serving and designated them as aid workers.[40]

Articles in *The Free Methodist* leading up to the 1907 General Conference also supported Ebey's position and were largely favorable towards a deaconess uniform. For example, a June 18, 1907, editorial, "Deaconess," discussed the dress issue, noting that the deaconess garb indicated their ministry role to the general public. However, the editorial went beyond just endorsing the deaconess uniform and suggested that women evangelists should also embrace a uniform or, at the very least, a "neat, modest suit, uniform in color and style."[41] In the May 21, 1907, issue, evangelist Eliza Haviland also wrote in favor of a uniform for women evangelists and deaconesses. Haviland was a licensed evangelist in the New York Conference since 1889.[42] Citing her missionary work in Brooklyn, New York, Haviland noted home visits were often challenging for her, and perhaps a uniform would help establish a woman evangelist's relationship with the church just as it did for a deaconess:

When calling at homes where I had to introduce myself, I have said, "I am the church missionary from Sixteenth street church, and your children attend our Sunday school," when a distinct garb would have greatly aided me in approaching strangers. Oftentimes I have told them "I fill the same position as the deaconess does in the Methodist Church."[43]

Haviland's argument was backed by other Free Methodist women, particularly minister's wives, who saw a uniform and a deaconess license as a way to illustrate their position within the church during visitation.[44] Haviland's views on women evangelists in uniform were also expressed by delegates at the 1907 General Conference, who called on the conference to approve the deaconess uniform and require women evangelists to wear it. Supporters in favor of requiring both the deaconess and the evangelists to wear a uniform cited the Methodist Episcopal Deaconess Order as their model.[45] However, the job of a Methodist and Free Methodist deaconess differed significantly. Methodist deaconesses could also engage in evangelistic work, including preaching, whereas the duties of Free Methodist deaconesses focused on social service.[46]

In defining the Free Methodist deaconess role, the 1907 General Conference outlined that she should have a clear spiritual calling and desire to serve in ministry. However, her ministry duties differed from a pastor or evangelist. Instead, a Free Methodist deaconess would engage in various social service enterprises that would help reduce suffering.[47] The 1907 *Free Methodist Book of Discipline* also outlined a uniform of a gray dress with a gray bonnet, and white ribbons, similar to the uniform other denominations had adopted for their deaconess orders.[48] In examining editorial articles discussing the deaconess uniform, it is essential to consider why a uniform was suggested and approved for women in ministry but was not suggested for men serving as elders or deacons. The Free Methodist Church already embraced simplicity of dress to make everyone feel welcome,[49] and early photos and ministry accounts by women evangelists illustrate that they were aware of the need to establish their authority and the need for simple fashion.[50] The cited reason for a deaconess uniform was to identify women in ministry to the public. However, a largely unspoken reason was that the uniform also illustrated separate spheres of ministry by gender. Fashion historian Ruth Rubinstein notes that this desire to uniform the female body was a centuries-old Christian concern, as women's attire could cause men's thoughts to stray from God.[51]

The Free Methodist apprehensions about women's fashion directly connected women's dress with indecency and immorality[52]—behavior that led to declining family life and increasing divorce rates.[53] Critiques on dress in *The Free Methodist* often focused on women's fashion and bodies and blamed society's moral failures on women. Starting in 1909, under the editorial control of Logan, *The Free Methodist* published twelve articles on dress between 1909 and 1915. None of the articles critiqued men and their fashion choices.[54]

Fig. 6.2. The 1907 General Conference delegates. C.W. Stamp (#113) is in the front row on the center-right, and Ada Hall (#119), delegate and one of the first Free Methodist female deacons, is in the first row to the far right. Source: Marston Memorial Historical Center

REGULATING FREE METHODIST
WOMEN THROUGH FASHION

When Logan became editor of *The Free Methodist* in 1907, he promised readers he would devote space in the paper to the "practical and experimental phases of the Christian life." While his predecessor Charles Ebey devoted space to support suffrage, Logan's tenure as editor defined "practical concerns" such as family roles, temperance, and condemnation of women's fashion as a temptation for godly men.[55] He often republished stories from other Christian periodicals that fit the themes he wished to highlight. For instance, in a May 6, 1913, article republished from the *Sunday School Times* in the reform section of the *Free Methodist*, the author called out women's fashion as one of the leading causes of men's moral failures and perceptions by men that such women were of questionable moral character. As the author explained:

> These women of better circumstances set the pace absolutely for the girl of small wages. The girl may have no home to which her friends may be invited; her social effort is expended in her dress. She follows the prevailing fashion of immodesty; she inflames the passions of the young men she meets; she may not be sheltered and safeguarded, and she is swept under.[56]

Placing responsibility on women for the thoughts and sometimes even choices of men was a theme Logan returned to on several occasions in *The*

Fig. 6.3. J.T. Logan, editor of *The Free Methodist,* 1907–1923 and 1927–1931. Source: Spring Arbor University White Library Archive

Free Methodist. In the October 7, 1909, editorial "Woman's Dress," he blamed women's fashion choices for leading men into adultery. The author cited David's "temptation" by Bathsheba in the Old Testament as the "one awful blot" on David's life. The article's conclusion cited early Methodist women such as Hester Ann Rodgers as the ideal model for modest womanhood.[57] The author's characterization of Rodgers is a classic illustration of shifting perceptions of appropriate expressions of Christian womanhood. Encouraged by Wesley to publish her journal, Rodgers' journal became one of the most widely published books by early Methodist presses and had well over fifty editions published in both the United States and Britain by the end of the nineteenth century. The widespread distribution of the *Account of the Experience of Hester Ann Rodgers* was partly because the Council of 100 chose her as their model for ideal womanhood. As a mystic, Rodgers had primarily lived her faith outside the public sphere, making her an ideal model of piety since she did not preach. In the nineteenth century, as new editions of Rodger's writings were published, editors included additional texts by men who praised Rodger's devotion as a wife and mother, further rewriting her experiences into the acceptable model the author uses in the 1909 *Free Methodist* article.[58]

Articles in *The Free Methodist* about dress and appropriate female role models were often directed toward young female readers, such as the 1913 *Sunday School Times* article urging young women not to tempt boys with their clothes. In 1914 and 1915, that emphasis continued in front-page editorials by Logan. For example, the March 3, 1914, *The Free Methodist* included an editorial entitled "The Girl Question." Logan warned families to keep an eye on their daughters as they grew older and became interested in "longer dresses and beaux." Citing an article from the Litchfield, Illinois, *News-Herald*, he encouraged parents to keep their daughters busy with home duties and only give them plain clothes to wear, and asked parents, "Where will you have their impression come from—from the riffraff of the streets or from the home?"[59] By 1907 the denomination sponsored rescue homes for young women, orphanages, and old folks' homes in New York, Illinois, Kansas, Nebraska, Texas, and Oklahoma. In particular, the Free Methodist Deaconess Order helped staff the Life Line Mission and Wichita Rescue Home in Kansas, the San Antonio Mission of Redeeming Love, the Gerry Homes in New York, the Omaha Rescue Home in Nebraska, and the Holmes Home of Redeeming Love in Oklahoma. The Free Methodist's fixation on women's apparel also helped justify the need for social service ministries in the denomination.[60] All these missions provided various social services to their respective communities, but many emphasized providing housing to unwed mothers and homes for orphans. As Logan's editorials on dress noted,

Free Methodists saw a direct connection between dress, sexual temptation, and moral failures.

FREE METHODIST DEACONESS RESCUE MISSIONS

In the first two decades of the twentieth century, the increasing insular focus of Free Methodist leaders resulted in fewer evangelistic endeavors. As Free Methodist historian Leslie Marston explains, the result was stagnation in church planting after 1903.[61] Only the denomination's global and home missionary endeavors bucked this trend. Home mission endeavors, including Free Methodist rescue missions, were concerned with promoting the social gospel initiatives of the denomination without sacrificing Free Methodist convictions about Christian living. Rescue work in the Progressive Era can be loosely grouped into three primary categories: settlement houses, rescue missions, and rescue homes. Settlement houses often had no underlying religious motivation, and, in fact, integrating religion into settlement houses was quite contentious, as many workers saw the work as separate from religious faith. Rescue missions, such as the Free Methodist missions, provided social services but also saw evangelism as central to bettering the lives of those they served.[62] Finally, like rescue missions, rescue homes often had an evangelistic focus and specifically cared for women. Free Methodist rescue missions combined traditional urban missions and rescue homes. One of the primary concerns of the rescue homes was drawing attention to "white slavery" or human trafficking as young women left home to pursue employment in the city. Since one motivation for establishing the deaconess order was to assist Free Methodist rescue homes in their work, these missions needed to be staffed by women who could fulfill the parental role many residents lacked. In 1907 General Conference discussions about the deaconess order, Bishop Wilson Hogue expressed deep concern about "white slavery." Referring to country girls and immigrant women led into prostitution when they went to the city looking for employment, Hogue explained:

> One of the most effective places of labor for a deaconess is at railway stations where many of our country girls and girls of foreign lands come, and many are decoyed away to disreputable places and taken into a white slavery that is much worse than black slavery ever has or could be.[63]

A 1922 overview of work at the Free Methodist Holmes Home of Redeeming Love in Oklahoma City also provides a glimpse into how the rescue homes addressed trafficking and immorality in their mission statements:

Holmes Home of Redeeming Love is an institution for the rescue of unfortunate girls, from lives of impurity and sin to lives of virtue and righteousness. The great majority of these girls have never entered a house of ill fame. They are very young and if left alone in their sad plight may commit suicide or destroy the lives of the unborn.[64]

According to records from the mission, that year, one hundred and forty-five girls were housed at Holmes Home of Redeeming love, with forty-five percent having no financial assistance except what the mission could provide them.[65] Life Line Mission in Kansas also worked with young women, as the 1913 report from S.V. Coe mentioned. A September 1914 report to *The Free Methodist* from Etta Chillson also calls attention to the other social endeavors Life Line regularly engaged in:

The Lord is blessing the work at Leavenworth and souls are being saved. We have a wide field here for mission work. If you have clothing, shoes or stockings or provisions to dispose of remember the Life Line Mission at Leavenworth, and God will reward and bless you for it. "Inasmuch as ye have done it unto one of the least of these, my brethren ye have done it unto me."[66]

In *Building Old Time Religion*, Priscilla Pope Levison notes that it was a common tactic for rescue homes to provide stark statistics to illustrate their success to benefactors and churches. Additionally, the emphasis on women's sexual promiscuity by mission reports illustrated a double standard also seen in *The Free Methodist* articles on dress. Men's promiscuity was overlooked, as women were held responsible for the moral behavior of men. Furthermore, the reports of the rescue homes pay little attention to wage discrepancies between men and women, which would often lead working women into prostitution.[67]

TRACKING FREE METHODIST
DEACONESS MINISTRIES

Because work at rescue missions was seen as a key ministry outlet for a deaconess, the deaconess training included a nursing manual and two different histories of deaconess orders. Since their duties did not include preaching, deaconesses were guided into ministry positions at Free Methodist rescue missions, Sunday school work, or mission work among immigrants, Native Americans, African-Americans, and Appalachian communities.[68] From annual conference records, it appears most deaconesses did not start as evangelists, choosing to pursue the deaconess license as their primary outlet for ministry. However, there were some exceptions, such as Kate Coe, the co-superintendent of Life Line Mission, who had been a licensed evangelist before becoming a deaconess.[69]

Outside of mission work, the ministries of Free Methodist deaconesses are challenging to track, as annual conferences did not designate deaconess appointments. Additionally, deaconesses did not regularly write ministry reports to *The Free Methodist* as women evangelists did. What ministry accounts remain are mostly from Rebecca Sellew and Ida Walsh's yearly mission reports. These reports noted several other influential deaconesses, including Kate Coe, Elizabeth Moreland, and Belle McCullough.[70] Perhaps one reason documenting Free Methodist deaconess history is problematic is that the order was not as popular as leaders anticipated. Unlike what Hogue and Webb predicted at the 1907 General Conference, women did not flock to the deaconess order. Because the coursework and oral examination was a two-year process, the first Free Methodist deaconesses did not even appear in the annual conference minutes until 1911.

Poor recruitment and access to the deaconess coursework also appear to have slowed the movement. In a September 5, 1916, article by Jessie McMurry entitled "The Deaconess Order," McMurry notes the only Free Methodist educational institution offering the deaconess course of

Fig. 6.4. (left to right) Rev. J.L. McCullough, Belle McCullough, and Florence Mitchell. Belle McCullough was a Free Methodist deaconess. You can see both Belle McCullough and Florence Mitchell are wearing the dark gray dresses assigned to the deaconess order. Source: Marston Memorial Historical Center

study was Evansville Junior College in Wisconsin, and the number of women who were pursuing that path was relatively small. If, as McMurry explained, other schools would begin offering the coursework, she was sure numbers would increase. McMurry urged denominational leaders to consider instituting a central committee to oversee the deaconess movement.[71] Another roadblock was the governance of the order; according to *The Free Methodist Discipline*, each annual conference's mission board oversaw that conference's deaconesses, and just as some conferences were more supportive of women evangelists than others, some conferences were also more supportive of the deaconess order. By far, the most significant number of deaconesses came from the Oil City Conference.[72] This was partly due to another issue McMurry outlined—the deaconess order needed older women to mentor and encourage younger women to join.[73] Annual conference records from 1910–1920 illustrate that conferences with several deaconesses continued adding one or two new deaconesses every few years. Those with no deaconesses saw women becoming evangelists and deacons instead of deaconesses.[74] However, even in conferences with strong deaconess mentorship, the numbers were not significant. By 1920, there were only fifty deaconesses in the entire denomination. In comparison, in 1920, four hundred and thirty-six women were licensed as evangelists.[75] Clearly, the deaconess order did appeal to some Free Methodist women, but the majority were still drawn to forms of public ministry that included evangelism and preaching.

GROWING TENSIONS AS WOMEN SEE
INCREASED ROLE IN CHURCH GOVERNANCE

While the 1907 General Conference had successfully approved a Free Methodist Deaconess Order with little opposition, another decision from the conference resulted in women's role in ministry becoming, once again, a heated topic. As the 1911 General Conference approached, ordination appeared to be something delegates would have to reconsider. However, the specifics of the ordination type would not be decided until the conference. The Southern California Conference had submitted a proposed amendment allowing women to become ordained deacons and ordained elders.[76] Tensions had been mounting since the 1907 General Conference granted appointed women evangelists the opportunity to become ministerial delegates for their quarterly and annual conferences. The 1907 decision also appears to have surprised some leaders, as governance changes were not among the legislative suggestions presented by the bishops in their 1907 pastoral address.[77] The change in governance rallied supporters and detractors of women's ordination and brought the topic back into the pages of *The Free Methodist*. Some of the harshest critiques of the 1907 General Conference came from a two-part editorial Logan published in September 1907. The critiques, written by an individual identified as only "Manetho," called the decision to allow women to become ministerial delegates "subversive." Manetho accused Free Methodist leaders of reducing the checks and balances between the lay and ministerial leadership.[78] Citing the decision as creating a third class within annual conference governance, Manetho outlined objections in both the September 17 and September 24 issues:

> It is class legislation, having its inception and support more in sentiment than justice. No man who is an evangelist under the same conditions, could be admitted into an annual conference and have a "voice and a vote." It is an unnecessary and an unjust decision against men evangelists.[79]

The anonymous editorials were divisive and caused so much speculation about their authorship that Hogue had to write an editorial denouncing those claiming he was Manetho. As Hogue explained, he owned his opinions and did not need to write under a pen name.[80] Indeed, Hogue was open with his criticism of the 1907 decision, publishing his two-part critique in April 1911, just months before the 1911 General Conference. Hogue also denounced the decision as "bad legislation" citing the 1890 General Conference ruling stipulating women could not be accepted on trial or in full connection to any annual conferences. However, the 1890 guidelines applied to accepting women on trial as ordained elders and said nothing about pastoral appointments or evangelist licensing. Nevertheless, Hogue vehemently argued that the older rule superseded the 1907 ruling. He claimed that by allowing women to become ministerial delegates, the denomination was on the verge of a crisis of jealousy. Women appointed as local pastors were sure to be viewed with envy, leading to no woman ever serving the two required years necessary to become a ministerial delegate.[81]

While Hogue denied being Manetho, his 1911 critiques made similar arguments. Both critiques relied on a specific interpretation of *The Free Methodist Discipline* that invalidated the 1907 decision. Both argued that the decision was not in the spirit of governance laid out by the denomination's founders, who saw the division between lay and ministerial delegates as an essential check and balance. The discussion about the 1907 decision and women's place in church governance continued in *The Free Methodist* throughout April, May, and June in the lead-up to the 1911 General Conference.[82] Just as Roberts did in *The Free Methodist* before 1890, supporters used the opportunity to publish numerous articles favorable towards women's ordination. However, besides Hogue's and Manetho's critiques, the articles were largely positive. Pro-ordination editorials often harshly critiqued opponents without directly calling out their colleagues. One such editorial was by C.W. Anguish entitled "Equal Representation." Anguish analyzed the exact breakdown of ministerial and lay delegates in each annual conference, indirectly disputing Hogue's and Manetho's concern that women as ministerial delegates would disrupt the balance of church governance. In fact, according to the 1910 Annual Conference Minutes, General Conference and annual conference committees were already heavily populated by ministerial representation, with an average of two ministerial representatives to one lay representative.[83] In the same issue, Rev. A.M. Adams of the Nebraska Conference also defended the 1907 decision, noting that too often, past General Conference decisions on women's ministry "grieved the Holy Spirit." As Adams explained, these past decisions "are revamped and put forward for the purpose of bolstering the male ego upon his pinnacle of supremacy."[84] *The Free Methodist*'s May 23, 1913, issue pushed those arguments even further. In an article written by Freeborn Brooke, "Do Women Preachers Ever Wear Out?," Brooke made a pointed critique of denominational policy, sometimes using a sarcastic tone to ridicule opponents. He called the decision to oppose women's ordination and their right to be ministerial delegates a decision based solely on sex and not on spiritual calling. Brooke drew attention to women's lack of financial support from the denomination, noting that the annual conferences gave superannuated (retired) elders financial support. However, without the right to be ordained, women evangelists could not access that support. Citing the 1907 decision, he critiqued the lack of denominational progress toward real gender equality in ministry:

> General Conference of the Free Methodist Church, soon to convene in Chicago, in the name of common honesty, answer, why this unwarranted (I almost said wicked) discrimination? Do not our devoted, toiling sisters in the ministry in time wear out? Do they not need "climate, water, and a place" on earth after they are worn out in "the work of the Lord?" Then why are they denied the support given by men who wear out in the same work that has won out the women?[85]

Brooke went on to note what "little favor" had been granted to women by the 1907 General Conference had been met with intense resistance. Emphasizing the word "little," Brooke lambasted critics of women's ordination who had denied women full enfranchisement as elders in the Free Methodist Church for the past thirty years. He also criticized articles in *The Free Methodist* that presented women as less than capable ministers while at the same time insisting that they were the harbingers of all things moral in the home:

Our women have been told publicly through the columns of the paper that the comparative width of their hips and shoulders proves they are better fitted for maternity than ministry. We have been asked with open-eyed astonishment, and with apparent sincerity, what a little woman who weighed but one hundred pounds would do if called upon to baptize a two hundred and fifty-pound man. (Of course, this two hundred and fifty-pound lubber would have conscientious scruples against anyone else baptizing him). We have been told that woman is the queen of the home, and some have hurrahed to keep her under her calico kitchen crown, but in spite of all, she has, by divine providence, pushed past and through the crowd of her opposers into the pulpit and "prophesied" as God ordained she should; and if the little favorable legislation she has received at the hands of the general conference looks so bunglesome to her opposers, they have themselves to thank for it, for her friends long ago would have put her at the side of her brother minister—his equal in all things in the church of God but for the stubborn resistance of the moral descendants of those who held women's most sacred mission was to raise children and cook man's meat.[86]

Brooke concluded by calling out the hypocrisy of those who used church policy under the guise of protecting women evangelists while at the same time refusing to pass better legislation giving them equal rights in governance and ministry. Free Methodists, such as Brooke, saw the denomination's treatment of women contradict Galatians 3:28: "There is neither Jew nor Greek, slave nor free, all are one in Christ."[87]

The second-tier status of women evangelists was summarized in a January 22, 1907, article by a woman evangelist, S.A.H. Writing a passionate defense of her ministry entitled "Rights of Women Pastors," S.A.H. argued that preaching authority was not enough. Women must be allowed to baptize and marry individuals who come to their church requesting it. As she explains:

All are aware that preaching alone is not the only way of reaching hearts, and to illustrate what I mean by handcuffs.[88] I give the following case. . . . A family of foreigners lived in the neighborhood of the Free Methodist Church. The babe was very ill. The Free Methodist pastor was sent to baptize it. She thought of the open door to the hearts of the parents to carry the gospel, but knowing the Discipline tied her hands, she had to refuse, saying, "Our church does not allow women to baptize." It was last in the evening. In the morning the pastor requested a brother in the ministry to go but it was too late; the babe was dead. The opportunity to reach that home through service in what seemed an opportune time was gone.[89]

S.A.H. expressed frustration over the lack of guidance from fellow Free Methodists, who advised her to ignore the *Free Methodist Discipline* and baptize when they heard her concerns. However, she argued, she and other female evangelists were asked if they would be governed by the *Discipline*

Fig. 6.5. Freeborn Brooke was a Free Methodist elder and vocal supporter of women's ordination. Source: Marston Memorial Historical Center

when they joined the denomination. As S.A.H. said, "I ask you which is better, to advise the sisters to violate the Discipline or make a Discipline which the sisters can be governed by and carry on the work of the Master where duty calls?"[90]

1911 GENERAL CONFERENCE GRANTS
WOMEN ORDINATION AS DEACONS

Pressure from advocates and the proposed Southern California Conference resolution brought the topic of women's ordination to the floor of the 1911 General Conference. In the nineteenth sitting on June 29, 1911, the Southern California Conference resolution was discussed. The resolution also included removing distinctions in the *Free Methodist Discipline* based on sex for the ordination of ministers.[91] It was almost identical to the original 1890 proposal set forth by Roberts with the exception of not including "race and condition" as well as gender.[92] The Southern California proposal failed in committee to get two-thirds of the votes either for or against, so it was brought to the entire General Conference for a vote.[93]

Some delegates immediately called for the proposal to be voted on without further discussion. As Rev. Alexander Beers noted, "this question has been debated throughout our denomination for twelve years and discussed in the paper and at our annual conferences."[94] He called for an immediate vote on the amendment. However, Bishop Sellew requested a chance to speak. He suggested amending it to read, "Annual conferences, once satisfied with a woman's call to preach, could receive her on trial in the same manner men were received on trial to become a deacon."[95] Sellew's amendment narrowed ordination to only the office of deacon. In explaining his proposed changes, Sellew outlined the same objections he had mentioned in *Why Not?*

> I am strongly in favor of the ordination of women. I think I can show to any-body, an unprejudiced person at least, that the New Testament shows clearly the cases of women who have been ordained deacons or ministers in the primitive and apostolic church, but there is no place where they have been ordained elders. The deacons were the original preachers of the gospel. The elders were the rulers of the church. I don't believe that God calls women to rule the church but God does call her to preach the gospel and as such she is entitled to be ordained a deacon.[96]

In concluding remarks, Sellew clarified his position further, noting if he could restrict women from ever being ordained an elder he would do so, because he could not find a single instance in the Bible showing women as ordained elders. However, he stopped short of suggesting such a resolution because he was unsure if delegates had the constitutional authority to do so.[97]

Opposition to the amendment was presented as a governance concern. Rev. W.N. Coffee worried that approving Sellew's revisions would still allow women a path to ordination as an elder.

The present polity of our church, with its constitutional rights guaranteed to every deacon, would insure her the right of successive steps into the order of an elder, and I think, inasmuch as that is so, we should go very slowly on this until such a time as this committee on our constitutional law shall have provided that a woman who is elected to the order of deacons is not necessarily eligible to the office of elder.[98]

As a solution, Rev. H.L. Crockett proposed inserting the word "only" after "deacon" to read "ordain her only a deacon." Following Crockett's suggestion, Coffee proposed a slightly different phrasing, suggesting a limitation clause noting that ordination as deacons would not be considered a step toward ordination as an elder.[99] Delegates were asked to vote on the wording, and Coffee's changes were approved. Sellew's changes limiting ordination to the office of deacon were then voted on and passed by a large majority.[100]

After the vote, the *General Conference Daily* reported that delegates favoring women's ordination broke into song, singing "Praise God from whom all blessings flow." As the nineteenth session concluded, some delegates were asked to share their thoughts on the vote.[101] Rev. Albert Sims, a delegate for East Ontario, noted supporters would see this decision as another step toward that ordination. "I consider it a very clever move. I do not mean anything as a reflection—I would prefer a straight vote. The demonstration that we had after the vote was taken shows how the brethren who are in favor of the ordination of women regard that measure."[102] Sims asked to be noted on record as opposing the proposal on principle. Indeed, Sims was correct; as the 1915 General Conference approached, rumors swirled that opponents of women's ordination were trying to roll back previous decisions at the next conference. Sellew was so concerned that he published a second edition of *Why Not?* in 1914, framing the 1911 decision as successfully bringing about complete gender equality in the denomination.

SELLEW'S INTERPRETATION VS. ROBERTS' VIEW OF ORDINATION

The decisions of the 1907 and 1911 General Conferences improved women's ministry opportunities. However, in the twenty years since Roberts' book *Ordaining Women*[103] had been published, denominational leadership's interpretation of women's roles in the church had dramatically shifted, as can be seen in Sellew's book, *Why Not?* Unlike Roberts, Sellew did not attempt to establish a biblical precedent for complete gender equality. In fact, Sellew dismissed such concerns. Citing the strict guidelines for those serving as district elder or bishop, Sellew rejected worries about women's lack of access to those roles. "Any person with ambitions for authority would be very much dissatisfied with these positions."[104] Sellew never directly addresses why he believes biblical ordination does not mean an individual also has a right to be an elder. However, he does wonder why ordination as an elder matters so much to women:

> She now has in our church all such openings she needs, and more than she uses. Ordination for women is not asked for her benefit, but for the benefit of the church. She can as, heretofore, get on very well without it; but the time has come when the church demands it both for the thing itself and for the consistency of our position before the world and before God.[105]

The inconsistency of his arguments was lost on Sellew, but the difference between his interpretation of women's ministry roles and Roberts' is stark. In *Ordaining Women*, Roberts laid out an argument for complete biblical equality and social equality for women. While he acknowledged that church elders govern, Roberts did not believe there was a biblical precedent limiting the ordination of elders by gender. Citing passages in Acts where women work alongside men in the Apostolic Church, both serving equally in governance and in preaching,[106] Roberts bluntly stated:

> The church has no right to forbid the free exercise of abilities to do good which God has given. To do so is usurpation and tyranny. Men had better busy themselves in building up the temple of God, instead employing their time in pushing from the scaffold their sisters, who are both able and willing to work with them side by side.[107]

Regarding Sellew's objection that women have no desire to govern and are satisfied picking qualified men to fill governance positions, Roberts argued that the ability to recognize the character of others is precisely why women are fit to govern in the church. Good leaders are good judges of character, and good leaders know when to delegate authority.[108] Additionally, *Ordaining Women* took a very different interpretation of a deaconess's role than Free Methodist leadership at the 1907 General Conference. Unlike the *Free Methodist Discipline*, which noted that a deaconess does not preach and is not to be seen as a substitute for a minister, Roberts provided New Testament examples where the terms "deacon" and "deaconess" are used. Arguing that a deaconess is simply a female deacon with no distinction in duties, he summarized the modern church's interpretation of a deaconess as only a lay worker:

> It is giving a stone to those who called for bread. It is conferring a shadow and withholding the substance; its bestowing a name and keeping back that which is implied in the name. In short it is a stupendous sham, of which any body of men

claiming common honesty should be ashamed. It is an insult to womankind and should be resented by them as such.[109]

Roberts argued that limiting the main ministry of a deaconess order to service was a disgrace. "Why give to the deacons the dignity and to the deaconess the drudgery?" The difference between the two roles was a differentiation based on sex alone.[110]

NOTES

1. S.V. Coe, "Life Line Mission," *The Free Methodist*, October 13, 1914, 12.

2. Free Methodist Church, *The Doctrines and Disciplines of the Free Methodist Church* (Chicago: Free Methodist Publishing House, 1908), 100–101.

3. Lori Ginzerberg, *Women and the Work of Benevolence* (New Haven, CT: Yale University Press, 1990), 25.

4. Annual conferences did not list appointments for deaconesses. However, by cross-referencing names with articles in *The Free Methodist*, the deaconesses were engaged in home missions, Life Line Mission in Kansas, and Gerry Home in Gerry, New York. Christy Mesaros-Winckles, *Data on Free Methodist Women Evangelists 1876–1920* (March 2022), distributed by Christy Mesaros-Winckles.

5. Janette Osmun, "Women's Influence," *The Free Methodist*, February 22, 1916, 3.

6. Betty DeBerg, *Ungodly Women: Gender and the First Wave of American Fundamentalism* (Minneapolis, MN: Fortress Press, 1990), 79–80.

7. R.L. Page, ed., "First Lady Elder in Free Methodism," *Pittsburg Conference Herald* 35, no. 1, September 1974, 1.

8. Ibid.

9. The duties of a bishop include serving as chairperson at annual and general conferences, helping establish new societies and conferences, upholding and promoting church policy, helping ministers transfer to other conferences, and to travel throughout the entire denomination. In *The Free Methodist Discipline* from 1911 or prior, the definition of a bishop and job duties uses the pronoun "they." However, other church positions, such as district elder, use the pronoun "he" when referring to job duties. Free Methodist Church, *The Doctrines and Disciplines of the Free Methodist Church* (Chicago: Free Methodist Publishing House, 1911), 85–89.

10. Walter Sellew, *Why Not? A Plea for Those Women God Has Called to Preach the Gospel*, 2nd ed. (Chicago: Free Methodist Publishing House, 1894), 11–12; and Walter Sellew, "Nineteenth Sitting, 1:30 p.m. Thursday, June 29," *General Conference Daily*, June 30, 1911, 4.

11. Ibid.

12. *The Discipline*'s section on dress notes that no one is to be accepted as a member of the Free Methodist Church unless they will forgo "superfluous ornaments." Additionally, everyone who oversaw a circuit was expected to read John Wesley's sermon on dress once a year, and the ministers oversaw enforcing dress on their

circuit. No indication of gender is given, which illustrates that *The Free Methodist* articles were not representing official church policy but instead reflected the views of those who upheld the cult of domesticity. Free Methodist Church, *The Doctrines and Disciplines of the Free Methodist Church 1911*, 27–28.

13. *The Doctrines and Disciplines of the Free Methodist Church* include a history of the denomination as an introduction. It is noted that "the church's mission is twofold—to maintain the Bible standard of Christianity and to preach the gospel to the poor." Church disciplines on dress and Christian living did not radically change from 1860 to 1914, but what did change was how *The Discipline* was interpreted. Free Methodist Church, *The Doctrines and Disciplines of the Free Methodist Church* (Rochester, NY: Free Methodist General Conference, 1870), ix.

14. Edward Hart, Burton Jones, Walter Sellew, and Wilson Hogue, "Pastoral Address Cont.," *The Free Methodist*, July 23, 1907, 9.

15. Vicki Tolar Collins, "Women's Voices and Women's Silence in the Tradition of Early Methodism," in *Listening to Their Voices: The Rhetorical Activities of Historical Women*, ed. Molly Meijer Wertheimer (Columbia: University of South Carolina Press, 1995), 244–46.

16. Judith Butler, "Performative Acts and Gender Constitution: An Essay in Phenomenology and Feminist Theory," *Theater Journal* 40, no. 4 (1988): 524.

17. Sellew, *Why Not?*, 29–30.

18. Hart, Jones, Sellew, and Hogue, "Pastoral Address Cont.," 9.

19. Ibid.

20. J.T. Logan, "Salutatory," *The Free Methodist*, July 23, 1907, 8.

21. Richard Hughes, *Christian America and the Kingdom of God* (Chicago: University of Illinois Press, 2009), 139.

22. Miriam King & Steven Ruggles, "American Immigration, Fertility, and Race Suicide at the Turn of the Century," *The Journal of Interdisciplinary History* 20, no. 3 (1990): 347–53.

23. J.T. Logan, "Roosevelt and the Pope," *The Free Methodist*, April 12, 1910, 1.

24. The Women's Congress was founded in 1897 by Alice McLellan Birney and Phoebe Apperson Heart. The women believed mothers were crucial advocates for the needs of children. In 1900 Theodore Roosevelt was named the chairman of the advisory council for the organization and remained in that role until 1919. National Parent Teacher Organization, "125 Years Strong," retrieved July 2, 2022, from https://www.pta.org/home/About-National-Parent-Teacher-Association/Mission-Values/National-PTA-History.

25. Theodore Roosevelt, "Remarks Before Women's Congress: March 13, 1905," The American Presidency Project, University of California Santa Barbara, accessed September 6, 2022, https://www.presidency.ucsb.edu/documents/remarks-before-the-mothers-congress.

26. Simone Caron, *Who Chooses? American Reproductive History 1830* (Gainesville: University Press of Florida, 2008), 48.

27. Ibid., 46.

28. Bill Leonard, *Christian Religious Experience in the United States* (Nashville, TN: Abingdon Press, 2014), 271–78.

29. C.E. Redeker, "The Value of the Deaconess Movement," *The Free Methodist*, December 10, 1907, 2.

30. Other Protestant denominations that had deaconess orders included the Methodist Episcopal Church both in the United States and the United Kingdom as well as the Lutheran, Mennonite, and Episcopal Churches. There also was an Evangelical Deaconess Order composed of women from numerous Protestant backgrounds. Ann Doyle, "Nursing by Religious Orders in the United States: Part V 1855–1928," *American Journal of Nursing* XXIX, no. 11 (November 1929): 1331–43; and United Methodist Church, "United Methodist Office of Deaconess and Home Missioner," retrieved July 1, 2022, https://dotac.diakonia-world.org/member-communities/united -methodist-office-of-deaconess-and-home-missioner/.

31. Hart, Jones, Sellew, and Hogue, "Pastoral Address," 9.

32. A 1914 *Free Methodist* report on the Gerry Homes in Gerry, New York, begins with a note about how Christianity cares more for "the unfortunate children" than other religions. It goes on to outline the daily operations at the orphanage, emphasizing the schooling and time for prayer and singing that was part of their daily routine. A 1915 report also noted that Chautauqua County had provided funding since the homes helped place children, but funding had recently ceased. Walter Sellew, "The Gerry Homes," *The Free Methodist*, March 2, 1915, 4; and W.B. Olmstead, "The Gerry Homes," *The Free Methodist*, June 30, 1914, 10–11.

33. J.T. Logan, "Eugenics," *The Free Methodist*, December 31, 1912, 9.

34. Roberts defined Christian living as setting oneself apart from the world, caring for the poor, opposing slavery and secret societies—things that would divide people by social class. As Free Methodism grew, what exactly the term "social gospel" meant varied greatly. Howard Snyder, *Populist Saints: B.T. and Ellen Roberts and the First Free Methodist* (Grand Rapids, MI: Wm. B. Eerdmans Publishing Co., 2006), 234–356.

35. William Olmstead, ed., "General Conference Proceedings: Eighteenth Sitting 2 p.m. Wednesday, June 26," *General Conference Daily*, June 27, 1907, 2.

36. Charles Ebey, "General Conference Proceedings Eighteenth Setting 2 p.m. Wednesday, June 26," *General Conference Daily*, June 27, 1907, 2.

37. Marston notes the first Free Methodist rescue homes were Holmes Home and Hospital in Guthrie, Oklahoma, and Life Line Children's Home in Kansas City, Kansas. Holmes was founded in 1900, and Life Line in 1907 by S.V. and Kate Coe. In addition, Free Methodists also founded Gerry homes to care for orphans and the elderly. The first Gerry Home was established in Gerry, New York in 1886 by Anna Chesbrough. Leslie Marston, *From Age to Age: A Living Witness* (Winona Lake, IN: Light and Life Press, 1960), 442–46.

38. Jessie McMurry, "Deaconess Training Course," *The Free Methodist*, August 24, 1915, 11.

39. Charles Ebey, "Free Methodist Deaconess," *The Free Methodist*, July 9, 1907, 1.

40. Ibid.

41. Charles Ebey, ed., "Deaconesses," *The Free Methodist*, June 18, 1907, 9.

42. Mesaros-Winckles, 2022.

43. Eliza Haviland, "The Deaconess Garb," *The Free Methodist*, May 21, 1907, 2.

44. Ibid.

45. Emily McGarvey, "Deaconesses," *The Free Methodist*, May 18, 1915, 2.

46. William Olmstead, ed., "Demands Made on the General Conference," *General Conference Daily*, June 12, 1907, 5–6.

47. Priscilla Pope Levison, "A Thirty-Year War and More: Exposing Complexities in the Methodist Deaconess Movement," *Methodist History* 47, no. 2 (2009): 103.

48. William Olmstead, ed., "Paper No. 149 Order of Deaconesses," *General Conference Daily*, June 27, 1907, 2.

49. Free Methodist Church, *1911 Discipline*, 27–28.

50. See photos of female evangelists in this book. In the photos, all the women wear dark colors and simple collars with no ordainment as per Free Methodist guidelines for dress in *The Free Methodist Discipline*.

51. Ruth Rubinstein, *Dress Code: Meanings and Messages in American Culture, 2nd edition* (Boulder, CO: Westview Press, 2001), 67 and 91.

52. Free Methodist Church, *1911 Discipline*, 27–28.

53. Deberg, *Ungodly Women*, 70–71 and 106–7.

54. Between 1910 and 1915 *The Free Methodist* had twelve articles on dress or blaming women for worldliness. Eugene Foster, "The Girl Part of the Boy Problem," *The Free Methodist*, May 6, 1913, 10; J.T. Logan, "The Girl Question," *The Free Methodist*, March 3, 1914, 1; J.T. Logan, "Fashion Slaves," *The Free Methodist*, October 5, 1909, 9; J.T. Logan, "Girls Read This," *The Free Methodist*, March 14, 1913, 1; & Nom De Plume, "Putting on of Apparel," *The Free Methodist*, March 29, 1910, 2.

55. Logan, "Salutatory," 8. For examples of the topics Logan favored, see J.T. Logan, "The Dress Question Again," *The Free Methodist*, August 3, 1915, 9; J.T. Logan, "Women Blamed," *The Free Methodist*, August 24, 1909, 1; Sarah Cooke, "The Bible and Dress," *The Free Methodist*, November 7, 1911, 3; Esther Meachem, "The Womanly Woman," *The Free Methodist*, December 6, 1910, 2; Sarah Cooke, "Woman's Dress," *The Free Methodist*, December 7, 1909, 11; and Eunice Budd Loomis, "Dress Reform for Free Methodism," *The Free Methodist*, June 15, 1909, 7.

56. Foster, "The Girl Part of the Boy Problem," 10.

57. Andrew Winckles, *Eighteenth-century Women's Writing and the Methodist Revolution* (Liverpool: Liverpool University Press, 2019), 142–75; Collins, "Women's Voices and Women's Silence," 239–49; & Cooke, "Woman's Dress," 11.

58. Cooke, "Woman's Dress," 11.

59. Logan, "Fashion Slaves," 9.

60. Mary McReynolds, *Redeeming Love: The Legacy of the Deaconess Ladies* (self-published by the Deaconess Hospital, 1999), 19–25.

61. Marston, *Age to Age*, 447.

62. Priscilla Pope Levison, *Building Old Time Religion: Women Evangelists in the Progressive Era* (New York: New York University Press, 2014), 149–69.

63. Wilson Hogue, "General Conference Proceedings Eighteenth Setting 2 p.m. Wednesday, June 26," *General Conference Daily*, June 27, 1907, 2.

64. McReynolds, *Redeeming Love*, 19–25.

65. Ibid.

66. When Etta Chillson wrote the Life Line Mission update in 1913–1914, she was not listed in annual conference minutes as a deaconess. She does appear in the 1917 Kansas Annual Conference Minutes as an ordained deacon that year. It is possible she was also a deaconess prior to becoming a deacon, as annual conference record-keeping was not incredibly accurate. McReynolds, *Redeeming Love*, 47.

67. Pope Levinson, *Building Old Time Religion*, 168–69.

68. McMurray's article promoted the deaconess training course at Evansville Junior College. In the article, she provides an overview of various forms of deaconess ministry. However, she notes the work of the Free Methodist deaconess is so varied and the need so great that it was hard to give prospective deaconesses direction on where they could go and serve. McMurry also noted the deaconess training program was incredibly rigorous and, to date, only a few students had completed it. This corresponds with annual conference reports on licensed deaconesses. By 1915 there were only 20 deaconesses listed in conference minutes, and the position had been available to women since 1907. McMurry, "Deaconess Training Course," 11.

69. In addition to becoming a licensed deaconess, Kate Coe also appears as a licensed evangelist in the 1904 Central Illinois Conference Minutes, where she was co-appointed with her spouse S.V. Coe to the Bingham and Bethel Circuits. In 1906 she was given a solo appointment to the Greenville Circuit in the Central Illinois Conference. She appeared between 1909 and 1912 in the Kansas Annual Conference Minutes as a conference evangelist appointed with S.V. Coe to Life Line Mission. In 1913 she became a deaconess and no longer appears as a licensed evangelist in conference minutes. Her choice to switch from evangelist to deaconess appears unusual, as other early deaconesses do not appear in minutes as evangelists before becoming deaconesses. Mesaros-Winckles, 2022.

70. Ibid.

71. McMurray, "Deaconess Training Course," 11.

72. Free Methodist Church, *Annual Conference Minutes: Proceedings of the Forty Annual Conference of the Free Methodist Church of North America* (Chicago: Free Methodist Publishing House, 1910), 189–211; & Free Methodist Church, *Annual Conference Minutes: Proceedings of the Forty-One Annual Conference of the Free Methodist Church of North America* (Chicago: Free Methodist Publishing House, 1912), 291–307.

73. McMurray, "Deaconess Training Course," 11.

74. The first deaconess was Rebecca Sellew in the Oil City Conference. From 1910 to 1912 all the deaconesses listed in annual conference minutes were in the Oil City Conference or New York Conference. By 1913 Michigan, Susquehanna, and Kansas all had at least one deaconess, and through 1920 conferences such as Susquehanna, New York, and Oil City consistently had more than one deaconess in their conference. Often women were listed for multiple years, implying that the first deaconesses in those conferences stayed active and served as an example that inspired other women to join. Mesaros-Winckles, 2022.

75. McMurray notes it is impossible to get accurate and up-to-date information on how many women are part of the deaconess order. Annual conference minutes do not

designate between women who are a deaconess on trial (completing their training and exam) and those with a permanent license. So, the number of licensed deaconesses is probably slightly lower than I report in this chapter since some women never completed their training. McGarvey also discussed how the deaconess training required "considerable work and quite strenuous exams," but she was not asking for standards to diminish; just to increase access to training by offering it at more Free Methodist educational institutions. McGarvey, "Deaconesses," 2.

76. Hart, Jones, Sellew, and Hogue, "Pastoral Address," 9. William Olmstead also noted in the *General Conference Daily* that the decision to allow women evangelists to be ministerial delegates caused the conference to be "thrown into confusion which lasted some time over the proposed amendment." The change to *The Discipline* was approved 73 for and 43 against. William Olmstead, ed., "Editorial," *General Conference Daily*, June 21, 1907, 1.

77. Manetho, "The General Conference—A Review," *The Free Methodist*, September 17, 1907, 2; and Manetho, "The General Conference—A Review V," *The Free Methodist*, September 24, 1907, 2.

78. Ibid.

79. Ibid.

80. Hogue also denied being another anonymous author, Veritas, who wrote an article before the 1907 General Conference denouncing the denomination's policy on no instrumental music in worship. Wilson Hogue, "To Whom it May Concern," *The Free Methodist*, October 15, 1911, 4.

81. Wilson Hogue, "Admission of Women to the Annual Conference No. 1," *The Free Methodist*, April 4, 1911, 2; and Wilson Hogue "Admission of Women to the Annual Conference No. 2" *The Free Methodist*, April 11, 1911, 2.

82. Ibid.

83. W.M. Adams, "The Woman Question," *The Free Methodist*, May 9, 1911, 2–3.

84. Ibid.

85. Brooks had advocated for women's ordination since at least the 1894 General Conference when he spoke in defense of their ordination. He made similar points to what he wrote in the 1911 article. Freeborn D. Brooks, "Do Women Preachers Ever Wear Out?," *The Free Methodist*, May 23, 1911, 3.

86. Ibid.

87. Hall, "Forward, Backward," 6.

88. Later in the article, S.A.H. clarified that what she means by "handcuffs" is the inability of women evangelists to fully serve their congregations by offering communion and the ability to marry and baptize. S.A.H., "Rights of Women Pastors," *The Free Methodist*, January 22, 1907, 3.

89. Ibid.

90. Ibid.

91. The Southern California petition read: "Whereas, our noble women who are called of God to preach the gospel, show gifts and graces in that direction; and, blessed in their labors as well as men. Therefore, we do petition your honorable body to make provision for their ordination on the same basis as the ordination of men." L.

Smith, J.B. Freeland, W.E. Shepard, "Paper No. 34," *The General Conference Daily*, June 19, 1911, 34.

92. Roberts' original resolution to ordain women in 1890 stated, "Resolved, That the Gospel of Jesus Christ, in the provision which it makes, and in the agencies which it employs for the salvation of mankind, knows no distinction of nationality, condition or sex: therefore, no person who is called of God, and who is duly qualified should be refused ordination on account of sex, or race, or condition." Wilson Hogue, *History of the Free Methodist Church: Volume 1* (Chicago: Free Methodist Publishing House, 1915), 192.

93. William Olmstead, ed., "Nineteenth Sitting, 1:30 p.m. Thursday, June 29," *General Conference Daily*, June 30, 1911, 4–5.

94. A. Beers, "Nineteenth Sitting, 1:30 p.m. Thursday, June 29," *General Conference Daily*, June 30, 1911, 4.

95. Sellew, "Nineteenth Sitting," 4.

96. Ibid.

97. W.N. Coffee, "Nineteenth Sitting, 1:30 p.m. Thursday, June 29," *General Conference Daily*, June 30, 1911, 4.

98. H.L. Crockett, "Nineteenth Sitting, 1:30 p.m. Thursday, June 29," *General Conference Daily*, June 30, 1911, 4.

99. Coffee, "Nineteenth Sitting," 4.

100. Ibid.

101. Olmstead, "Nineteenth Sitting," 5.

102. Albert Sims, "Nineteenth Sitting, 1:30 p.m. Thursday, June 29," *General Conference Daily*, June 30, 1911, 5.

103. Benjamin Titus Roberts, *Ordaining Women* (Rochester, NY: Earnest Christian Publishing House, 1891).

104. Sellew, *Why Not?*, 11.

105. Ibid., 12.

106. Roberts, *Ordaining Women*, 139–41.

107. Ibid., 148–49.

108. Ibid., 108–10.

109. Ibid.

110. Ibid.

Chapter 7

A Twist & Then Finally Acknowledgment

The 1915 and 1974 General Conferences

The 1911 General Conference decision to ordain women as deacons was lauded by supporters of women's ordination. However, it soon became apparent that detractors would not allow the decision to go uncontested. Rumblings of plans to try and revoke women's ordination as deacon at the 1915 General Conference were confirmed by Bishop Walter Sellew in his revised second edition of *Why Not? A Plea for Those Women God Has Called to Preach the Gospel*. Published in 1914, Sellew's introduction noted that the new edition was intended to remind Free Methodists that there was biblical justification for ordaining women as deacons.[1] Nevertheless, while Sellew had been instrumental in helping pass women's ordination as deacons, he was resistant to their ordination as elders; both in *Why Not?* and in his judiciary role as bishop, he often favored limitations on women's access to ordination and leadership positions within the denomination. As the 1915 General Conference approached and annual conferences published their proposed amendments in *The Free Methodist*, it became clear that at least the New York Annual Conference intended to protest the 1911 ordination decision. An additional hurdle would emerge in a judiciary case from the California Annual Conference. While the New York Conference's protest appeared to be the primary cause of concern among supporters of women's ordination before the conference, the real threat to women's rights was the California appeal case. The annual conference requested the 1915 General Conference to review an earlier ruling by Sellew, stating that married women deacons could not be brought into full connection in the same annual conference if their spouse was also an ordained deacon or minister. Sellew argued that to do so was a violation of *The Doctrines and Disciplines of the Free Methodist Church*. Allowing both a husband and wife to be ordained and serve in the

same annual conference would disrupt the balance of lay and ministerial delegates and allow a single family to draw two stipends from the conference's
superannuated (retirement) funds. Denominational governance was laid out
in the *Discipline*, and according to the 1911 *Discipline*, Free Methodist bishops were charged with presiding over all trials of appeal from quarterly and
annual conferences and deciding how to interpret questions related to The
Discipline.[2] Annual conferences had the right to appeal the bishop's decisions
at the next general conference, which California chose to do in 1915.

THE CALIFORNIA CONFERENCE APPEAL

In the lead-up to the 1915 General Conference, *The Free Methodist* featured
several editorials by members arguing for revisions to annual conference
superannuated funds. The superannuated fund was used to financially support
retired ordained ministers in each annual conference. Since the approval of
ordaining women as deacons in 1911, some conferences were increasingly
concerned about the long-term financial health of their funds. A complete
breakdown in superannuated funds was also one of Sellew's concerns, and
it influenced his decision in the California case to restrict married ordained
women deacons from having full conference membership just as their
spouses did. In explaining his decision to the appeal's committee at the 1915
General Conference,[3] Sellew noted that even Free Methodist elders opposed
to women's ordination now realized that there was a chance to collect additional retirement funds if their wife became an ordained deacon:

Fig. 7.1. The 1915 General Conference delegates. Source: Marston Memorial
Historical Center

You know I have been strongly in favor of ordaining women, but I have been trying to keep this system which has been working for four years from being broken down. They all want to be ordained, everyone of the wives of the evangelists want to be ordained. I have a letter from one man who said, "I have always been opposed to having women ordained, but I would like to have my wife ordained." They all want to break it down to get in their wives, and what I want to do is keep this system from being broken down. After it has been working from six to ten years it may be all right to reconsider it, but so far it has not had a fair trial. We must see to it that we do not overload it with ordaining the wives of preachers who already belong to the conference.[4]

Sellew also argued his decision was based on past precedent, as in 1908 Bishop Burton Jones had ruled that the Ohio Conference could not allow a woman serving a circuit a seat as a delegate at the annual conference because her husband was also a preacher. Sellew's decision to deny full ministerial rights to married women deacons was controversial, and the appeals committee was evenly split, with some members siding with the bishop and others siding with the appellant. As General Conference Delegate Lewis[5] noted:

I cannot see how it would be consistent to base ordination on the marriage or single relation. I should think it would be on the call of God and the endorsement of the church and not on any family relation. A point in hand; there is a man and woman with whom I am personally acquainted. One is a pastor in one place and the other in the other. She goes to her circuit and he to his, and they both are entitled to recognition. Regarding the conference claim, if we have a discipline that does not provide for this, we should change our discipline. If we do not want the women who are wives of husbands to receive the conference claim, change the discipline. The ruling of Bishop Jones was before it was the policy of the church to give women a vote.[6]

Lewis noted that in the 1911 *Discipline*, paragraph 100 clearly stated that whenever an annual conference was satisfied that a woman was called to preach, they could receive her into full connection as a deacon in the *same* manner the conference received men as deacons.[7]

Freeborn Brooke also spoke up in favor of allowing married women deacons full annual conference membership, noting that in reviewing Sellew's decision, the bishop's argument that allowing a married couple to both to be full conference members violated the *Discipline* was an incorrect interpretation. As Brooke argued, it came down to fairness. Flipping the script, Brooke asked committee members to consider if the situation was reversed and the wife ordained before the husband, would the husband then not be eligible for full membership, too?

> Suppose a case; Miss Blank is an ordained deacon in the Free Methodist church, twenty-five years old. She exercised that office for five years; she reaches the age of thirty and then Mr. John Doe, a young man twenty-six years or thirty-one years old joins the conference on trial. During his trial period, he takes a fancy to Miss Blank and after serving his time, he marries her. Now Miss Blank has been ordained deacon for five years. After this young man has served two years, having lived one year as her husband, he is elected to the deacon's orders, and joins the conference in full connection. According to this providing if they are on the level you will have to set John Doe aside. He can not be ordained because former Miss Blank, now his wife, has been ordained and it will make two ministers in the family and the Free Methodist church has decided that is too many.[8]

In response to Brooke's supposition, Sellew protested that ordination was not up for debate. What was up for debate was conference membership. Dodging the gender issue, Sellew used female pronouns to refer to the spouse who should not have full conference membership.[9]

The appeals committee debate sparked accusations of breaches in governance at the 1911 General Conference from committee members who supported Sellew's decision. C.E. Harroun, a ministerial delegate from the Oklahoma Conference, noted the decision to ordain women deacons had resulted in four years of embarrassment for him as he continually saw ongoing issues with governance as a result of the decision:

> I think now, as I did then, that this whole question should have gone the rounds of the annual conferences as it did twenty years ago when the ordination of women was up. It was sent to the conferences and returned. The general conference practically admitted that it was a matter for them [annual conferences] to decide, but it was hurried through and we did not have time to discuss it as we should have and now we have what we have.[10]

Interestingly, Wilson Hogue, another long-time vocal opponent of women's ordination, actually sided with Brooke on women's right to full conference membership. Noting in opening his personal opposition, Hogue nevertheless worried that denying full membership to married, ordained women would be a public relations nightmare for the denomination. Disagreeing with Sellew's argument to the committee that the issue of women's membership was not the same as their right to ordination, Hogue stated:

> My brother [Sellew] said he did not mean the question of ordination, but the question of ordination is just as clearly involved as though he had said it. That is just where I stood. I opposed it stoutly during the long years of our contention, and if you were to try to reverse it I would oppose it, for I don't believe in being so changeable as to give the impression to the world that we have no mind of our own from one general conference to another. I think it would very

seriously injure the work. I think my colleague wrote me about this thing the first year or the first fall after the conference passed upon this matter, and I stand now where I did then. I replied to him that I didn't believe in any arbitrary ruling and I could not see how he could rule a woman out of her constitutional rights except by an arbitrary ruling, and I don't see, even if this substitute passes, how you could force a woman into the local ranks if she were to be properly recommended for admission in the ministry and deacon's relations. The law says, "If any woman"—it doesn't say, "any woman except the wife of a clergyman or minister."

The appeals committee could not agree, with half voting in support of Sellew's earlier decision and half voting to send the appeal to the entire General Conference for a decision. It ultimately did not matter since the committee was split. The case automatically went to the main floor for discussion and a vote.[11]

THE GENERAL CONFERENCE DECISION ON MARRIED WOMEN DEACON

The issue of married women deacon's conference membership rights came to the main floor for discussion six days after the committee deadlocked on the issue. Presented as paper no.193, delegates were asked to vote either for or against Sellew's original ruling, which would change the ordination of deacon section to include a caveat that no woman "whose husband is a member on trial or in full connection shall be eligible to be received by the conference."

Sellew spoke in favor of his ruling, acknowledging the work of Free Methodist women and reminding delegates that the decision to approve their ordination as deacons did not pass by a slim majority but by a margin of nearly two to one. He urged delegates to vote in favor of the limitation so conference leadership would have more time to address financial concerns with the superannuated funds. He did not mention how the ruling would also restrict ordained women's right to serve as ministerial delegates to their quarterly and annual conferences.[12] Hogue, as well, spoke up on the matter. Speaking directly after Sellew and in opposition to his proposal, Hogue expressed his belief that women should not be ordained. Reiterating his arguments made to the appeals committee, Hogue proposed another solution:

The discipline states that they shall be ordained in all respects on the same basis men are ordained, and I maintain that to make a change on this point would be to arbitrarily take away the constitutional rights of the preacher's wife. There is a different way and place to correct this thing, and the way and place to correct it will be with some distribution of the superannuated fund. If the minister and his wife are both in the conference and they come up as claimants, we can limit the amount that they should have.[13]

Speaking after Hogue, D.J. Santmier, a ministerial delegate from the New York Conference who had opposed women's ordination in 1894, used the discussion to bring his annual conference's memorial opposing the 1911 decision to ordain women as deacons to the floor.

Interestingly, Santimer prefaced his arguments by noting his own wife was a long-time Free Methodist evangelist who some Free Methodists said was a better preacher than her spouse. However, despite supporting his wife's right to *preach*, Santmier wanted delegates to note the New York Conference's memorial objecting to their right to *ordination*. Addressing his fellow delegates, Santimer read the entire memorial from his conference on the floor:

Whereas, The question of ordaining women was twice referred back to the constituency of the general conference and twice rejected by the same; and. Whereas, ordination of women was rejected by the general conference at Greenville in 1894 by more than two-thirds vote after it had been submitted and rejected by its constituency; and. Whereas, The general conference four years ago, in the rush and closing hours of said conference and after a goodly number of the delegates had been excused and returned home, voted to ordain women; and. Whereas, The committee on revision at this conference buried the memorial of the New York Conference, asking for a reconsideration and resubmitting of the question; and. Whereas, We believe that such burying of a memorial of a conference praying for a reconsideration of a subject is not showing proper respect for such conference constituency, especially under the above mention circumstances. We, the delegates of said New York conference wish to register our protest against the procedure of which we complain.

In addition to Santmier, the memorial was signed by New York delegates A.W. Myer, Jos. F. Eberhard, and M.F. Boring. Following his address, a motion was made to return to the discussion of married-ordained women's right to conference membership. The motion passes, essentially burying the New York memorial and ending the discussion.

Ultimately, it was not the New York memorial that detrimentally affected Free Methodist women in ministry, as Sellew had feared in his 1914 introduction to *Why Not?* However, ironically, his own judicial decision restricting married, ordained women deacons' right to full conference benefits caused the most significant setback to gender equality in ministry. A day after discussing the changes to the *Discipline*, conference paper no. 193 passed with little further discussion, essentially preventing a married woman evangelist or deacon from participating in denominational governance. The 1915 decision illustrated that women's place within the denomination was far from secure. For the next fifty-nine years, married Free Methodist women deacons were extremely limited in their denominational role. When the 1974 General Conference considered the question of women's ordination as an elder, women's second-class status put in place by the 1915 General Conference was often cited by supporters as one of the main reasons the denomination needed to grant women full access to all forms of ordination.

1974: FREE METHODIST WOMEN
FINALLY ORDAINED AS ELDERS

In the Free Methodist Church, denominational publications played a crucial role in allowing members to share their opinions and promote the views of various denominational leaders. Just as *The Free Methodist* was used as a rhetorical device, particularly by Roberts during his tenure prior to the 1890 General Conference, its twentieth-century successor, *Light and Life*, was utilized in a similar manner prior to the 1974 General Conference. In May 1974, just a few months before the General Conference, editors of *Light and Life* used the May Mother's Day issue as a chance to advocate for women's ordination. Using editorial tactics like Roberts, editors solicited original articles by women advocating for their rights. Just as Roberts did in the 1890s, *Light and Life* editor Robert Fine also wrote an editorial defending women's right to ordination. In explaining the denominational history of the issue, Fine astutely assesses Sellew's 1911 push to grant women ordination as deacons:

> Bishop Sellew offered a resolution maintaining the subordination of women while providing for their ordination. . . . Today apart from the opening words of Bishop Sellew's resolution concerning women's call to preach, this measure stands as the law of the church. Its passage, despite strong efforts to defeat it, expressed the uneasy conscience of the church concerning the place of women in the pulpit. They cannot aspire to the higher ordination because of their sex. [14]

Fine noted that by 1974 more than eighty denominations ordained women. However, within the Free Methodist Church, unmarried women still had limited opportunities for leadership. For married women, the continued refusal to grant them conference membership was also a significant obstacle to women's involvement. As Fine summarized:

> The further refusal of the church to grant conference membership to married women who are ordained raises problems than cannot be ignored or easily resolved. Can the church justify its implicit demand that women remain unmarried in order to vote in the conference? The celibacy of the clergy ought not to be implied for women while never demanded for men. [15]

In the same issue Viola Walton, president of the Free Methodist Women's Missionary Society of North America, wrote an article, "Women in the Church," noting the significant contributions of women to the spread of Christianity. Pointing to women's mission involvement, Walton reminded readers that most missionaries had been women for nearly a century. Thirty percent of those women travel to the mission field as a single person. In comparison, nearly one hundred percent of male missionaries were married and entered mission work with a woman by their side.[16] Concluding her article, Walton wondered what had happened to the Free Methodist egalitarian ethos:

> What has happened to the conviction of B.T. Roberts relating to women in the ministry in the fullest sense? Tragic, but nonetheless true, today's female seminarians still face opposition and discrimination. Women should sit on administrative boards in the church, not because they are women, but because they are persons with abilities and insights.[17]

Approving women's ordination as elders at the 1974 General Conference appears to have received widespread support from leadership and denominational publications before the conference. The 1974 *General Conference Daily* continued *Light and Life*'s coverage of the upcoming discussion and vote. However, unlike Fine's May 1974 editorial in *Light and Life*, the *General Conference Daily*'s editorial coverage illustrated the power of organizational culture to construct public memory contrary to fact. The June 22, 1974, *Daily* editorial "Women's Ordination: An Issue Past and Present" reflected on the 1894 General Conference debates and painted Wilson Hogue as an advocate of women's ordination who continued Roberts' quest to see women ordained. Touting Hogue's influence as editor of *The Free Methodist* and then as bishop, the editorial credited him with being a vocal supporter of women's rights. Hogue's numerous speeches and articles opposing women's ordination appear to be long forgotten as he was made a Free Methodist founder with the same egalitarian ideology as Roberts.

Fortunately, unlike earlier General Conferences, the 1974 General Conference had few delegates opposed to ordination, and on July 1, 1974, women's ordination as an elder was approved unanimously.[18] Shortly after General Conference approval, the first two Free Methodist women were ordained elders. Jean Parry, the pastor of Sunnyside Free Methodist Church in Monongahela, Pennsylvania, was ordained on July 19, 1974, and Ina Ellis from the Wabash Conference was ordained on August 14, 1974. Parry had been the local pastor at Sunnyside for seven years before her ordination, five of those years working full-time in ministry. Ellis, who was eighty-one when she was ordained, had devoted much of her life to evangelism and was an ordained deacon. However, her spouse was an ordained Free Methodist elder

Fig. 7.2. The 1974 General Conference delegates. Source: Marston Memorial Historical Center

in the same conference. *Light and Life*, the denominational magazine, noted Ellis' ordination came as soon as the restrictions on women's ordination as elders were lifted, for herself and the Wabash Conference, ordaining Ellis served as a recognition of her lifetime of service to the denomination and an acknowledgment of the restrictions church policy had placed on her ministry and denominational involvement.[19] In total, nineteen women were ordained as elders between 1974 and 1978 in the North American Free Methodist Church, and when also considering ordination as a deacon, there were sixty-five ordained women.[20] The number of women ordained in 1974 was a far cry from the hundreds of women serving as evangelists at the turn of the twentieth century and illustrated the steep decline in women's involvement with preaching ministries since the sedimentation of secondary ministries categories for women in 1911. The denomination continued to make changes that would place men and women on equal ministerial footing. At the next General Conference in 1979, delegates voted to redefine lay leadership positions, eliminating the ministry categories of local deacon, the deaconess order, and local elders and providing local church flexibility in lay leadership appointments so churches could select leaders in areas that fit the specific needs of their congregations.[21]

CONCLUSION

The decision of the 1974 Free Methodist General Conference to ordain women corresponded with larger social trends regarding women's advancement, just as decisions made at the 1890, 1894, 1907, 1911, and 1915 General Conferences also reflected larger cultural debates about women's leadership roles. In his research on the history of women's ordination from 1830 to 1980, sociologist Mark Chaves traces most advancements in women's ordination to two particular decades—the 1880s and the 1970s. Both periods in Free Methodist history can be informally tied to the first-wave suffrage movement and the second-wave feminist movement of the 1960s and 1970s. While the first-wave movement focused on getting women the right to vote and the right to work outside the home, the second wave focused on increasing gender equality and passing the Equal Rights Amendment (ERA) to guarantee women their rights constitutionally.[22] Decisions and debates on women's roles in the Free Methodist Church also fall within this window and illustrate how organizational policy and member opinions operate in conversation with larger social trends.

Nevertheless, just as anti-suffrage rhetoric ramped up before the passage of the Nineteenth Amendment in 1919, so did anti-feminist rhetoric in the 1970s. The 1974 General Conference decision should be viewed not as a turning point that resulted in scores of women pursuing ordination in the Free Methodist Church, but as a brief moment that made that goal possible. The 1974 decision came immediately after two major historical events for women's rights advocates and detractors. First, the ERA was passed by Congress in 1972 and sent to the states for ratification; then in 1973 the historic U.S. Supreme Court case *Roe v. Wade* legalized abortion. Both the ERA and *Roe v. Wade* served as a rallying cry for conservatives who saw efforts to advance women's rights as an attempt to turn the country away from its Christian heritage. The underlying premillennialism which emerged during Progressive Era debates on gender was now fully embraced by many conservative Americans, including Protestant Christians.

While Catholic activist Phyllis Schlafly is perhaps the most well-known anti-feminist activist of the 1970s and 1980s, perhaps the activists with the most far-reaching and long-lasting influence emerged from the Moral Majority movement of the late 1970s and early 1980s. Notably, James Dobson, who began his Focus on the Family radio show in 1977 and quickly became the leading Protestant voice on all "family issues," took his cues from the rhetorical arguments of Progressive Era anti-suffragists, arguing that there were God-given gender roles for men and women.[23] The ERA, the passage of *Roe v. Wade*, and other advancements for women were seen as a direct threat to family life and Christian values. As the rhetoric of the Moral Majority gained traction in Protestant, and particularly evangelical, culture, it became increasingly challenging for denominations such as the Free Methodist Church to convince members to welcome women who wanted to pursue full-time ministry. The challenges female seminarians faced in the 1970s did not diminish with the approval of women's ordination, as Walton had hoped in her 1974 *Light and Life* article. Instead, increasingly blurred denominational lines and a prolific Christian publishing industry (spearheaded by Dobson and his organizations) popularized unbiblical gendered divisions of labor in both the home and church, which made it more difficult for denominations that did ordain women, such as the Free Methodist Church, to find women willing to enter ministry and churches willing to accept them as pastors.

As Chaves explains, when organizations come into contact with larger social movements, such as the women's liberation movement, organizational members will be more likely to interpret internal organizational tensions using the terminology of larger social movements.[24] Thus, in the case of women's ordination within the Free Methodist Church, the tradition of biblical egalitarianism that could be traced back to Roberts got conflated with supposedly "secular" conversations about women's rights and roles in society. As a result, ordained Free Methodist women who are appointed as lead pastors are still rare and when they are appointed often face resistance to their leadership because congregants see them as an anomaly and not a norm.

NOTES

1. Walter Sellew, *Why Not? A Plea for Those Women God Has Called to Preach the Gospel*, 2nd ed. (Chicago: Free Methodist Publishing House, 1894).

2. Free Methodist Church, *The Doctrine and Disciplines of the Free Methodist Church* (Chicago: Free Methodist Publishing House, 1911), 86.

3. The debate regarding married, ordained women deacons right to conference membership was complicated by complex denominational governance structures, but according to the 1911 *Book of Discipline*, the topic came about through a complex appeals process that is outlined in the annual conference, executive committee, and bishop sections of the *Discipline*. It outlines the job duties of the bishop to include overseeing sessions of general conference, executive committee, and annual conference meetings as well as to preside over any appeals from quarterly or annual conference and "to decide all question of law therein, subject to an appeal to the general conference." The denomination's executive committee was tasked with hearing the appeals from quarterly and annual conferences and met once a year to hear such appeals in the years General Conference did not meet. Membership included one elder and one lay representative from each annual conferences. Executive committee members were selected at each General Conference. The California case regarding married women deacons was an appeal by that annual conference to the 1915 General Conference for reconsideration since Bishop Sellew based his ruling on a previous 1908 ruling by Bishop Jones. Because 1908 was prior to the 1911 approval of women's ordination as deacons, California felt the decision went against current church law. Ibid., 43–44, 47, and 85–86.

4. Ibid., 86.

5. There were two delegates at the 1915 convention with last name "Lewis." The *General Conference Daily* does not provide initials or first name in the (issues) so it is

impossible to know which delegate was quoted. Both came from annual conferences that could conceivably have been sympathetic to women's ordination.

6. The 1915 General Conference had two ministerial delegates with the last name of Lewis. L.G. Lewis was a ministerial delegate from the Kansas Conference and F.G. Lewis from North Minnesota. The *General Conference Daily* does not include initials so it is not possible to discern which ministerial delegate is quoted. Lewis, "Eighteenth Session June 24, 1915," *General Conference Daily*, June 25, 1915, 4.

7. Ibid.

8. Freeborn Brooke, "Eighteenth Session June 24, 1915," *General Conference Daily*, June 25, 1915, 3.

9. Walter Sellew, "Eighteenth Session June 24, 1915," *General Conference Daily*, June 25, 1915, 3.

10. C.E. Harroun, "Eighteenth Session June 24, 1915," *General Conference Daily*, June 25, 1915, 4.

11. A.D. Zahniser, "Eighteenth Session June 24, 1915," *General Conference Daily*, June 25, 1915, 4.

12. Ibid.

13. Ibid.

14. Robert Fine, Donald Demarray, U. Milo Kaufmann, H. Frank VanValin, eds., *Light and Life Magazine: Woman* (Winona Lake, IN: Free Methodist Publishing, May 1974).

15. Robert Fine, "Can Rachel Stand in the Pulpit?," *Light and Life Magazine* (Winona Lake, IN: Free Methodist Publishing, May 1974), 5.

16. Viola Loder Walton, "Women in the Church," *Light and Life Magazine* (Winona Lake, IN: Free Methodist Publishing, May 1974), 7.

17. Ibid., 8.

18. Robert Fine, Donald Demarray, U. Milo Kaufmann, H. Frank VanValin, eds., *Light and Life Magazine: Free Methodist Conference* (Winona Lake, IN: Free Methodist Publishing, July 23, 1974), 7.

19. George Ford, "Ina Ellis, Mother & Minister," *Light and Life Magazine* (Winona Lake, IN: Free Methodist Publishing, October 22, 1974), 12–13; Robert Fine, Donald Demarray, U. Milo Kaufmann, H. Frank VanValin, eds., "First Woman Elder Is Elected," *Light and Life Magazine* (Winona Lake, IN: Free Methodist Publishing, September 10, 1974), 16; and David McKenna, *A Future with a History* (Indianapolis, IN: Light and Life Communication, 1997), 256.

20. Evelyn Mottweller, "Letter to Doris Schrock Regarding Free Methodist Women in Ministry Research," March 15, 1979.

21. Free Methodist Church, "Fourth Sitting," Minutes of the 1979 Free Methodist General Conference, 493.

22. Mark Chavez, *Ordaining Women: Culture and Conflict in Religious Organizations* (Cambridge, MA: Harvard University Press, 1997), 64–65.

23. Christy Mesaros-Winckles and Andrew Winckles, "Focus on the (Changing) Family: A Hot Message Encounters a Cool Medium," in *The Electronic Church in the Digital Age*, ed. Mark Ward Sr. (Santa Barbara, CA: Praeger, 2016), 42–43.

24. Chavez, *Ordaining Women*, 66.

Chapter 8

Where We Are Now

Current Concerns about Women's Acceptance in Ministry

It was 2011, and I had just finished preaching a sermon at my local church. As a consecrated Free Methodist deacon, we were often asked to step into the pulpit when our pastor was away. Both my husband and I had preached on occasion. "Great talk, the stories of those women preachers were really interesting," a well-meaning gentleman told me after the service. *Talk*? Why was I thanked for my *talk* when I preached, but when my spouse preached, he was thanked for his *sermon*? This might seem like semantics, but the underlying differences in word choice reflect deeply rooted perceptions of gender. In this concluding chapter, I want readers to recognize that the debates on women's roles in the church have not really changed. In particular, I want to emphasize the ongoing struggles women in ministry face, especially in evangelical Christian congregations. The hurdles the women in this book faced are often the same struggles women pastors face today. Ida Gage, Clara Wetherald, Ada Hall, Laura Lamb, Anna Grant, and many more had to prove their qualifications and spiritual calling continually. They faced criticism for stepping into nontraditional roles for women and did not have access to the most senior leadership positions within the denomination. Today's women pastors still face questions about their qualifications, struggle to be considered qualified for denominational leadership positions, and even face questions about their ability to balance family and ministry—something that their male counterparts are never asked. Numerous reasons exist for these ongoing issues, including blurred denominational boundaries, a prolific complementarian material culture, and little historical reflection in even the most egalitarian Protestant traditions. Understanding denominational history is crucial if denominational leaders wish to stop repeating the mistakes of the past. Free Methodist theologian Kristina LaCelle-Peterson aptly summarizes the dilemma:

> Many evangelicals believe that only "liberal" churches ordain women and that women had never been in ministry until the feminist movement prodded these "liberal" women and "liberal" churches to move in that direction. They are unaware of the long and rich history of women's participation in the church's leadership: the deacons, the widows, those called priests, and bishops on their tombstones in the early centuries of the church.[1]

Because the fantastic contributions of women have all but been written out of many Free Methodist denominational histories, whether intentionally or not, few members are aware of the rich history of women's leadership within their denomination; this lack of awareness is not a uniquely Free Methodist concern. As LaCelle-Peterson explains, many evangelicals still do not view gender equity as a pressing concern facing the church. This is partly due to a lack of historical context and acknowledgment that women have participated in ministry and church leadership since the first century.[2] Acknowledging and re-integrating women's narratives into denominational histories is challenging. Particularly since such a move likely would be labeled "feminist" (aka secular) by many evangelicals. Over twenty years ago, powerful gender essentialists such as James Dobson, John Piper, Stu Weber, and Wayne Grudem successfully crafted a narrative labeling egalitarian theology as an extension of secular feminism. As sociologist Sally Gallagher explains, these men have successfully defined biblical feminism "as a version of theological liberalism, teetering on the edge of Biblical relativism's slippery slope."[3] This narrative has so effectively been integrated into evangelical culture that it will be difficult for individual denominations to get rhetorical buy-in on a new narrative. However, as evangelical denominations wrestle with cultural relevancy and wonder why so many young adults are permanently leaving, dealing with gender equity can no longer be pushed aside. A 2021 study of over 10,000 young adults aged eighteen to twenty-five found that seventy-seven percent of respondents said gender equity was incredibly important to them. However, respondents also felt that Christian culture did not share this value or only marginally cared about it.[4]

SEEING SOMEONE LIKE YOU

When people do not see visible leaders who look like them and share similar cultural experiences, they are less likely to feel included and more likely to seek spiritual fulfillment elsewhere. This is particularly problematic as young adults say they do not engage in organized religion because they feel they cannot be themselves and must fit an organizational mold they do not feel comfortable with.[5] Representation and inclusion are still significant concerns for the next generation of women. As of 2019, only three percent of evangelical churches were led by women. That three percent reflects women in senior leadership positions in local churches, not women serving as assistant pastors or deacons.[6] Within Free Methodism, the root of current issues with gender equity can be traced back to the 1894 General Conference decision not to ordain women as elders and the subsequent 1907 and 1911 General Conferences, which established a deaconess order and approved women's ordination as deacons. Free Methodist leaders sent a clear message that women were welcome to serve but *not* at the most senior levels.[7] This continued for sixty-three years as Free Methodist women essentially only had denominational support in secondary forms of ministry. Even though the Free Methodist Church theoretically rectified this gender equity issue in 1974, allowing women to be ordained as elders, over a hundred years of sedimented gender roles is not easy to overcome. Once members accept a narrative vision, it is very difficult to change.[8] The effects of these nineteenth-century decisions are still apparent, as the Free Methodist Church is embarking on a campaign to empower women pastors and help create a culture where they can thrive.[9] This is primarily due to a 2011 study by Free Methodist scholar Beth Armstrong, which repeated research from 1997 tracking how many Free Methodist women were serving as senior pastors. In 1997 only sixteen percent of ordained women served as senior pastors, and when the study was replicated in 2011, it had only increased by a percentage point.[10]

These challenges are not unique to the Free Methodist Church. As of 2019, women in white evangelical churches still primarily serve in secondary ministry positions, making up thirty-six percent of secondary ministry roles.[11] Changing perceptions about gender roles is a massive rhetorical challenge requiring creative thinking and courage if denominational leaders want to see substantive change. As the 2021 National Congregations Study illustrates, leadership is often very localized within Protestant traditions. While many senior pastors attend seminary or other denominational training for their positions, secondary ministerial positions often come from within a congregation and rely on the senior pastor to educate these ministers in the denomination's theology.[12] If there is not already a robust egalitarian tradition in the local church, then complementarian views on gender will be perpetuated.

PUSHING BACK AGAINST
COMPLEMENTARIAN MASS MEDIA

The reasons why so few women are senior pastors can also partly be traced to the prolific complementarian media industry in Protestant American culture. Mainly since the 1980s, with the formation in 1987 of the Council on Biblical Manhood and Womanhood, the publication of John Piper's best-selling book *Recovering Biblical Manhood and Womanhood: A Response to Evangelical Feminism*, and the rise of Bill Gothard's Institute in Basic Life Principles, there has been a concerted effort in Christian media to discount egalitarian theology and downplay the history of women's leadership in many denominations.[13] Believing that men and women are functionally different—and, thus, have different roles to play in the church and the home—has become a cornerstone of evangelical culture. As Julie Ingersoll's research into Christian bookstores illustrates, Christian popular culture is intrinsically gendered:

> By looking at the material culture that evangelicals produce, we can discern a much-overlooked dimension of who these people are. The culture they have produced is profoundly gendered, suggesting that evangelicalism, as a religious movement, is itself essentially gendered.[14]

Ingersoll goes on to note the challenges Christian egalitarians face in overcoming the functional difference argument popularized by complementarian theologians:

> While there is evidence that evangelical feminists have gained significant ground on the institutional and theological fronts, the fact remains that gendered dualism is perpetuated on a popular level by virtue of the fact that the material culture that gives shape to everyday life reproduces it.[15]

This gendered dualism is present in church life as well. Gender-specific retreats and speakers help entrench already established beliefs that men and women are inherently different. Evangelical girls grow up believing that a career and motherhood are not compatible, and if forced to choose between a career and family, young women are likely to choose motherhood, in part due to complementarian views that men are the financial and spiritual leaders in the home.[16] The immense power of Christian publishing and evangelical organizations such as Focus on the Family, which promotes functional complementarianism, should not be discounted.[17] Because this theology is so entrenched in the day-to-day lives of many evangelical Christians, denominations should evaluate every avenue of messaging—Sunday school curriculum, visual representations of church participation, social media messaging, and the structure of gender-specific ministries are just a few areas that should be interrogated.

Leaders should never assume church members are savvy enough to recognize functional complementarianism. As rhetorician Mark Ward notes in his study of visual media in evangelical Christian culture, most content reinforces gender dualism. It requires little cognitive interpretation or reflection from the audience.[18] Indeed, media ecologist Neil Postman warned decades ago of the immense power of visual media, cautioning that when religion and visual media combine, a potentially dangerous relationship develops where religion is stripped of everything that makes it "historic, profound and sacred." There is no longer "ritual, no dogma, no tradition, no theology, and above all no sense of spiritual transcendence."[19] As today's media landscape extends into every area of life, we are more connected through technology than ever before. The pseudo-community created through social media, television, radio, and print recreates an experience similar to what Christians encounter when attending church.[20] These mediated narratives have the potential to reinforce gender dualism through constant immersion, a phenomenon that denominations will struggle to compete with when members only engage with their denominational theology a few hours a week, as compared to seven days a week of other Christian media sources.

HURDLES IN PERCEPTIONS OF LEADERSHIP

In addition to Christian popular culture, women clergy continue to face skepticism about their qualifications and struggle to personify strong leadership without being perceived as pushy or bossy. Moreover, negative perceptions of women leaders go beyond women clergy. Research on leadership has shown that people, especially men, respond best to women leaders who can balance a warm and friendly personality with a subtle approach to taking leadership. A direct, commanding personality is met with repulsion.[21] It does not help matters that Christian self-help books for women rarely focus on courage and leadership.[22] The lack of strong, accepted female leaders results in many women downplaying their leadership strengths as they work to rhetorically gain acceptance as nurturing, warm, and non-threatening, thus suppressing their direct leadership style.

In an ethnographic study of Free Methodist women clergy, Roberta Moiser-Peterson found that Free Methodist women clergy were aware of this gender tightrope. The women interviewed acknowledged that they faced the impossible role of appearing both strong and capable but not overtly "masculine" or aggressive in their speech and nonverbal behavior. As one participant explained:

Several people have told me . . . that if I were a man I would be leading a church of several thousand. But because I am a woman, I am not permitted. And there is no law that says I'm not permitted. I'm just not permitted. Can I use a word that is? . . . All right, when a woman is a strong leader she is a bitch, and when a man is a strong leader, he is courageous and noble and all of that.[23]

These unrealistic gender performance expectations come from men and women who, like their male counterparts, have grown up in a culture steeped in gender essentialism. Church leaders must go beyond just acknowledging this problem and recognize their own complacency. In a 2022 study of egalitarian churches, leaders were found to be aware of gender disparities but would downplay the need to develop concrete policies to address the issue.[24] As shown in the earlier chapters of *Silenced*, denominational rhetoric is a powerful tool that can either help or hinder cultural acceptance. A denominational publication such as *The Free Methodist* had immense rhetorical influence. It is crucial that denominations, such as the Free Methodist Church, use every tool available, including more modern forms of communication, such as social media, to promote an egalitarian narrative.

Moreover, denominations must also work on creating a cohesive organizational narrative highlighting the historical contributions of women within the denomination. Denominational websites and literature also need to include imagery of women clergy intentionally, and women speakers should be regularly included in denominational leadership events.[25] If perceptions of women in ministry are ever going to change, it will take a concerted effort to evaluate every aspect of organizational life. Furthermore, if women are ever going to feel empowered and accepted in ministry, they must begin to see women leaders as the norm, not the exception.

Inclusion begins Sunday morning in the local church as the pastor gives the sermon. Pastors must be intentional with the language and examples they use in sermons. Biblical examples and metaphors referring to God often are masculine, systematically excluding women from seeing themselves as biblical leaders.[26]

Moiser-Peterson's ethnography of Free Methodist women clergy saw this in the biblical examples with which women choose to identify. Most of the women in the study chose to identify with male figures, such as Moses, and some women went so far as to reject outright choosing a female biblical figure for fear of appearing "too feminine." This illustrates a concerning rhetorical trend; if women clergy are afraid to identify with biblical examples of women leaders, what is the likelihood that the young girl sitting in the pew will do so? Sermon metaphors for God should reflect both masculine and feminine characteristics. As LaCelle-Peterson explains, this does not diminish the power of God: "Remembering that God is pictured as female as well as male will keep us from imagining that God *is* male, it will guard us from reducing God to someone quite a bit more like us, that is, a gendered being."[27] It is crucial that clergy are intentional with the metaphors and examples they use.

Ultimately, what must happen if denominations genuinely want to address gender equity is a willingness to disrupt culture. Historically, the most radical changes occur when individuals are willing to push back against the status quo. B.T. Roberts pushed back against the gender norms of his day and pushed for women's equal inclusion in ministry. Women such as Clara Wetherald- Buell-Harbridge did not give up when the Free Methodist Church would not ordain her. Instead, she continued her ministry in a denomination that would. As Nazarene theologian C.S. Cowles explains, any social movement that has brought about significant change has been subversive. The abolitionist movement, the Civil Rights Movement, and Martin Luther's Reformation were subversive; even Jesus' ministry was subversive though, asking his followers to evaluate cultural practices in Judaism and the Roman Empire in light of his teachings. As B.T. Roberts so eloquently put it in *Ordaining Women*:

> Christian men and women should not wait until a righteous cause is popular before they give it their influence. Those who do so, are simply following fashion, while they think they are following the Lord. . . . It is not enough to say that the right will ultimately triumph; if we claim to be righteous we should help the right triumph.[28]

Imagine what could have happened if Free Methodist leaders at the turn of the twentieth century had not given into fundamentalism and continued pursuing the radical path of social equality Roberts had set forth. Even today, it is not too late for the Free Methodist Church and other egalitarian denominations to return to the ideals espoused by Roberts. However, to do so requires the courage and conviction to stay the course and not be silenced.

NOTES

1. Kristina LaCelle-Peterson, *Liberating Tradition: Women's Identity and Vocation in Christian Perspective* (Ada, MI: Baker Academic, 2008), 193–94.

2. Ibid., 151–52.

3. Sally Gallagher, "The Marginalization of Evangelical Feminism," *Sociology of Religion* 65, no. 2 (2004): 232.

4. The 2021 Springtide Research study used survey data for their "State of Religion & Young People" report. Young adults ages 18–25 also helped construct survey questions and provide additional focus group data. In the report, 77% of respondents said gender equity was very important, while they felt only 52% of religious institutions

(denominations) shared their values. Additionally, 55% of respondents did not attend religious services because they did not feel they would be accepted for who they were and could not be their "full self." Springtide Research Organization, "State of Religion and Young People: Navigating Uncertainty, 2021," 35 and 72, retrieved September 28, 2022, from https://springtideresearch.org/the-state-of-religion-2021 -digital-edition/.

5. Ibid., 72–73.

6. Mark Chavez, Mark Roso, Anna Holleman, and Mary Hawkins, "Religious Congregations in 21st Century America," in *National Congregations Study* (Durham, NC: Department of Sociology, Duke University, 2021), 38.

7. J.T. Logan, ed., "General Conference Proceedings," *The Free Methodist*, June 27, 1911, 1; and Wilson Hogue, "General Conference Proceedings Eighteenth Setting 2 p.m. Wednesday, June 26," *General Conference Daily*, June 27, 1907, 2.

8. Earnest Borman's Symbolic Convergence Theory is a useful framework for understanding rhetorical buy-in and narrative in organizational communication. Christian culture is a storytelling culture that uses biblical narratives, personal testimonies, and media to retell key theological messages. As Symbolic Convergence Theory explains, these "fantasy themes," once embraced, spiral into a chain that creates a rhetorical vision and community. Zachary Sheldon, "The Limits of Faith-Based Organizations: Lessons from a Big Idea," *Communication Studies* 71, no. 4 (2020): 568–83.

9. The executive leadership team in the Free Methodist Church of North America acknowledged the concerns of Free Methodist women pastors in an August 2022 e-newsletter. In speaking with Fraser Venter, who is on the team leading the initiative, he acknowledged that the issues women clergy face are more than just an issue of access but also social justice issues. The denomination has embarked on an intensive listening campaign to hear women nationwide. It is collecting data on gender equity in all ministry positions, including senior pastors and annual conference leadership positions. Free Methodist Church, "Free Methodist Women," e-newsletter, August 22, 2022; and Fraser Venter, Zoom meeting, September 14, 2022.

10. Beth Armstrong, "The Stained Glass Ceiling: Description, Debate and Discussion" (Ph.D. diss., Gonzaga University, 2011), 13.

11. Chavez, Roso, Holleman, and Hawkins, "Religious Congregations in 21st Century America," 38–39.

12. Ibid., 42.

13. Bill Gothard's Institute in Basic Life Principles (IBLP) taught attendees tenets of Christian living (according to Gothard's interpretation). Emphasizing a separation from the world, IBLP encouraged attendees to shy away from non-Christian forms of media, public schools, and dating. Additionally, Gothard's IBLP curriculum emphasized "God-Given" authority—a strict hierarchy that placed God at the top, followed by church leaders, employers, and, for women, their husbands. The concepts taught in IBLP extended beyond just those who took the course. Both my spouse and I grew up in the late 1980s and 1990s, which was the height of Christian music and television programming as well as anti-dating books that, instead, emphasized courtship, such as Joshua Harris' bestselling book *I Kissed Dating Goodbye*. We both grew

up attending Free Methodists churches. My local church heavily emphasized living separate from the rest of society out of concern that we would be "tempted" and lose our faith. My husband's home church went even further and had members who had attended IBLP and firmly followed Gotthard's teachings. Church leadership did not insist that members believe the egalitarian theology espoused in the Free Methodist Church, almost resulting in a church split when in the 1990s, the congregation elected a woman to the pastor's cabinet. IBLP views were still popular in the early 2000s and gained national attention. TLC shows *17 Kids and Counting, 18 Kids and Counting, 19 Kids and Counting,* and *Counting On* as the Duggar family; the show's stars regularly shared their complementarian views and modeled this lifestyle to their audience. Today, IBLP says over 2.5 million people have completed its course. Bill Gothard is no longer associated with the organization, stepping down in 2014 after allegations that he harassed and molested women. Christy Mesaros-Winckles, "Christian Patriarchy Lite: TLC's *19 Kids and Counting*," in *Media Depictions of Brides, Wives, and Mothers,* ed. Alena Rugerio (Lanham, Maryland: Lexington Books, 2012), 63–76; Carolina Radnofsky, "Ministry that Once Nourished the Duggar's Family Faith Falls from Grace," *NBC News,* February 6, 2022, https://www.nbcnews.com/news/us-news/ministry-nourished-duggar-familys-faith-falls-grace-rcna14024; & Mark Ward, Sr. "'Men' and 'Ladies': An Archeology of Gendering in the Evangelical Church," *Journal of Communication and Religion* 41, no. 4 (2018): 127.

14. Julie Ingersoll, *Evangelical Christian Women: War Stories in the Gender Battles* (New York: NYU Press, 2003), 106.

15. Ibid., 107.

16. Colleen Warner Colaner & Steven Giles, "The Baby Blanket or the Briefcase: The Impact of Evangelical Gender Role Ideology on Career and Mothering Aspirations of Female Evangelical College Students," *Sex Roles* 58 (2008): 526–34.

17. Christy Mesaros-Winckles & Andrew Winckles, "Focus on the (Changing) Family: A Hot Message Encounters a Cool Medium," in *The Electronic Church in the Digital Age,* ed. Mark Ward Sr. (Santa Barbara, CA: Praeger, 2016), 31–37.

18. Mark Ward, Sr., "Head Knowledge Isn't Enough: Biblical Visualization and Congregational Culture in an Evangelical Church," *Interdisciplinary Journal of Research on Religion* 14 (2018): 23.

19. Neil Postman, *Amusing Ourselves to Death* (New York: Penguin Books, 2005), 116–17.

20. Terézia Roncáková, "Media as Religion, Stardom as Religion. Really? Christian Theological Confrontation," *Religions* 11, no. 1 (2020): 9–10.

21. Alice Eagly and Linda Carli, "Women and Men as Leaders," in *The Nature of Leadership,* ed. John Atonaskis, Anna Cianciolo, and Robert Sternberg (Thousand Oaks, CA: Sage Publications, 2004), 294.

22. Ingersoll, *Evangelical Christian Women,* 123.

23. Roberta Mosier-Peterson, "Lived Experiences of Female Pastors in The Free Methodist Church, USA: An Ethnographic Study" (Ph.D. diss., Northeastern Seminary, 2016), 136–37.

24. Heather Matthews, "Uncovering and Dismantling Barriers for Women Pastors," *Priscilla Papers,* February 3, 2022, accessed September 3, 2022, https://www

.cbeinternational.org/resource/article/priscilla-papers-academic-journal/uncovering
-and-dismantling-barriers-women.

25. In my content analysis of Focus on the family's website and other media entities, I found a concerted effort by the organization to push functional complementarianism through various media platforms, making it essential that egalitarian denominations counter this messaging whenever possible. Mesaros-Winckles and Winckles, "Focus on the (Changing) Family," 40–44.

26. Helen Sterk, "Faith, Feminism and Scholarship: *The Journal of Communication and Religion*, 1999–2009," *The Journal of Communication and Religion* 33, no. 2 (2010): 30.

27. LaCelle-Peterson, *Liberating Tradition*, 206.

28. Benjamin Titus Roberts, *Ordaining Women* (Rochester, New York: Earnest Christian Publishing House, 1891), 13.

Appendix One

1894 Free Methodist Annual Conference Vote on Ordaining Women

Conference	*Yes*	*No*
Texas	5	6
Louisiana	3	3
Oregon and Washington	22	10
California	22	14
Southern California	15	6
North Michigan	13	65
West Iowa	14	23
West Kansas	39	10
Nebraska	21	3
Iowa	21	11
East Michigan	17	56
Colorado	15	12
Michigan	11	32
Kansas	24	24
Minnesota and North Iowa	13	11
Genesee	17	57
Ohio	18	14
Missouri	12	9
Illinois	31	27
Wisconsin	22	22
Susquehanna	17	40
Canada	9	36
New York	3	34
Central Illinois	31	27
South Dakota	10	22
North Minnesota	24	3
Wabash	24	20
North Indiana	7	9
Pittsburgh	42	18
Total:	503	633

J.G. Terrill, ed., *General Conference Daily*, October 11, 1894, 8.

Appendix Two

Longitudinal Data on Free Methodist Women Evangelists 1880–1920

Year	Number of Women Evangelists	Number of Women Deacons	Number of Deaconesses	Number of Appointed Female Evangelists*
1880	3			0
1881	10			4
1882	13			8
1883	20			13
1884	25			16
1885	28			16
1886	35			12
1887	26			12
1888	43			21
1889	49			23
1890	41			12
1891	56			20
1892	61			23
1893	57			23
1894	48			12
1895	84			17
1896	88			40
1897	113			40
1898	147			57
1899	170			65
1900	174			61
1901	204			48
1902	206			64
1903	295			78
1904	307			82
1905	316			85
1906	376			98

Year	Number of Women Evangelists	Number of Women Deacons	Number of Deaconesses	Number of Appointed Female Evangelists*
1907	366			86
1908	406			97
1909	403			111
1910	387		1	84
1911	403		1	87
1912	435		11	100
1913	406		18	89
1914	414		15	105
1915	429	6	20	101
1916	435	7	27	101
1917	397	19	25	85
1918	446	19	22	114
1919	425	20	34	101
1920	436	21	50	83

*Women who held an evangelist license were not guaranteed a ministry appointment. Mesaros-Winckles, Christy. *Data on Free Methodist Women Evangelists 1876–1920.* March 2022. Distributed by Christy Mesaros-Winckles.

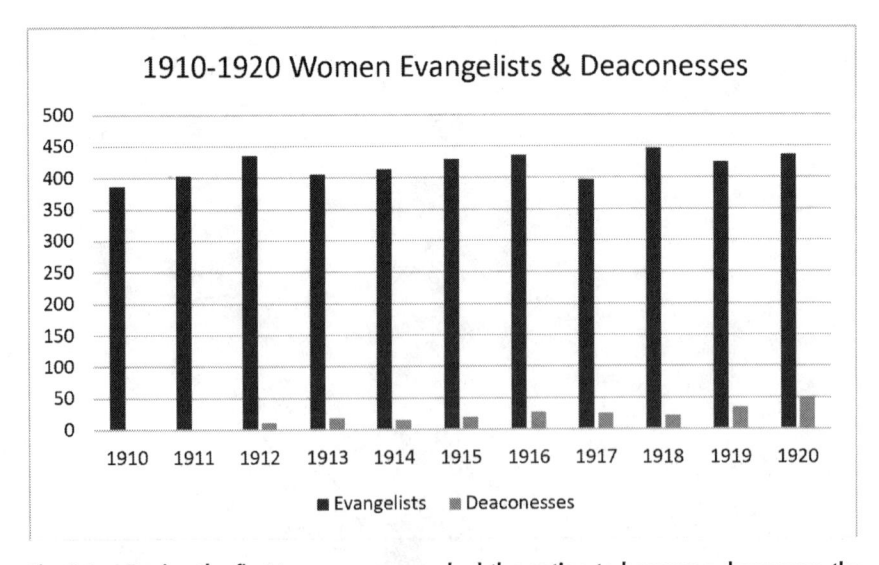

Fig. 9.1. During the first ten years women had the option to become a deaconess, the majority of women still chose to participate in ministry roles that emphasized preaching, such as evangelist. Source: Created by Christy Mesaros-Winckles

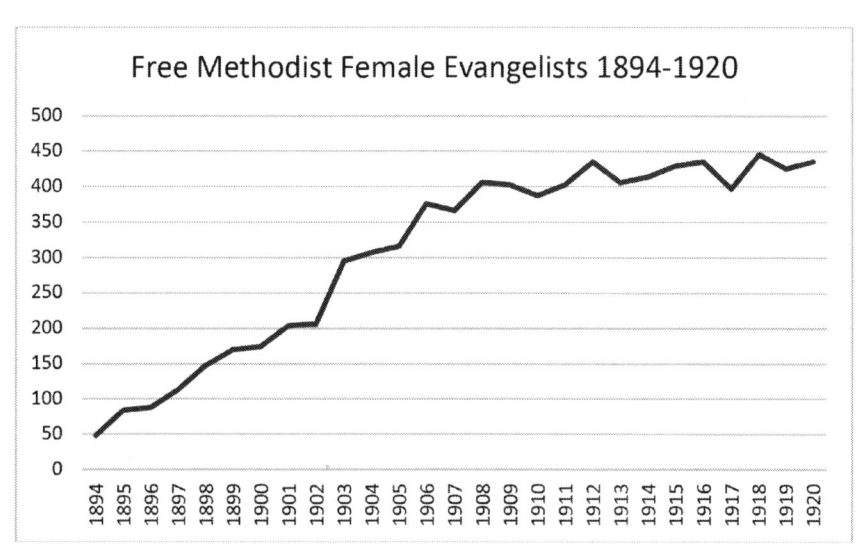

Fig. 9.2. Even though women's ordination was voted down at the 1894 General Conference, women continued to serve as Free Methodist evangelists, and the number of women serving as evangelists actually increased steadily after 1894 and continued to increase through 1920. Source: Created by Christy Mesaros-Winckles

Appendix Three

Free Methodist Deaconesses and Female Deacons 1907–1920

FREE METHODIST DEACONESSES 1907–1920

1910 Rebecca Sellew—Oil City*
1911 Viletta Dairymple—Oil City
1912 Elizabeth Moreland—New York
1912 Ruth Sandys—New York
1912 Martha Shoup—New York
1912 Gladis Gates—Oil City
1912 Mary Edwards—Oil City
1912 Mary Hogan—Oil City
1912 Harriet Schuler—Oil City
1913 Katie Coe—Kansas
1913 Clara Lutgen—Michigan
1913 Katie Booth—New York
1913 Mrs. J. Frances Sheldon—New York
1913 Margaret VanNess—New York
1913 Laura Brevard—West Kansas
1913 Susie Osborne—Susquehanna
1913 Jennie Lane—Susquehanna
1913 Lulu Champion-Hessler—Susquehanna
1913 Esther Hockenberger-Vandermillen—Susquehanna
1913 Nell Bricklay—Oil City
1913 Stella Conkle—Oil City
1913 Elizabeth Collins—Oil City
1913 Lizzie Franell—Oil City
1913 Estella Havelycheck—Oil City

1914 Mrs. M.L. MacGregor—Oil City
1914 Ida Schell—Oil City
1915 Bessie Danskin—Oregon
1915 Ida Walsh—Southern California
1915 Mrs. B.H. Edwards—Southern California
1915 Emma Linn—Kansas
1915 Margaret Ross—Susquehanna
1915 Emily Shattuck—Susquehanna
1915 Emily McGarvey—Oil City
1915 Minnie Potter—Texas
1915 Almeada Finger—Texas
1916 Belle McCullough—Genesee
1916 Ethel Alexander—Genesee
1916 Mary Edwards—Kansas
1916 Ida Schell—Oil City
1916 Estella Shannon—Oil City
1916 Margaret Thompson—Oil City
1916 Lila Shott—Iowa
1916 Mary Backenstoe—New York
1916 Anna Bessemer—North Michigan
1917 Mary DeFoe—Washington
1917 Julia Marston—Southern California
1917 Nellie Loomis Southern California
1918 Winnie Nickolson—Oregon
1918 Agnes Waer—Southern California
1918 Pearl Adams—Southern California
1918 Margaret Thompson—Oil City
1918 Harriet Brodhead—Oil City
1918 Jeannette Gray—Oil City
1918 Anna Bessemer—North Michigan
1918 Lily McConkey—North Dakota
1918 Edith Lewzadar—North Dakota
1919 Edith Abbott—Saskatchewan
1919 Ida Aiken—Ohio
1919 Edith Snyder—East Ontario
1919 Alice Redmond—East Ontario
1919 Ella Cole—Illinois
1919 Nellie Eakins—New York
1920 Lucy Green—Oregon
1920 Winnina Johnston—Oregon
1920 Mrs. B.A. Elliott—Washington
1920 Flora Fisher—Washington

1920 Grace Tiffany—Washington
1920 Anna Prose—Washington
1920 Maggie Logan—Washington
1920 Lillian Graves—Southern California
1920 Mary McGSherman—Ohio
1920 Handa Trimble—Iowa
1920 Emily Hampton—Iowa
1920 Catherine Eaton—Iowa
1920 Minnie Dickson—Iowa
1920 Cora Smith—Iowa
1920 Alma Frederick—New York

WOMEN DEACONS 1913–1920

1913 Bersha Green—Central Illinois*
1913 Anna Bright—North Indiana
1913 Laura Lamb—Pittsburg
1913 Ada Hall—Minnesota and Northern Iowa
1913 Minnie Beers—Nebraska
1914 Mattie Stoll—Wisconsin
1915 Hattie Handyside—Colorado
1915 Nellie Haskins—Kansas
1916 Rozella Douglas—Washington
1916 Aurelia Moore—Wisconsin
1916 Bertha Brown—West Iowa
1916 Pearl Wells—Oklahoma
1917 Mary Hillis—Oregon
1917 Anna Northrup—Platte River
1917 Maud Wallace—West Iowa
1917 Etta Chillson—Kansas
1917 Mary Jones—Wabash
1917 Helen Potter—North Minnesota
1918 Rhoda Burnett—Southern Oregon
1918 Mrs. M.E. Buckbee—Southern Oregon
1918 Myrtle Young—Palmer—Columbia River
1918 Anna Bates—Michigan
1918 June Horning—Oil City
1918 Ida Helgen—Wisconsin
1919 Alice Walls—West Ontario
1919 Nellie Lillard—Oil City
1919 Elsie Parker—Oil City

1919 Mrs. E.R. Sherman—Oil City
1919 Ida Robbins—North Michigan
1919 Mary Noyes—Southern California
1919 Lillian Graves—Southern California
1920 Rhoda Burnett—Southern Oregon
1920 Lilian Poole—California
1920 Anna May Belcher—Colorado
1920 Maud Jackson—Susquehanna
1920 Dana Dimmick—New York
1920 Lotta Babcock—Saskatchewan

*Conference location follows name. Mesaros-Winckles, Christy. *Data on Free Methodist Women Evangelists 1876–1920.* March 2022. Distributed by Christy Mesaros-Winckles.

Bibliography

Adams, Judith. *Against the Gates of Hell: The Glenn Tingley Story*. Harrisburg, PA: Christian Publications, 1977.

Adams, W.M. "The Woman Question." *The Free Methodist*, May 9, 1911.

Altick, R.D. *The English Common Reader: A Social History of the Mass Reading Public, 1800–1900*. Chicago: University of Chicago Press, 1957.

Anderson, W.H. "San Diego." *The Free Methodist*, January 7, 1913.

"Apollo PA Is Chosen for 1923 Meeting." *East Liverpool Evening Review*, October 9, 1922.

Apostol, Jane. "Why Women Should Not Have the Vote: Anti-Suffrage Views in the Southland in 1911." *Southern California Quarterly* 70, no. 1 (1988): 29–42.

Armstrong, Beth. "The Stained Glass Ceiling: Description, Debate, and Discussion." Ph.D. diss., Gonzaga University, 2011.

Arnold, T.B., ed. 1886 *General Conference Daily*. Coopersville, MI.

Aslanian, Artour. "The Use of Rhetoric in Anti-Suffrage and Anti-Feminist Publications." *The Journal of Transdisciplinary Writing and Research from Claremont Graduate University* 2, no. 1 (2013): 1–17.

"At the Free Methodist Church." *Cedar Rapids Evening Gazette*, June 6, 1913.

Baker, Walter. "Sweet Are the Uses of Adversity." *The Religious Telescope*, July 14, 1909.

Ballenger, E. "Nineteenth Sitting, 1:30 p.m. Thursday, June 29." *General Conference Daily*, June 30, 1911.

Ballew, M.C. "Price-Laura Lamb." *The Free Methodist*, August 26, 1938.

Bastian, Donald. "Does Theology Matter?" Indianapolis, IN: Life and Life Communication. Pamphlet.

"Bates, Missouri." U.S. Census 1900.

Beers, A. "Nineteenth Sitting, 1:30 p.m. Thursday, June 29." *General Conference Daily*, June 30, 1911.

"Begin Revival Services at Free Methodist Church." *Daily Inter Lake*, October 9, 1916.

Bendroth, Margaret. *Fundamentalism and Gender 1875 to Present*. New Haven, CT: Yale University Press, 1993.

Benjamin, Anne Myra. *Women Against Equality: The Anti Suffrage Movement in the United States from 1895 to 1920*. Piedmont, NC: Lulu Press, 2014.

Berkus, Catherine. *Strangers and Pilgrims: Female Preaching in America 1740–1845*. Chapel Hill: University of North Carolina Press, 1998.

Birmingham, Elizabeth. "'I See Dead People': Archive, Crypt, and an Argument for the Researcher's Sixth Sense." In *Beyond the Archives: Research as a Lived Process*, edited by Gesa Kirsch and Liz Rohan, 139–46. Carbondale: Southern Illinois University Press, 2008.

Birney, James. "Divorce Petition: Esther A. Miller vs. Harvey Miller." Saginaw County, MI, March 1862.

"Bits of Scripture." *Rock Island Argus*, December 14, 1912.

Bizzell, Patricia. "Frances Willard, Phoebe Palmer, and the Ethos of the Methodist Woman Preacher." *Rhetoric Society Quarterly* 36 (2006): 377–98.

Bizzell, Patricia, and Bruce Herzberg, eds. "Phoebe Palmer." In *The Rhetorical Tradition: Readings from Classical Times to Present*, 1085–94. Boston: Bedford/St. Martin's Press, 2001.

Blews, Richard. *Master Workman: Biographies of Late Bishops of the Free Methodist Church During Her First Century 1860–1890*. Winona Lake, IN: Light and Life Press, 1960.

"Boone, Arkansas." U.S. Census 1910.

Bormann, Earnest. "Fantasy and Rhetorical Vision: The Rhetorical Criticism of Social Reality." *Quarterly Journal of Speech* 54, no. 4 (1972): 396–407.

Bourgeois, Michael. *All Things Human: Henry Codman Potter and the Social Gospel in the Episcopal Church*. Champaign: University of Illinois Press, 2004.

Brooke, Freeborn. "Monday—Ordination Speeches." *General Conference Daily*, October 18, 1894.

———. "Shall We Commit the Church to Premillennialism?" *The Free Methodist*, March 9, 1915.

———. "Do Women Preachers Ever Wear Out?" *The Free Methodist*, May 30, 1911.

Browne, Stephen. *Angelina Grimke: Rhetoric, Identity, and the Radical Imagination*. Lansing: Michigan State University Press, 1999.

Buchanan, Linda, and Kathleen Ryan. "Walking and Talking through the Field of Feminist Rhetorics." In *Walking and Talking Feminist Rhetorics*, edited by Linda Buchanan and Kathleen Ryan, xiii–xx. West Lafayette, IN: Parlor Press, 2010.

Buell, Le Grand. "Holly and Germany." *The Free Methodist*, May 27, 1891.

Burton, Vicki Tolar. *Spiritual Literacy in John Wesley's Methodism*. Waco, TX: Baylor University Press, 2008.

Burton, Vincent. "Ida L. Wood." *The Free Methodist*, May 25, 1915.

Butler, Judith. "Performative Acts and Gender Constitution: An Essay on Phenomenology and Feminist Theory." *Theater Journal* 40, no. 4 (1988): 519–31.

By a Woman. "The Other Side of the Question." *The Free Methodist*, June 17, 1891.

"C. Perry Miller vs. I.S. Ferguson and the Estate of H. Miller Deceased." Court Records. Stockbridge, MI, July 15, 1867.

Cahill, Cathleen, Crystal Feimster, and Kimberly Hamlin. "Expanding the Suffrage Archive: Chronology, Region, Ideology, Biography, and Memory." *The Journal of the Gilded Age and Progressive Era* 19 (2020): 533–41.

Calkins, J.F. "John Wetherald." *The Free Methodist*, January 13, 1903.

Campbell, Karlyn Kohrs. *Man Cannot Speak for Her, Vol. II.* Westport, CT: Praeger Publishing, 1989.

Campbell, Olivia. *Women in White Coates: How the First Female Doctors Changed the World of Medicine.* Toronto: Park Row, 2021.

Carman, William. "Women in the Pulpit." *The Woman's Column* 5, no. 2, January 9, 1892.

Carpenter, Adella. *Ellen Roberts: Life and Writing.* Chicago: Free Methodist Publishing House, 1926.

Caron, Simone. *Who Chooses? American Reproductive History 1830.* Gainesville: University Press of Florida, 2008.

Cayton, Mary Kupiec. "Part 2: Harriet Newell's Story: Women, the Evangelical Press, and the Foreign Mission Movement." In *A History of the Book in America, vol. 2*, edited by Robert Gross and Mary Kelly, 408–15. Chapel Hill: University of North Carolina Press, 2010.

Chaves, Mark. *Ordaining Women: Culture and Conflict in Religious Organizations.* Cambridge, MA: Harvard University Press, 1997.

Chavez, Mark, Mark Roso, Anna Holleman, and Mary Hawkins. "Religious Congregations in 21st Century America." *National Congregations Study.* Durham, NC: Department of Sociology, Duke University, 2021.

"Church Announcements." *Charleroi Mail*, June 30, 1919.

"Church Notices." *Simpson Daily Leader*, December 24, 1921.

"Circuit Court." *Flushing Observer,* July 9, 1891.

Clair, Robin Patric. *Organizing Silence: A World of Possibilities.* Albany: New York University Press, 1998.

"Clarissa Wetherald." *Genesee Democrat*, February 28, 1891.

Clarke-Stewart, Alison, and Cornelia Brentano. "The Social Context of Divorce." In *Divorce Consequence and History*. New Haven, CT: Yale University Press, 2006.

Cloud, Dana. "The Null Persona: Race and the Rhetoric of Silence in the Uprising of '34." *Rhetoric and Public Affairs* 2, no. 2 (1999): 177–209.

Coe, S.V. "Life Line Mission." *The Free Methodist*, October 13, 1914.

Coffee, W.N. "Nineteenth Sitting, 1:30 p.m. Thursday, June 29." *General Conference Daily*, June 30, 1911.

Coleman, G.W. "Ordination of Women." Supplement to *The Free Methodist*, June 17, 1891.

Collins, J.H. "Bible Defense of Woman's Ministry." *The Free Methodist*, January 8, 1901.

Collins, Vicki Tolar. "The Speaker Respoken: Material Rhetoric as Feminist Methodology." In *Walking and Talking Feminist Rhetorics*, edited by Linda Buchanan and Kathleen Ryan, 144–67. West Lafayette, IN: Parlor Press, 2010.

———. "Women's Voice and Women's Silence in the Tradition of Early Methodism." In *Listening to Their Voices*, edited by Molly Meijer Wertheimer, 233–51. Columbia: University of South Carolina Press, 1997.

Colt, W.B.M. "Why Not?" *The Free Methodist*, October 1 and 8, 1890.

Colton and Co. Railroad Map of Michigan Prepared for the Commissioner of Railroads. Philadelphia, PA: 1876. Map. https://www.loc.gov/item/98688498.

Cooke, Sarah. "The Bible and Dress." *The Free Methodist*, November 7, 1911.

———. "Woman's Dress." *The Free Methodist*, December 7, 1909.

Coontz, Stephanie. *Social Origins of Private Life.* New York: Verso, 1988.

Coughron, G. Leonard. "Woman in Her Place." *The Free Methodist*, May 6, 1902.

"Cousin Nell: A Love Story." *Connersville Examiner*, July 17, 1877.

Cram, George Franklin. *Cram's Township and Rail Road Map of Indiana.* Chicago, 1888. Map. https://www.loc.gov/item/98688474/.

Cram and Stebbins Co. *Official Map of Michigan, Railroad, Township, and Sectional, Prepared Under the Direction of the Commissioner of Railroads.* Chicago, 1885. Map. https://www.loc.gov/item/98688499/.

Crocket, H.L. "Nineteenth Sitting, 1:30 p.m. Thursday, June 29." *General Conference Daily*, June 30, 1911.

Cross, Whitney. *The Burned-over District: The Social and Intellectual History of Enthusiastic Religion in Western New York, 1800–1850.* Ithaca, NY: Cornell University Press, 1950.

Cruea, Susan. "Changing Ideals of Womanhood in the 19th-century Women's Movement." *American Transcendental Quarterly* 19, no. 3 (2005): 187–204.

Cullum, Douglas. "Fanatical Women." In *Earnest: Interdisciplinary Work Inspired by the Life and Teachings of B. T. Roberts*, edited by Andrew C. Koehl and David Basinger, 3–29. Eugene, OR: Pickwick Publications, 2017.

Damon, C.M. "The Woman Question." *The Free Methodist*, September 19, 1894.

Dayton, Donald. *Discovering an Evangelical Heritage.* Peabody, MA: Hendrickson Publishers, 1976.

———. *Holiness Tracts Defending the Ministry of Women.* New York: Garland Publishing, Inc., 1985.

DeBerg, Betty. *Ungodly Women: Gender and the First Wave of American Fundamentalism.* Minneapolis, MN: Fortress Press, 1990.

De La Mater, Myrtle, ed. "Role of Ministers." *The First Hundred Years—Gaylord Congregational Church (United Church of Christ).* Self-published, June 1974.

Demaray, Door C. "Rev. Frank A. Miller: Special Number." *Evangel: The Children's Evangelistic Union*, October 1938.

De Plume, Nom. "Putting on of Apparel." *The Free Methodist*, March 29, 1910.

De Voist, M. *History of the Eastern Michigan Conference of the Free Methodist Church.* Owosso, MI: Times Printing Company, 1925.

"Double Funeral." *The Goshen Democrat*, March 21, 1913.

Doyle, Anne. "Nursing by Religious Orders in the United States: Part V 1855–1928." *American Journal of Nursing* XXIX, no. 11 (November 1929): 1331–43.

Dryer, Ollie. "Salida, Colorado." *The Free Methodist*, March 2, 1915.

D.W., Harriet. "Woman's Debt to Christ." *The Free Methodist*, August 7, 1889.

Eagly, Alice, and Linda Carli. "Women and Men as Leaders." In *The Nature of Leadership*, edited by John Atonaskis, Anna Cianciolo, and Robert Sternberg, 279–301. Thousand Oaks, CA: Sage Publications, 2004.

Ebey, Charles. "The Millennium." *The Free Methodist*, June 26, 1906.

———. "Woman's Suffrage." *The Free Methodist*, March 8, 1904.

———. "Lay Preachers." *The Free Methodist*, May 21, 1902.

———. "Free Methodist Deaconesses." *The Free Methodist*, July 9, 1907.

———. "General Conference Proceedings." *The Free Methodist*, July 2, 1907.

———. "General Conference Proceedings Eighteenth Setting 2 p.m. Wednesday, June 26." *General Conference Daily*, June 27, 1907.

Ede, Lisa, Cheryl Glenn, and Andrea Lunsford. "Border Crossings: Intersections of Rhetoric and Feminism." In *Walking and Talking Feminist Rhetorics*, edited by Linda Buchanan and Kathleen Ryan, 54–79. West Lafayette, IN: Parlor Press, 2010.

"Ellington, Michigan—Tuscola County." U.S. Census 1870.

Ellis, Franklin. *History of Genesee County, Michigan*. Philadelphia, PA: Everts and Abbott, 1879.

"Here and There." *Elyria Reporter*, November 14, 1901.

"Here and There." *Elyria Reporter*, March 11, 1902.

E.M. "More About Women in Her Place." *The Free Methodist*, June 17, 1901.

Epstein, Barbara. *The Politics of Domesticity*. Middletown, CT: Wesleyan University Press, 1986.

"Fell from Grace: Result of Clio Pastor's Visit to Saginaw." *Saginaw News*, February 25, 1891.

"Female Doctor." *Sullivan Democrat*, March 17, 1885.

"The First Female Medical College: 'Will You Accept or Reject Them?' Doctor or Doctress?" Drexel University Legacy Center College of Medicine. Accessed May 3, 2021. https://doctordoctress.org.

"First Meeting of District." *South Haven Daily Tribune*, October 2, 1914.

Fisher, Walter. *Human Communication as Narration: Toward a Philosophy of Reason, Value and Action*. Columbia: South Carolina Press, 1987.

Foster, Eugene. "The Girl Part of the Boy Problem." *The Free Methodist*, May 6, 1913.

Freeland, Mariet Hardy. "Why?" *The Free Methodist*, September 5, 1894.

"Free Methodist." *The Covina Argus*, October 15, 1926.

"Free Methodist Church." *The Corvina Argus*, May 22, 1925.

Free Methodist Church. "1984 General Conference Roll Call." Unpublished meeting minutes 1894, transcript.

———. *Annual Conference Minutes: Proceedings of the Forty Annual Conference of the Free Methodist Church of North America*. Chicago: Free Methodist Publishing House, 1910.

———. *Annual Conference Minutes: Proceedings of the Forty-One Annual Conference of the Free Methodist Church of North America*. Chicago: Free Methodist Publishing House, 1912.

———. *The Doctrine and Disciplines of the Free Methodist Church*. Chicago: Free Methodist Publishing House, 1908.

———. *The Doctrine and Disciplines of the Free Methodist Church*. Chicago: Free Methodist Publishing House, 1912.

———. *The Doctrine and Disciplines of the Free Methodist Church*. Chicago: Free Methodist Publishing House, 1914.

———. "1995 FMC Statement on Women in Ministry." Updated December 20, 2016. https://scod.fmcusa.org/fmc-statement-on-women-in-ministry/.

———. "The Free Methodist Way." Accessed July 14, 2021. https://fmcusa.org/.

"Free Methodist Pastors Named." *Centralia Evening Sentinel*, August 31, 1925.

Gage, Ida. "Hume, Ohio." *The Free Methodist*, March 6, 1895.

———. "Sixth Sitting-Monday Morning." *General Conference Daily*, October 17, 1894.

———. "Bowling Green, Ohio." *The Free Methodist*, February 1, 1893.

———. "Experience." *The Free Methodist*, February 8, 1893.

Gale Isenberg, Nancy. "Co-Equality of the Sexes: The Feminist Discourse of the Antebellum Women's Rights Movement in America." Ph.D. diss., University of Wisconsin Madison, 1990.

Gallagher, Sally. "The Marginalization of Evangelical Feminism." *Sociology of Religion* 65, no. 2 (2004): 215–37.

"General Affidavit: Original Widow's Claim No. 670760." Genesee County, MI, April 21, 1891.

Gere, Anne Ruggles, and Sarah Robbins. "Gendered Literacy in Black and White: Turn of the Century African-American and European American Club Printed Texts." *Signs* 21, no. 3 (1996): 643–78.

Ginzerberg, Lori. *Women and the Work of Benevolence*. New Haven, CT: Yale University Press, 1990.

Grammer, Elizabeth. *Some Wild Visions: Autobiographies by Female Itinerant Evangelists in 19th-century America*. New York: Oxford University Press, 2003.

Grant, Annie S. "Waterloo Indiana March 2." *The Free Methodist*, March 14, 1892.

———. "West Iowa." *The Free Methodist*, August 21, 1894.

———. "Aurelia, Cherokee County, Iowa." *The Free Methodist*, November 30, 1897.

———. "San Diego, California." *The Free Methodist*, March 11, 1912.

Grant, F.F. "Mrs. S. Anne Grant." *The Free Methodist*, July 11, 1916.

Griffith, G.W, ed. *1915 The General Conference Daily*. Chicago: Free Methodist Publishing House.

Gring-Premble, Lisa. "Writing Themselves into Consciousness: Creating a Rhetorical Bridge between Public and Private Spheres." *Quarterly Journal of Speech* 84 (1998): 41–61.

Gould, William. "Ought Women to Govern in the Church? No. 4." *The Free Methodist*, July 7, 1886.

Hadley Circuit Meeting Minutes (1875–1890). Retrieved August 2011 from the Marston Memorial Historical Center Archives, Indianapolis, IN.

Hall, Ada. "Mason City, Iowa." *The Free Methodist*, April 25, 1911.

———. "Forward, Backward, Which?" *The Free Methodist*, April 26, 1911.

———. "Gleanings: Mason City, Iowa." *The Free Methodist*, April 25, 1911.

———. "Spring Valley, Minnesota." *The Free Methodist*, July 27, 1915.

Hanmer, W.G. "Granite Oklahoma." *The Free Methodist*, March 24, 1903.

Hassey, Janette. *No Time for Silence*. Minneapolis, MN: Christians for Biblical Equality, 1986.

Harbridge, Clara. "Obituary: Esther Smith." 1903.

―――. "To the Commission on Pensions." Letter dated January 17, 1916.

Harroun Jr., C.E. "Oklahoma Letter." *The Free Methodist*, October 9, 1900, 12.

Hart, Edward, Jones Burton, Sellew Walter, and Wilson Hogue. "Pastoral Address Cont." *The Free Methodist*, July 23, 1907.

Hart, Edward Payson. *Reminiscences of Early Free Methodism*. Chicago: Free Methodist Publishing House, 1903.

Haviland, Eliza. "The Deaconess Garb." *The Free Methodist*, May 21, 1907.

Hawley, C.F. "Miss Willard and the Minor Secret Orders." *The Free Methodist*, February 25, 1888.

"He Sold Buckwheat." *The Democrat*, July 4, 1891.

Hempton, David. *Methodism and Politics in British Society, 1750–1850*. London: Hutchinson and Co., 1984.

Hindmarsh, Bruce. *The Evangelical Conversion Narrative: Spiritual Autobiography in Early England*. New York: Oxford University Press, 2008.

Hogue, Emma. *Adella P. Carpenter: In Memory of a Beautiful Life*. Winona Lake, IN: Light and Life Press, 1939.

Hogue, Wilson. "Educate Women for Higher Womanhood." *The Free Methodist*, August 22, 1899.

―――. "Mrs. Jane B. Coleman." *The Free Methodist*, November 30, 1897.

―――. *History of the Free Methodist Church, Volume II*. Chicago: The Free Methodist Publishing House, 1915.

―――. "Seventh Sitting." *General Conference Daily*, October 17, 1890.

―――. "Women's Legal Rights." *The Free Methodist*, August 27, 1901.

―――. "General Conference Proceedings Eighteenth Setting 2 p.m. Wednesday, June 26." *General Conference Daily*, June 27, 1907.

―――. "Was it Wise? No. 1." *The Free Methodist*, February 7, 1911.

―――. "Was it Wise? No. 2." *The Free Methodist*, February 14, 1911.

―――. "Admission of Women to Annual Conferences no. 1." *The Free Methodist*, April 4, 1911.

―――. "Admission of Women to Annual Conferences no. 2." *The Free Methodist*, April 11, 1911.

―――. "To Whom it May Concern." *The Free Methodist*, October 15, 1911.

"Holly, Michigan—Oakland County." U.S. Census 1880.

Hughes, Richard. *Christian America and the Kingdom of God*. Chicago: University of Illinois Press, 2009.

Hummel, Michael. "The Attitudes of Edward Bok and The Ladies Home Journal Towards Women's Roles in Society 1889–1913." Ph.D. diss., University of North Texas, 1982.

Ingersoll, Julie. *Evangelical Christian Women: War Stories in the Gender Battles*. New York: NYU Press, 2003.

Jarratt, Susan. "Speaking to the Past: Feminist Historiography in Rhetoric." In *Walking and Talking Feminist Rhetorics*, edited by Linda Buchanan and Kathleen Ryan, 19–35. West Lafayette, IN: Parlor Press, 2010.

Johnson, Nan. "Reigning in the Court of Silence: Women and Rhetorical Space in Postbellum America." In *Walking and Talking Feminist Rhetorics*, edited by Linda Buchanan and Kathleen Ryan, 274–90. West Lafayette, IN: West Parlor Press, 2010.

Jones, Burton. "Women Ordained to Office of Deacon." *The Free Methodist*, November 25, 1913.

J.S. "Women's Work." *The Free Methodist*, February 20, 1900.

Kelly, Mary. "Introduction." In *A History of the Book in America vol. 2*, edited by Robert Gross and Mary Kelly, 53–57. Chapel Hill: University of North Carolina Press, 2010.

Killon, J.T. "Blanche Stamp." *The Free Methodist*, April 20, 1945.

Kimmel, Michael. "Men's Responses to Feminism at the Turn of the Century." *Gender and Society* 1, no. 3 (1987): 261–83.

King, Miriam, and Steven Ruggles. "American Immigration, Fertility, and Race Suicide at the Turn of the Century." *The Journal of Interdisciplinary History* 20, no. 3 (1990): 347–69.

Krueger, Christine. *The Reader's Repentance: Women Preachers, Women Writers, and Nineteenth-century Social Discourse*. Chicago: University of Chicago Press, 1992.

LaCelle-Peterson, Kristina. *Liberating Tradition: Women's Identity and Vocation in Christian Perspective*. Ada, MI: Baker Academic, 2008.

Lamb, Laura. "Greenburg, Pennsylvania." *The Free Methodist*, March 23, 1915.

———. "Greensburg, Pennsylvania." *The Free Methodist*, December 14, 1915.

Leonard, Bill. *A Sense of the Heart: Christian Religious Experience in the United States*. Nashville, TN: Abingdon Press, 2014.

Lerner, Neil. "Archival Research as a Social Process." In *Working in the Archives: Practical Research Methods for Rhetoric and Composition*, edited by Alexis Ramsey, Wendy Sharer, Barbara L'Elplattenier, et al., 195–205. Carbondale: Southern University of Illinois Press, 2010.

Lloyd, Jennifer. *Women and the Shaping of British Methodism: Persistent Preachers, 1807–1907*. New York: Palgrave, 2009.

"Local Items." *Wood County News*, October 21, 1892.

Logan, J.T., ed. "General Conference Proceedings." *The Free Methodist*, June 27, 1911.

———. "Salutatory." *The Free Methodist*, July 23, 1907.

———. "Women Blamed." *The Free Methodist*, August 24, 1909.

———. "Fashion Slaves." *The Free Methodist*, October 5, 1909.

———. "Roosevelt and the Pope." *The Free Methodist*, April 12, 1910.

———. "General Conference Proceedings." *The Free Methodist*, June 27, 1911.

———. "Eugenics." *The Free Methodist*, December 31, 1912.

———. "Girls Read This." *The Free Methodist*, March 14, 1913.

———. "The Girl Question." *The Free Methodist*, March 3, 1914.

———. "The Dress Question Again." *The Free Methodist*, August 3, 1915.

Loomis, Eunice Budd. "Dress Reform for Free Methodism." *The Free Methodist*, June 15, 1909.

Mack, Phyllis. *Heart Religion in the British Enlightenment: Gender and Emotion in Early Methodism.* New York: Cambridge University Press, 2008.

MacKinnon, Catherine. *Only Words.* Cambridge, MA: Harvard University Press, 1994.

Manetho. "General Conference—A Review." *The Free Methodist*, September 17, 1907.

———. "General Conference—A Review V." *The Free Methodist*, September 24, 1907.

Marshall, Susan. *Splintered Sisterhood: Gender and Class in the Campaign against Women's Suffrage.* Madison, WI: University of Wisconsin Press, 1997.

Marston, Leslie Ray. *From Age to Age: A Living Witness: Free Methodism's First Century.* Indianapolis, IN: Light and Life Communications, 1960.

Matthews, Heather. "Uncovering and Dismantling Barriers for Women Pastors." *Priscilla Papers*, February 3, 2022. Accessed September 3, 2022. https://www.cbeinternational.org/resource/article/priscilla-papers-academic-journal/uncovering-and-dismantling-barriers-women.

Mattingly, Carol. "Telling Evidence: Rethinking What Counts in Rhetoric." *Rhetoric Society Quarterly* 32, no. 1 (2002): 99–108.

Mayfield, Judy, ed. "Riverview Cemetery, Arkansas City, Kansas: Eliza C. Witherspoon (1855–1932)." Accessed August 20, 2021. https://www.findagrave.com/memorial/47339038/eliza-c-witherspooon.

McCold, Merle. "Ada Hall Marsh." *The Free Methodist*, June 24, 1938.

McGarvey, Emily. "Deaconesses." *The Free Methodist*, May 18, 1915.

McKenzie-Stearns, Precious. "Venturesome Women: Nineteenth-century British Women Travel Writers and Sport." Ph.D. diss., University of South Florida, 2007.

McMillen, Sally. *Seneca Falls and the Origins of the Women's Rights Movement.* New York: Oxford University Press, 2008.

McMurry, Jessie. "Deaconess Training Course." *The Free Methodist*, August 24, 1915.

McReynolds, Mary. *Redeeming Love: The Legacy of the Deaconess Ladies.* Self-published by the Deaconess Hospital, 1999.

M'Culloch, George. "Ordaining Women." *The Free Methodist*, September 12, 1894.

Meachem, Esther. "The Womanly Woman." *The Free Methodist*, December 6, 1910.

Mendenhall, Edward. *Map of Iowa Exhibiting the Townships, Cities, Villages, Post Offices, Railroads, Common Roads and Other Improvements.* Cincinnati, Ohio, 1855. Map. https://www.loc.gov/item/98688478/.

Mesaros-Winckles, Christy. "Christian Patriarchy Lite: TLC's *19 Kids and Counting.*" In *Media Depictions of Brides, Wives and Mothers*, edited by Alena Rugerio, 63–76. Lanham, MD: Lexington Books, 2012.

———. *Data on Free Methodist Women Evangelists 1876–1920.* March 2022. Distributed by Christy Mesaros-Winckles.

———. "Hear Our Plea: Voices of Early Free Methodist Women in Denominational Print Culture." *Westminster Papers in Communication and Culture* 8, no. 3 (2011): 25–46.

———. "Why Not Now? The 1890 and 1894 Free Methodist Debates on Ordaining Women." *Wesley and Methodist Studies* (Winter 2021): 45–68. https://doi.org/10.5325/weslmethstud.13.1.0045.

Mesaros-Winckles, Christy, and Andrew Winckles. "Focus on the (Changing) Family: A Hot Message Encounters a Cool Medium." In *The Electronic Church in the Digital Age*, edited by Mark Ward, Sr., 31–56. Santa Barbara, CA: Praeger, 2016.

Meyers, Burton. *The History of Medical Education in Indiana*. Bloomington, IN: Indiana University Press, 1956.

Michigan Legislature. *Journal of the House of Representatives of the State of Michigan*. December 31, 1864.

Miller, Eric. "Phyllis Schlafly's 'Positive' Freedom: Liberty, Liberation and Equal Rights." *Rhetoric and Public Affairs* 18, no. 2 (Summer 2015): 277–300.

Miller, Frank A. "Clara Harbridge." *The Free Methodist*, December 13, 1921.

Miller, Gertrude Evangeline. *Adam Miller Known Progenitor of the Branch of the Miller Family*. Evanston, IL: Miller Family Genealogy Collection, 1961.

Miller, Sarah. "Letter about Father Harvey Miller." Family correspondence to Mr. Geo W.G. Smith, Genesee County, MI.

M'Kinney, A.J. "Woman's Suffrage." *The Free Methodist*, November 17, 1903.

Minutes of the Methodist Conferences, Vol. 1. London: Mason, 1862.

Minutes of the Michigan Congregational Congress at the Eightieth Annual Meeting. "Clara Harbridge Nercology Report." May 1922.

Montgomery, Hiram. "Experience." *The Free Methodist*, March 2, 1887.

Morgan, Sue, and Jacqueline deVries. "Introduction." In *Women, Gender and Religious Cultures in Britain 1800–1940*, edited by Sue Morgan and Jacqueline deVires, 1–10. New York: Routledge, 2010.

Morris III, Charles. "Pink Herring and the Fourth Persona: J. Edger Hoover's Sex Crimes Panic." *Quarterly Journal of Speech* 88, no. 2 (2002): 228–44.

Mosier-Peterson, Roberta. "Lived Experiences of Female Pastors in The Free Methodist Church USA: An Ethnographic Study." Ph.D. diss., Northeastern Seminary, 2016.

Mottweiler, V.H. "Minnie Beers." *The Free Methodist*, February 4, 1958, 13.

National Parent Teacher Organization. "125 Years Strong." Accessed July 2, 2022. https://www.pta.org/home/About-National-Parent-Teacher-Association/Mission-Values/National-PTA-History.

Niebuhr, Richard. *The Kingdom of God in America*. Middletown, CT: Wesleyan University Press, 1988.

Noll, Mark. *Old Religion in a New World*. Grand Rapids, MI: Wm. B. Eerdmans Publishing Co., 2001.

"Of General Interest." *Ames Intelligencer*, October 16, 1890.

Offen, Karen. "Defining Feminism: A Comparative Historical Approach." *Signs* 14, no. 1 (1998): 119–57.

"Ohio." U.S. Census 1850.

Oklahoma Historical Society. "El Reno Homesteader Filings." Accessed May 12, 2022. https://www.okhistory.org/research/elreno.

———. "Homestead Applications." Accessed May 12, 2022. https://www.okhistory .org/research/applications.

Olmstead, W.B. "Hume, Ohio." *The Free Methodist*, February 6, 1895.

———.1903. *General Conference Dailies.*

———. 1911. *General Conference Dailies.*

———. "The Gerry Homes." *The Free Methodist*, June 30, 1914.

"Ordaining Women." *The Free Methodist*, June 3, 1891.

Osborne, Zenas. "Model Woman." *The Free Methodist*, November 21, 1899.

Osmun, Janette. "Women's Influence." *The Free Methodist*, February 22, 1916.

Owen, O.M. "Sixth Sitting." *General Conference Daily*, October 15, 1894.

Page, R.L., ed. "First Lady Elder in Free Methodism." *The Pittsburgh Conference Herald* 35, no. 1.

Palmer, Phoebe. "Tongue of Fire on the Daughters of the Lord." In *The Rhetorical Tradition: Readings from Classical Times to Present*, edited by Patricia Bizzell and Bruce Herzberg, 1100–13. Boston: Bedford St. Martin's Press, 2001.

Payne, Lea. "Pants Don't Make Preachers' Fashion and Gender Construction in Late-Nineteenth- and Early-Twentieth-century American Revivalism." *Fashion Theory* 19, no. 1 (2015): 83–113.

"Pennsylvania Girl." *The Indianapolis Journal*, June 21, 1884.

Pope Levinson, Priscilla. "A 'Thirty Year War' and More: Exposing Complexities in the Methodist Deaconess Movement." *Methodist History* 47, no. 2 (2009): 101–16.

———. *Building the Old Time Religion: Women Evangelists in the Progressive Era.* New York: New York University Press, 2014.

Postman, Neil. *Amusing Ourselves to Death*. New York: Penguin Books, 2005.

Radnofsky, Carolina. "Ministry that Once Nourished the Duggar's Family Faith Falls from Grace." *NBC News,* February 6, 2022. https://www.nbcnews.com/news/us -news/ministry-nourished-duggar-familys-faith-falls-grace-rcna14024.

R.B.S. "Women in the Pulpit." *The Free Methodist*, April 24, 1900, 2.

Redeker, C.E. "The Value of the Deaconess Movement." *The Free Methodist*, December 10, 1907.

"Revival Meetings." *LeMars Semi-Weekly Sentinel*, March 29, 1912.

Reynolds, David. *Mightier than the Sword*. New York: W.W. Norton and Company, 2011.

Richardson, Jack D. "B.T. Roberts and the Role of Women in Ministry in Nineteenth-century Free Methodism." M.Div. thesis, Colgate Rochester Divinity School, 1984.

Ringenberg, William. *Taylor University: The First 150 Years*. Upland, IN: Taylor University Press, 1996.

Roberts, Benjamin Titus, ed. *The Doctrines and Discipline of the Free Methodist Church*. North Chili, NY: Earnest Christian Publishing House, 1875.

———. "Ought Women to Govern in the Church? Reply to W. Gould's Fourth Article." *The Free Methodist*, August 11, 1886.

———. *The Doctrines and Disciplines of the Free Methodist Church*. North Chili, NY: Earnest Christian Publishing House, 1887.

———. "Ordination of Women: A Review of an Article by Rev. G.W. Coleman." In supplement to *The Free Methodist*, August 12, 1891.

———. *The Doctrines and Disciplines of the Free Methodist Church of North America.* North Chili, NY: Earnest Christian Publishing House, 1891.

———. *Ordaining Women.* North Chili, NY: Earnest Christian Publishing House, 1891.

Roberts, Benson. *Benjamin Titus Roberts Late General Superintendent of The Free Methodist Church: A Biography.* North Chili, NY: Earnest Christian Publishing House, 1900.

———, ed. 1898 *General Conference Daily.* Chicago: Free Methodist Publishing House.

Roberts, Emma Sellew. "Help it On!" *The Free Methodist*, October 22, 1890.

Roncáková, Terézia. "Media as Religion, Stardom as Religion. Really? Christian Theological Confrontation." *Religions* 11, no. 1 (2020): 1 of 16.

Roosevelt, Theodore. "Remarks before Women's Congress: March 13, 1905." The American Presidency Project, University of California Santa Barbara. Accessed September 6, 2022. https://www.presidency.ucsb.edu/documents/remarks-before -the-mothers-congress.

Royster, Jacqueline Jones. *Traces of a Stream: Literary and Social Change among African American Women.* Pittsburgh, PA: University of Pittsburgh Press, 2000.

Rubinstein, Ruth. *Dress Code: Meanings and Messages in American Culture*, 2nd edition. Boulder, CO: Westview Press, 2001.

Sage, Clara. "Denominational News." *The Free Methodist*, May 11, 1897.

———. "Experience." *The Free Methodist*, June 15, 1897.

———. "Decker Indiana." *The Free Methodist*, May 11, 1897.

S.A.H. "Rights of Women Pastors." *The Free Methodist*, January 22, 1907.

"San Diego, California." *The Free Methodist*, March 12, 1912.

Santmier, D.J. "Sixth Sitting." *General Conference Daily*, October 15, 1894.

Schultze, Quentin. "The Nature and Future of Religions Communication Scholarship." *Journal of Communication and Religion* 33, no. 2 (2010): 190–205.

Sellew, Walter. *Clara Leffingwell: A Missionary.* Chicago: The Free Methodist Publishing House, 1913.

———. *Why Not? A Plea for the Ordination of Those Women Whom God Calls to Preach His Gospel,* 2nd edition. Chicago: Free Methodist Publishing House, 1914.

———. "Nineteenth Sitting, 1:30 p.m. Thursday, June 29." *General Conference Daily*, June 30, 1911.

———. "The Gerry Homes." *The Free Methodist*, March 2, 1915.

Sheldon, Zachary. "The Limits of Faith-Based Organizations: Lessons from a Big Idea." *Communication Studies* 71, no. 4 (2020): 568–83.

Shuter, Robert. "The Cultures of Rhetoric." In *Rhetoric in Intercultural Contexts*, edited by Alberto Gonzalez and Dolores Tanno, 11–18. Thousand Oaks, CA: Sage Publications, Inc., 2000.

Sims, Albert, T.B. Arnold, and Walter Sellew, et al., "General Conference Report of the Committee on the State of the Work." *The Free Methodist*, January 30, 1895.

Sims, Albert. "Nineteenth Sitting, 1:30 p.m. Thursday, June 29." *General Conference Daily*, June 30, 1911.

Skylar, Kathryn Kish. "Organized Womanhood: Archival Sources on Women and Progressive Reform." *The Journal of American History* 75, no. 1 (1988): 176–83.

Smith, S.L., J.B. Freeland, and W.E. Shepard. "Paper No. 34." *General Conference Daily*, June 19, 1911.

Smith, Timothy. *Revivalism and Social Reform: In Mid-Nineteenth-century America.* New York: Abingdon Press, 1957.

Snyder, Howard. *Populist Saints: B.T. and Ellen Roberts and the First Free Methodist.* Grand Rapids, MI: Wm. B. Eerdmans Publishing Co., 2006.

Southworth, C.F. "Woman." *The Free Methodist*, June 1, 1887.

Spencer, O.L. "Dedication at Cridersville, Ohio." *The Free Methodist*, February 9, 1897.

Springtide Research Organization. "State of Religion and Young People: Navigating Uncertainty 2021." Retrieved September 28, 2022, from https://springtideresearch .org/the-state-of-religion-2021-digital-edition/.

Stamp, Blanche. "Gallatin, Tennessee." *The Free Methodist,* August 30, 1904.

———. "A Remarkable Conversion." *The Free Methodist*, May 16, 1911.

Stamp, C.W. "A Statement." *The Free Methodist*, June 15, 1915.

Stamp, C.W., and Mrs. B.E. "Parma Center, New York." *The Free Methodist*, December 17, 1907.

"State of Michigan Marriage Records." Montcalm County, 1879.

Sterk, Helen. "How Rhetoric Becomes Real: Religious Sources of Gender Identity." *Journal of Communication and Religion* 12 (1989): 24–33.

Stone, Lucy, ed. *The Woman's Column* 5, no. 46, November 12, 1892.

———. "The Progress of Fifty Years." Speech to the Congress of Women at the World's Fair, 1893.

Strange, Lisa. "Elizabeth Cady Stanton's Woman's Bible and the Roots of Feminist Theology." *Gender Issues* (Fall 1999): 17–36.

"Sunday Services." *The Bradford Era*, February 24, 1917.

Taylor, M. "Woman's Christian Temperance Union." *The Free Methodist*, July 27, 1887.

Terrill, J.G., ed. *General Conference Daily.* Chicago, IL, 1890.

———. *General Conference Daily.* Greenville, IL, 1894.

"The Churches." *Emporia Gazette*, April 15, 1911.

"The City." *The Daily Sentinel*, March 3, 1885.

"The Free Methodists." *The Dubuque Daily Herald*, October 11, 1890.

"The Week's Doings." *Palo Alto Reporter*, December 9, 1915.

Thompson, James. "Bersha Green." *The Free Methodist*, March 8, 1955.

Thompson, Robert. "Should Women be Ordained?" *The Free Methodist*, April 10, 1892.

Tingley, Edith Gage. *Memoirs I.* Unpublished manuscript.

"To Preach Her Husband's Funeral." *New York Times*, June 25, 1895.

"Training Our Girls." *The Free Methodist*, October 4, 1904.

"Tributes to Ada Hall Marsh." *The Free Methodist*, June 24, 1938.

Tuchman, Barbara. *Practicing History.* New York: Ballantine Books, 1981.

United Methodist Church. "United Methodist Office of Deaconess and Home Missioner." Accessed July 1, 2022. https://dotac.diakonia-world.org/member -communities/united-methodist-office-of-deaconess-and-home-missioner/.

———. "Timeline of Women in Ministry." Last modified February 22, 2019. https:// www.umc.org/en/content/timeline-of-women-in-methodism.

Ward, Mark, Sr. "'Men' and 'Ladies': An Archeology of Gendering in the Evangelical Church." *Journal of Communication and Religion* 41, no. 4 (2018): 114–34.

———. "Head Knowledge Isn't Enough: Biblical Visualization and Congregational Culture in an Evangelical Church." *Interdisciplinary Journal of Research on Religion* 14 (2018): 2–29.

Warne, A.G. "Woman's Work in the Church." *The Free Methodist*, July 11, 1888.

Warner-Colaner, Colleen, and Steven Giles. "The Baby Blanket or the Briefcase: The Impact of Evangelical Gender Role Ideology on Career and Mothering Aspirations of Female Evangelical College Students." *Sex Roles* 58 (2008): 526–34.

Webb, Lynn. "Women's Ordination." *The Free Methodist*, May 30, 1911.

———. 1907 *General Conference Daily.* Chicago: Free Methodist Publishing House.

Wells, Sarah. *Out of the Dead House: Nineteenth-century Women Physicians and the Writing of Medicine.* Madison: University of Wisconsin Press, 2001.

Wesley, John. *The Works of John Wesley.* Edited by Thomas Jackson. Grand Rapids, MI: Baker, 2007.

Wetherald, Clara. "Sixth Sitting." *General Conference Daily*, October 13, 1890.

———. "Shall Women be Ordained?" *The Free Methodist*, May 14, 1890.

———. "Tuesday Night at May Street Church." *General Conference Daily*, October 22, 1890.

———. "Letter to Benjamin Titus Roberts—Biographical Sketch of Brother and Sister Lincoln." October 4, 1888.

Wetherald, Mary. "Mary Wetherald, South Lyon, Mich." *The Free Methodist*, April 1888.

"What Is Said about this Book." Supplement to *The Free Methodist*, August 12, 1891.

Wheatlake, S.K. "Hume, Ohio." *The Free Methodist*, October 3, 1894.

Willard, Frances. "Woman in the Pulpit." In *The Rhetorical Tradition: Readings from Classical Times to Present*, edited by Patricia Bizzell and Bruce Herzberg, 1124–35. Boston: Bedford/St. Martin's Press, 2001.

Williams, W. *A New Map of the United States upon Which Are Delineated Its Vast Works of Internal Communication, Routes Across the Continent.* Philadelphia, PA, 1852. Map. https://www.loc.gov/item/98688314/.

Witherspoon, Eliza. "Virginia Missouri." *The Free Methodist*, July 8, 1895.

———. "Phelps Missouri." *The Free Methodist*, August 15, 1905.

———. "Experience." *The Free Methodist*, October 17, 1911.

Woman's Foreign Missionary Society. *Mariet Hardy Freeland: A Faithful Witness.* Chicago: Free Methodist Publishing House, 1913.

Woods, Dale. *East Michigan's Great Adventure: A History of the East Michigan Conference of the Free Methodist Church 1884–1894.* Winona Lake, IN: Light and Life Press, 1984.

Yocum, A.D. "The Crown of Womanhood." *The Free Methodist*, June 17, 1891.

Young and Delleker and Finley, A. *Ohio*. Map. Philadelphia, PA: 1828. Map. https:// www.loc.gov/item/91681725/.

Young, Jeremy. "Transformation in the Tabernacle: Billy Sunday's Converts and Emotional Experience in the Progressive Era." *The Journal of the Gilded Age and Progressive Era* 14 (2015): 367–85.

Zaeske, Susan. "The 'Promiscuous Audience' Controversy and the Emergence of the Early Woman's Rights Movement." In *Walking and Talking Feminist Rhetorics*, edited by Linda Buchanan and Kathleen Turner, 234–36. West Lafayette, IN: Parlor Press, 2010.

Zahniser, A.D. "Greensburg District Camp Meeting Pennsylvania." *The Free Methodist*, August 16, 1898.

Zink-Sawyer, Beverley. *From Preachers to Suffragists: Woman's Rights and Religious Conviction in the Lives of Nineteenth-century American Clergywomen*. Louisville, KY: Westminster John Knox Press, 2003.

Index

About the Author

Christy Mesaros-Winckles, PhD, is an associate professor in the Communication Arts and Sciences Department at Adrian College. Mesaros-Winckles has been interviewed about evangelical culture and gender for *Good* and *Marie Claire*, and her blog *Free Methodist Feminist* has had over 100,000 views. Her 2013 dissertation, "Only God Knows the Opposition We Face: The Rhetoric of Nineteenth-century Free Methodist Women and Their Quest for Ordination," won the Religious Communication Association's Dissertation of the Year Award and served as the starting point for *Silenced*. Additionally, her research has also been published in *The Journal of Religion and Popular Culture*, *Wesley and Methodist Studies*, *Westminster Papers in Communication and Culture*, and *The International Review of Qualitative Inquiry*. She resides in Adrian, Michigan, with her husband, three children, and six cats and is a member of the Adrian United Methodist Church.